A FRAGILE EDEN

A Fragile Eden

Portraits of the Endemic Flowering Plants of the
Granitic Seychelles

WRITTEN AND ILLUSTRATED BY

ROSEMARY WISE

WITH "THE BIOGEOGRAPHY OF THE
SEYCHELLES ISLANDS" CONTRIBUTED BY

MALCOLM COE

PRINCETON UNIVERSITY PRESS, PRINCETON, NEW JERSEY

Copyright © 1998 by Princeton University Press
Illustrations copyright © 1998 by Rosemary Wise
Published by Princeton University Press, 41 William Street,
Princeton, New Jersey 08540
In the United Kingdom: Princeton University Press,
Chichester, West Sussex

Library of Congress Cataloging-in-Publication Data

Wise, Rosemary, 1941–
A fragile Eden : portraits of the endemic flowering plants of the
granitic Seychelles / written and illustrated by Rosemary Wise ;
with "The biogeography of the Seychelles Islands"
contributed by Malcolm Coe.
p.   cm.
Includes bibliographical references and index.
ISBN 0-691-04817-7 (cl : alk. paper)
1. Endemic plants—Seychelles.   2. Botanical
illustration.   I. Title.
QK429.S4W57   1998
581.9696—dc21   97-27815

This book has been composed in Berkeley
Designed by Jan Lilly
Composed by Gretchen Oberfranc

Princeton University Press books are
printed on acid-free paper, and meet the guidelines for
permanence and durability of the Committee on Production
Guidelines for Book Longevity of the
Council on Library Resources

http://pup.princeton.edu

10 9 8 7 6 5 4 3 2 1

*Dedicated to many dear friends in
Britain and Seychelles,
my mother Marienne, and my late father Peter Haynes,
but especially to my children,
Richard and Rebecca Wise*

CONTENTS

As is the case with many isolated archipelagos, the Seychelles has a large number of fascinating and unusual endemic species of plants. It is not often that an artist has sought out all the endemic species of an island and painted them so beautifully. In this case the artist has also demonstrated that she is a good botanist because she has written her own text to accompany the paintings. In addition to the accurate botanical descriptions, much interesting local information is given about each of these species. In this volume we are seeing some of the rarest and most threatened species of plants on earth. Many of them are now surviving in out-of-the way places inaccessible to agriculture or feral animals. It is to be hoped that this book is not only one for us to enjoy the fine paintings, but also one that stimulates and challenges the local people to realize the value of the botanical treasures that are held in the Seychelles. Here we see illustrated the world's largest seed of the extraordinary double coconut *Lodoicea maldivica* from a large palm tree to the minute saprophytic *Seychellaria thomassetii*. Even the tropical Asian pitcher plant genus *Nepenthes* has found its way to the Seychelles and speciated there. These plants are illustrated by paintings of such a quality because of the many trips the artist has made to study them in the field. Here is a most welcome addition to the botanical literature because it brings to us a collection of such rare and little-known botanical treasures.

Prof. Sir Ghillean Prance, F.R.S.
Director
Royal Botanic Gardens, Kew

ACKNOWLEDGMENTS

So many have helped me in so many ways during the years that I have spent on this project in my spare time.

Dr. Barrie Juniper, who in 1984 was chairman of the Expeditionary Council at the University of Oxford, suggested that I should accompany the students of the Oxford University Biological Expedition to Seychelles in 1985. I thank him for this and also for subsequent advice and support for many aspects of this project, the idea of which was formulated during this expedition. My very grateful thanks go to the Churchill Trust for awarding me a Winston Churchill Travelling Fellowship, which enabled me to visit the islands for the first time as an associate member of this expedition and to return for a further five weeks in 1986. At the end of the 1985 expedition, Mr. Lindsay Chong Seng, then current conservation officer, knowing that I would be returning, suggested that my time would be better spent concentrating on painting the endemic flowering plants of Seychelles rather than the variety of indigenous and introduced species that I had hitherto depicted. (This was my first visit to the tropics and practically every plant was new to me and there to be painted.) Lindsay, his wife Katy Beaver, and his colleagues have helped me on many visits. In the early years, my parents, Peter and Marienne Haynes, looked after my two children, Richard and Rebecca, in my absence, enabling me to travel.

After months of quiet thoughts on the feasibility of finding and painting all the endemic flowering plants of Seychelles, I eventually spoke to Dr. Frank White, Department of Plant Sciences, Oxford. Over the years he gave me so much time, so much good advice, and most of all, encouraged me not only to work toward a publication, but eventually to write the text myself. Without his input and continual interest this book would not have materialized. His untimely death in September 1994 meant that he did not see the finished project. In the initial stages, Professor F. R. Whatley took great interest in the project and gave me a lot of valuable advice. I could not have added so much information on plant families without Dr. David Mabberley's superb and invaluable dictionary of higher plants, *The Plant Book*. My colleagues in the Oxford herbaria have helped in many ways. They have heard all my stories and have aided in the processing of my collections. Dr. Malcolm Coe, for many years a lecturer in the Department of Zoology, University of Oxford, was, with Dr. White, a referee for my application for a Churchill Fellowship. Malcolm has talked "Seychelles" with me on countless occasions, given much inspiration, and written this account of the biogeography for me. Mrs. Ann Robertson, now living in Malindi, Kenya, who wrote *Flowering Plants of Seychelles*, has offered many valuable suggestions from the earliest stages. I have looked forward to her annual visits to Oxford. Dr. Francis Friedmann of the Muséum de Phanérogamie, Paris, has helped me with a myriad of questions, lent me specimens, and offered much advice. As my visits to Seychelles had never coincided with the flowering of the orchid *Hederorchis seychellensis*, he kindly lent me photographs from which I was able to paint. In Seychelles, I have had many constructive discussions with Dr. Annette Carlstrom, a visiting botanist.

Financing such a project has not been easy, as it has not really fallen into any particular funding category. Mr. G. M. Ricci of G. M. R. Seychelles, Ltd., who has generously supported all Oxford University expeditions to Seychelles, saw my early paintings and offered accommodation and financial help for visits in 1989 and 1990. The ten weeks spent on Mahé in 1989 was obviously the most productive time, as almost all the endemics needed to be painted. (I had completed just three during my first two visits.) I am grateful beyond words to him. Although mostly self-funded, I have also received grants and financial donations from the following: The Linnean Society of London (Percy Sladen Trust and N.E.R.C. Taxonomic Publications Fund), New York Explorers Club, the Claridge Druce Trust and Nancy Lindsay Trust of the University of Oxford, *Annals of Botany*, and Mrs. Lorna Polunin.

Very special thanks go to all who gave up time to help with the plant searching. Initially in 1989, Lindsay Chong Seng and the forestry officers kindly provided me with excellent specimens, as I was then recovering from a car accident. Dr. Maureen (Mo) Kirkpatrick, of Anse Royale Hospital, accompanied me on my first and many other expeditions into the hills and shared my enthusiasm for the breathtaking scenery and the color of the forest. I stayed with Mo in the final stages of writing and am very grateful for much advice. Ron, Gill, and Justin Gerlach have offered me accommodation on many occasions, often for weeks on end, and gave up their very limited free time to go collecting with me, discussed the project at all stages, read the text, and made many suggestions. Adrian and Judith Skerrett offered me their house in 1990 in return for animal-sitting in their absence. Painting on their veranda, with wonderful views of Beau Vallon Bay, gave me much inspiration. I stayed with Katy Beaver and Lindsay Chong Seng on several occasions. Along with their two children, Karen and Zoe, we had several memorable walks in the hills. Alison and Bryant Marriott were also keen plant-searchers during their two-year stay in Seychelles. I thank them for their help and hospitality.

On the other islands, I would like to give many thanks to all who helped me. In 1985, the warden on Aride, Sue Tyzack, offered much assistance with the expedition's vegetation survey and helped to make our stay on Aride very enjoyable. Sue's friendship, help, and advice to me extended way beyond this first visit. I looked forward to the weekly arrival of Betty Beckett in 1986 during the four weeks I spent on Aride. We had long talks on many aspects of the natural history of Seychelles, a subject on which Betty is unrivaled. I thank Betty for endless help on all my visits, for the loan of reference books, and for the fresh water that she always left for me on Aride! I have learned so much from her.

On Praslin, Victorin Laboudallon collected various plants for me over the years. On one visit an enormous fruit of *Pandanus sechellarum* was cut for me, with special permission, as the Vallée de Mai is a World Heritage site. The old sack in which it traveled back to Mahé did not compare too favorably with the smarter luggage of the Italian tourists!

Many thanks to Mr. Atteville Cedras on Curieuse for showing me the island, including the "speciality," *Secamone schimperianus* (formerly *Toxocarpus schimperianus*). I thank the members of the Oxford University Expedition to Curieuse, 1990, especially Clive Hambler, for their hospitality. Clive and I have since had many hours of discussions over sandwich lunches in Oxford. I thank Victorin and Gemma for collecting leaves of *Gastonia sechellarum* var. *curieusae* during a visit I made in 1994.

I visited Silhouette on four occasions. I am grateful to the Island Development Company, Ltd. (I.D.C.) for permission to stay in the Guest House and Mme. Belmond for arranging travel on the I.D.C. schooner. My first visit coincided with the Oxford University Expedition of 1990, and I am indebted to the members for bringing Silhouette's "own plants" down for me from the high-altitude forests. Justin Gerlach, the leader, Caroline Awmack, the botanist on the team, along with the two Seychelles residents, Mo Kirkpatrick and Pat Matyot, all found good specimens for me to paint. With permission, some of these plants were put into the Guest House refrigerator for storage. Thank you, Caroline, for collecting more after one of the well-meaning young men of the island thought that they would all be better stored in the freezer! I have very fond memories of this first visit to Silhouette in 1990 with the late Elaria Gates Smith, a dynamic American who was, at that time, conservation officer. She, too, offered me accommodation on Mahé on several occasions, and we had many laughs and great games of Scrabble in the evenings! On subsequent visits, Pat Matyot accompanied and collected for me. In the evenings I have spent many exciting hours insect-hunting with him, frequently finding species not seen since the Percy Sladen Expedition of 1908. My very limited time on Silhouette on all visits was taken up with the paintings, and I am very grateful indeed for all this valuable help with collecting, which allowed me prime working time in the daylight hours.

On two occasions I was extremely fortunate to have professional botanists with me. Dr. Alistair Hay of the Royal Botanical Gardens, Sydney, Australia, (formerly of Oxford University) and I spent day after day up in the hills of Mahé in 1992. At this time we found many of the rarest plants, some of which I had previously not expected to see, notably both species of *Hypoxidia* in flower and fruit. Alistair and Pat Matyot also climbed to the high peaks of Silhouette and brought back various plants that I still needed, including a perfect fruit of the aroid *Protarum sechellarum*. Alistair has also read this text and offered plentiful advice and criticism. I am so grateful for this. Dr. Mark Large of the University of Massey, Palmerston, New Zealand (a Royal Society visitor to the Department of Plant Sciences, Oxford University, 1992–95), accompanied me to Seychelles in 1993. Again, our time was spent principally in the hills, both on Mahé and on Silhouette. I learned a lot of botany from both of these very dear friends and appreciated their assistance greatly.

Many others in Seychelles have shown interest in this project and have given assistance. A succession of conservation officers have provided permission for me to collect plant material. I have had much help from the Ministry of Agriculture and Fisheries; the Ministry of Education; the Ministry of Environment, Economic, Planning, and External Relations (including the Forestry Division and the Botanic Gardens); and the Ministry of Tourism and Transport. At the Bastille and more recently at the new National Archives, the staff, particularly Mr. MacGaw, Mr. Julian Deroup, and Mr. Charles Morel, have allowed me to use the herbarium and the reading room. The Medicinal Plant Group, headed by Mr. Marcel Rosalie, have helped with the suggested medical uses of these particular plants. I was also lucky to meet a charming, elderly herbalist up in the hills, who gave me more information.

I would also like to thank the staff of the British High Commission and Mr. Willie Andre, Mr. John Colley, Mr. Joe Four, Mr. Guy Lionnet, Mr. Kantilal Jivan Shah, Mr. Nirmal Jivan Shah, Mr. Peter Wilcockson, and many, many others who have made this rather daunting project easier in a variety of ways.

I have always been made welcome at the herbarium of the Royal Botanic Gardens, Kew, and have enjoyed my visits there over many years. Professor Sir Ghillean Prance has given me continuous encouragement, especially after Dr. Frank White's death, and has very kindly written the foreword. Many other members of the staff at Kew have given me invaluable help and advice on writing this book. Professors Grenville Lucas and Robert Johns, Mrs. Diane Bridson, Drs. Phillip Crib, David Frodin, Terry Pennington, Roger Polhill, Charles Radcliffe-Smith, David Simpson, and Bernard Verdcourt, and Mr. Steven Renvoize and Mr. Aljos Farjon have all discussed various aspects of the project with me. To be greeted with a smile and an enquiry on the progress of this book from so many there has been heartwarming.

My thanks go to Dr. John Akeroyd, botanical consultant and editor of the plant conservation magazine, *Plant Talk*, for encouragement from the very beginning, for discussions on writing a flora, and for much help in editing the text.

Minolta U.K. kindly awarded me a grant in 1996, with which the Photographic Unit of the Department of Nuclear Physics, Oxford, headed by Mr. Cyril Band, produced two sets of superb color photocopies of the paintings. Mr. Band and Mr. Paul Flint undertook this task. Now professionally mounted, these photocopies provide a colorful exhibition, which has supported my lectures on the project.

I thank Ms. Emily Wilkinson, Senior Science Editor at Princeton University Press, and her colleagues, especially Ms. Beth Gianfagna and Ms. Gail Schmitt, for endless help and for allowing me so much time to complete this "holiday" project.

Lastly, but certainly not least, many, many thanks again to my family, especially my two dear children, Richard and Rebecca Wise, for managing without my presence during frequent trips to the tropics when they were younger. Richard has very patiently taught me techniques of word processing. Both have visited Seychelles and fully understand the attraction! Unfortunately, my father did not live to see the completion of this book.

DONORS

I would like to thank the following people, who have contributed most generously to the publication costs of this book.

LADY H. Y. BULLOCK, M.A., J.P., an honorary fellow of St. Catherine's College, Oxford, is a keen amateur gardener. She has been an ardent campaigner for preserving the green environment and natural habitats around Oxford.

The late CHRISTOPHER CADBURY, CBE, allowed me to stay on Aride Island while carrying out a vegetation survey. He acquired the island in 1973 as a nature reserve and was dedicated to the conservation of its special wildlife. Although he donated Aride to the Royal Society of Nature Conservation to manage, he continued to be heavily involved in the island's management until his death in 1995. I am also extremely grateful for his provision of accommodation on two further visits, for his interest, financial help, and encouragement.

VALERY FINNIS was first a student, then a staff member at Waterperry Horticultural School for Women in Oxfordshire, where she stayed for almost thirty years. Her great specialty was the growing of alpine plants. She traveled extensively, lecturing on the subject, and also exhibited her plants at Chelsea and other shows. In 1975, Valerie received the Victoria Medal of Honour, the highest award given by the Royal Horticultural Society. After the death of her husband, Sir David Scott, she established the Merlin Trust in memory of his son, a gifted naturalist who was killed in World War II. The purpose of the trust is to help young people expand their knowledge and love of gardening.

PETER PLACITO graduated from Wadham College, University of Oxford, with a degree in natural sciences. He has been the technical director of Phoenix Petroleum since 1965 and is also a qualified European Chemist, chartered chemist, and Fellow of the Royal Society of Chemists. Peter is chairman of the management boards of two university funds concerned with improved patient care and is an active member of the President's Committee of the Campaign for Oxford. A man with wide interests, including music, archeology, entomology, agricultural history, and botany, Peter helps organize the annual Oxford University field trip to the Algarve, Portugal, where he has had a second home since 1974. With Dr. David Mabberley, he wrote *Algarve Plants and Landscape.*

B. E. SMYTHIES read first-year botany at Cambridge and tropical botany at Oxford, where he also received an MA in forestry. He is a Fellow of the Linnean Society and of the RGS. He was in the Colonial Service in Sarawak and Brunei from 1949 to 1964 and wrote *The Birds of Burma, The Birds of Borneo, Common Sarawak Trees, A Checklist of the Flora of Spain and the Balearic Islands,* and with Oleg Polunin, *Flowers of South-West Europe.* In honor of his wife, in 1988 he funded the Jill Smythies Award for Botanical Illustration at the Linnean Society of London, an annual award given for accurate and artistic illustrations. He is currently working with Dr. Chris Wemmer of the National Zoological Park, Front Royal, Virginia, on a database of all naturalists who have ever worked in Burma.

The late PRIMROSE WARBURG was an exceptional plantsman. Her ability as a collector and grower of plants was based on a very sound knowledge of botany. Her specific areas of interest were bulbs, aroids, older roses, and older vegetable varieties. She never tired of looking for plants new to her, and her support of young gardeners is legendary.

A FRAGILE EDEN

INTRODUCTION

In July 1985, from the window seat of a plane, I watched the sun rise over the Indian Ocean and, as the light became more intense, saw a collection of emerald-green, mountainous islands, seemingly floating on the turquoise sea, a magical sight that will be in my memory forever. It is this amazing vista, "a thousand miles from anywhere," that has brought such a sense of elation to the start of all my subsequent visits. Everything was new to me. I had never been further south than Morocco before. I had never seen bananas growing, or mangoes, papaya, coconuts, breadfruit, cashews, or avocado for that matter. The gardens around the picturesque wooden houses were a riotous kaleidoscope of color. Plants familiar to us at home on windowsills were growing wild, bigger, better, and healthier than any I had ever seen before. Swiss-cheese plants and philodendrons raced together to the treetops. Orchids, hibiscus, crotons, and bougainvillea graced almost every garden, growing in gay profusion. Even our "Christmas special," the red-bracted poinsettias, were tree-sized! Ropes of violet-flowered thunbergias festooned and hung from trees, which often were covered with colored blooms of their own.

The Republic of Seychelles is an equatorial island group in the Indian Ocean. The archipelago is scattered over a sea area of 1.3 million km², ranging from 4° to 10° south of the equator and from 46° to 56° east. The 115 islands, of which only 32 are inhabited, can be divided into two types, granitic and nongranitic. The latter can be subdivided into atolls, coral islands, and sand cays. In the far south is one of the world's largest atolls, Aldabra, a World Heritage Site, which is situated 420 km northwest of Madagascar and 1,000 km southwest of Mahé, where the small capital of Seychelles, Victoria, is situated. Aldabra Atoll is composed of four main islets surrounding a shallow lagoon, which is large enough to accommodate Mahé, the largest of the granitic islands. The present population of these islands is approximately 70,000, with some 95 percent living on Mahé, Praslin, and La Digue.

The 32 granitic islands are (with the exception of the coralline islands of Bird and Denis) the most northerly and represent fragments of the ancient supercontinent Gondwanaland. Their 60-million-year-long isolation from other landmasses has resulted in an extremely interesting flora and fauna with high degrees of endemism—species occurring naturally nowhere else on earth except on these remote granitic islands. The two highest islands, Mahé and Silhouette, rising respectively to 905 m (Morne Seychellois) and 750 m (Mt. Dauban), support tropical rainforest vegetation.

Victor S. Summerhayes was the first botanist to prepare a complete taxonomic study of the flora of the granitic islands and

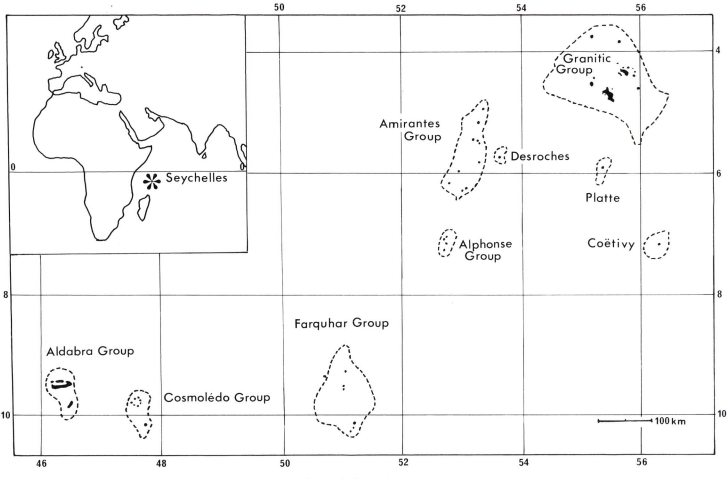

The Seychelles archipelago

estimated that there were 230 species of indigenous plants. (Summerhayes 1931). Dr. Francis Friedmann, in his book *Flore des Seychelles* (1994), suggests 200 species (130 dicotyledons and 70 monocotyledons), of which 80, or 40 percent, are endemic. Within this endemic group are nine monotypic genera, *Glionnetia* (Rubiaceae), *Northia* (Sapotaceae), *Protarum* (Araceae) and *Deckenia*, *Lodoicea*, *Nephrosperma*, *Phoenicophorium*, *Roscheria*, and *Verschaffeltia*, all of which are in the Palmae. The one monotypic family, Medusagynaceae, has *Medusagyne oppositifolia* as the sole representative.

Unlike most locations on our overpopulated planet, these tiny islands, with an overall land area of 450 km², have known the destructive powers of people for only about 230 years. (The first settlers landed in 1770.) But in this short time, the original forests that clothed the islands have all but disappeared, except for small areas on Silhouette, which are protected only by the rugged terrain. Approximately 18 percent of the land area remains as forest and woodland.

In the eighteenth century, the larger trees at all altitudes were felled for timber to construct the first settlements, for boat building, and for export to Isle de France and Bourbon (the present-day Mauritius and Réunion). Many of the larger endemic hardwood trees previously growing at low altitude, for example, *Vateriopsis seychellarum*, were all but exterminated at this time. Some remaining ones must have disappeared in this century to fuel the insatiable appetite of the furnaces of the cinnamon-oil distilleries, which were active until the 1960s. Now, with more imported timbers, the closure of the distilleries, and a greater awareness of the need for conservation, the woodlands, especially those at high altitudes, are regaining their peaceful existence. They are visited, as in the past, more often by birds, bats, rodents, and reptiles than by humans. Some areas have the added protection of National Park status, and the endemic flora and fauna can hopefully flourish again.

Most of the plants depicted in this book cling tenuously to existence in places too rocky, too inaccessible, or too high for human cultivation. But a threat to the endemic population far greater than people has come on the scene, even threatening these secure areas: the seemingly unstoppable, introduced, invasive plants. These can spread naturally, changing ecosystems and degrading areas. Introduced plants are often fast-growing, unlike the majority of endemic species, which are far slower. They change the pH value of the soils and imperil biodiversity by smothering native species. The late Al Gentry noted how, with worldwide climatic changes over the last few decades, there has been an increase in tree fall, creating more gaps into which the invasive plants can move. It is estimated that, worldwide, every day five species of plant that might have untold pharmacological properties become extinct, some almost certainly before they have been discovered and described.

In 1772, Pierre Poivre, an agent of Louis XVI, king of France, attempted to create a spice garden at the Jardin du Roi, Anse Royal, in the south of Mahé, with imports that included nutmeg (*Myristica fragrans*), cloves (*Syzygium aromatica*), and cinnamon (*Cinnamomum verum*). Owing to the unsettled political situation of the day, with the English and French playing a cat-and-mouse game for ownership of the islands, the garden was eventually abandoned. The French were afraid that the gardens might have fallen into the hands of the British, and, on seeing warships out in the bay, they hurriedly burned the site. They eventually realized that the ships were in fact French.

Whereas occasional isolated trees of nutmeg and cloves can be seen, cinnamon, or "cannelier," to give its creole name, is found everywhere, from sea level to the highest peaks on most islands, a most successful alien colonizer. The slate blue fruits are attractive to and distributed by indigenous birds. Cinnamon is easily recognized by its dark green leaves alone, with their characteristic trinerved venation. Another common feature is the presence of bright red flush leaves, both in young plants and older ones that have sustained damage. (Flush leaves are young leaves that have either a different color, a different texture, or a different growth form from those typical of the plant in question. This may be an adaptation by the plant to safeguard new growth, by presenting leaves sufficiently different to ensure that they will be overlooked by predators with conditioned recognition of a particular food plant.) In all habitats it is intriguing to try to imagine what the scenery must have been like before the introduction of cinnamon. With the distilleries long since redundant and a much reduced

trade in both cinnamon powder and "quills," the trees and bushes are spreading unchecked.

From low to midaltitude, bushes of *Chrsysobalanus icaco* (commonly called coco plum or prune de France) grow alongside the cinnamon. These have lighter green, oval leaves and brilliant pink fruits, enjoyed by children but tasting to most adults like wet cotton wool. *Tabebuia pallida*, with the vernacular name calise du pape, is also common, having distinctive crumpled, pale pink flowers; but at least this species is of economic importance to the carpenter as an attractively grained timber. Parts of Mahé, notably the northwest peninsula and areas of Praslin, are now covered with impenetrable thickets of *Memecylon caeruleum*, prohibiting the growth of all other plants. The beautiful cream flowers and the large bronze-tinged leaves of the creeper *Merremia peltata* were mainly confined to the south of Mahé, but in the last decade this plant has spread rapidly and it now blankets trees at low altitude in many parts of the island. Bushes of the attractively flowered *Lantana camera* densely colonize mainly lowland areas, forming thickets similar in habit to the British brambles. *Leucaena leucocephala* has been introduced to many tropical locations. These nitrogen-fixing plants are fast-growing and are used as shade plants for crops, as animal fodder, as green manure, and as soil stabilizers—wonder plants. But maybe these also are too successful here? Large areas of these plants now dominate the landscape, especially at low altitudes. The forest tree *Paraserianthes falcataria* (formerly *Albizia falcata*) is as great a threat as any of these on most of the islands. Its flat-topped, wide-spreading crowns can be seen colonizing and dominating all valleys, in many places being by far the commonest tree. Jackfruit, *Artocarpus heterophyllus*, is another widespread colonizer of mid-altitude, and in some locations seedlings densely cover large areas of the understory. The young leaves of these are often deeply lobed, bearing little resemblance to the simple leaves of the parent plants. When areas are cleared of trees, the bracken fern *Dicranopteris linearis* soon takes over, prohibiting germination of all plant species beneath it.

Silhouette, a small, almost circular island, approximately 5 km across, has Mt. Dauban, which at 750 m is the second highest mountain in Seychelles. (Morne Seychellois on Mahé is 905 m.) Silhouette is a naturalist's paradise, with strong probabilities of new species of flora and fauna still to be discovered. A species of *Piper*, a creeper, has been collected from the high-altitude forests, and with more research, it may later be determined as an endemic species. Here on Silhouette, amid exceedingly steep slopes, rocky peaks, and boulder fields, exists a small, almost untouched area of primary forest, supporting no fewer than five of its own endemic plant varieties. Dr. Friedmann discovered this area, which is high above Anse Mondon, in 1983. In 1990, this forest became the study site of an Oxford University expedition led by Justin Gerlach.

But an alien introduction to Silhouette presents the most tragic story of all. The South American herb *Clidemia hirta* was first recorded on Silhouette in 1987. In 1990, members of the Oxford expedition noted its distribution over the higher parts of the island. Some of us have since returned and have been perturbed to see how rapidly the carpet-forming, meter-high plant has spread, inhibiting the germination and growth of everything beneath it. In November 1992 I found many plants at sea level, and my companion, Dr. Alistair Hay of the Royal Botanic Gardens, Sydney, reported that at high altitude it was now growing on the trunks and branches of other plants, often the endemic species. Silhouette's rocky terrain is the most difficult to explore, and the eradication of this highly destructive pest seems an impossibility. So what then is to be the future of Silhouette's rare treasures?

The majority of research on biological evolution has been centered on islands. Long-term isolation is conducive to endemism but, in contrast, these small "pockets" are all too easily destroyed, be it by human, animal, or climatic conditions. The extinction of the dodo on Mauritius in the fifteenth century is a case in point. These enormous flightless birds existed happily on this one island until man arrived with accompanying animals, and very soon the poor dodo was no more. Hillaire Belloc wrote, "The voice that used to squawk and squeak is now forever dumb; But you can see his bones and beak, all in the museum." (The "museum" is the University Museum, Oxford, where that is in fact just about all that has survived.)

No one can say how many species have come and gone here during the turmoil of fluctuating climate and geological change. That an endemic flora has survived so long on these tiny islands indicates its tenacity. Yet the human exploitation of the last two hundred years accentuates its great fragility. Were there perhaps generally more plant species in Seychelles in the eighteenth century before man arrived and the destruction of the forests began? Unfortunately no plant checklist exists from those very early years of habitation. The only two to be mentioned at this time were *Lodoicea maldivica*, the legendary double coconut, and *Curculigo sechellensis*, a small palm-like plant (Procter, 1984).

The earliest surviving plant collection from Seychelles is that of the French gardener and explorer Auguste Pervillé, who visited the islands in 1841. John Horne, director of Pamplemousses Botanic Garden in Mauritius, carried out the first thorough survey of the vegetation in 1871 and 1874. In 1877 Baker published *The Flora of Mauritius and Seychelles*, which was to be the only full

account until 1994, when the first volume of *Flore des Seychelles (Dicotylédons)*, by Dr. Francis Friedmann, was published. Most of the plants described last century are still to be found but many are becoming increasingly rare. Some have only a few individuals left. At least two known herbaceous plants have become extinct. *Vernonia sechellensis* (Compositae) was collected at Forêt Noire (Herbarium sheet: Horne 497, 1874), and *Bakerella clavata* subsp. *sechellensis* (Loranthacea) was recorded by Thomasset at Cascade Estate in the early years of this century and never seen again. Many plants that were known to be common at this time are no longer to be found on Mahé but still occur on the relatively undisturbed heights of Silhouette. In her report of 1996, Dr. Carlström considered 20 species (mainly endemic) to be critically endangered, 13 endangered, 20 vulnerable, and 38 near-threatened. Only 5 of the endemic plants does she suggest are at low risk.

In the short time that these beautiful islands have been colonized, crocodiles, sea cows, and the local giant tortoises have been eradicated. (The tortoises seen nowadays on these islands are from Aldabra.) Two species of land birds, the Green Parakeet and the Chestnut-Flanked White-Eye, are known to us now only as sad-looking little skins in museums. These losses are, of course, irretrievable.

It is the endemic plants that have occupied my thoughts and most of my holiday times throughout the past ten years. These plants have close affinities with species in the Americas, Africa, Madagascar, the Mascarene Islands, India, Malesia, and Papuasia to the Pacific islands—links going back to the mists of time and Gondwanaland. My original intention was to find all of the endemic plants of the granitic islands and to record them in detailed watercolor paintings, just as a personal collection. The late Dr. Frank White, distinguished research curator in the Department of Plant Sciences, University of Oxford, a world authority on the vegetation of Africa and my supervisor for twenty-nine years, persuaded me to write an accompanying text and to produce this book, allowing others to see the result of my labors.

I have purposely kept the botanical descriptions as short and simple as possible. The family order is alphabetical, with genera and species following alphabetically. The authorities of the endemic species and details of publication are recorded in full, mainly because I have found it more interesting this way. Where possible, I have included the local medicinal uses. Long before the advent of modern drugs, generation after generation had handed down their knowledge of medicinal plants and their healing powers. There is today a renewed interest in ethnobotany, and it is amazing as to how it could be known that certain plants prepared in certain ways had specific beneficial uses. Modern science and chemical analysis often demonstrate that our ancestors certainly did know the curative properties of their plants well.

Most plates feature both flowering and fruiting habits, and enlargements have been added where necessary. With limited time on the islands, obviously I was not always in the right place at the right time and in a very few cases I was unable to portray all the stages that ideally I would have liked. But what has been painted is always sufficiently characteristic to ensure identification. All the plants considered to be endemic species at the moment are represented. The orchid *Agrostophyllum occidentale* was never seen in flower, but the leaves and fruits are unlike any other Seychelles orchid likely to be encountered in the wild. Readers will note that the creeper presently referred to as *Piper* sp. is completely vegetative. Leaves are all that have been collected so far, but again, it is different enough for Dr. Friedmann to suggest that it is almost certainly an endemic plant.

The last ten years have enriched my life in so many ways. Primarily, I have learned a lot of botany! (My training was in the fine arts, not science.) I have been moved by the mysterious light and atmosphere of the mist forest; experienced indescribable joy when finding the flowers of *Northia seychellana* after a five-year search; watched flying fish and dolphins from the schooner during my first journey over to Praslin; dashed over to Aride in a leaky pirogue at the height of the rough southwest monsoon in response to the radio message, "*Rothmannia* is in bloom," continuously bailing-out all the way, so there was no time to think of sea sickness; felt abject frustration on another visit to paint the newly recognized *Peponium*, finishing the plate under cover owing to a million seabirds wheeling overhead and forgetting that the geckos on the ceiling function in the same way as the birds; searched for *Secamone schimperianus* on the bare, burning heights of Curieuse; sat sketching palms in complete silence in the cathedral-like Vallée de Mai; jumped at loudly dehiscing fruits of *Excoecaria benthamiana*; looked and not believed that I really was seeing the infrequent, ephemeral inflorescences of the *Hypoxidias* and *Protarum sechellarum*; filled my senses with the wonderful scents of *Rothmannia annae*, *Glionnetia sericea*, and *Ixora pudica*. Every picture certainly has a story attached to it!

But I have also looked on these plants as old and valued friends and have enjoyed meeting up with them again and again during my visits. I hope that I can pass a little of my enthusiasm on to you. These are very special plants.

Rosemary Wise
Finstock, Oxfordshire
November 1996

THE BIOGEOGRAPHY OF THE SEYCHELLES ISLANDS
BY MALCOLM COE

It was largely his association with the animals and plants found on oceanic islands that convinced Charles Darwin to formulate his theory of evolution, which was published in 1859 as *On the Origin of Species by Means of Natural Selection*. In addition to his well-known evolutionary work, Darwin was also greatly intrigued by the coral reefs and atolls that he encountered in the Indo-Pacific. Indeed his views as expressed in *The Structure and Distribution of Coral Reefs* regarding the effects of subsidence (and changing sea levels) on their formation are still extremely important. The closest that Darwin got to the Seychelles was his visit to and his observation of corals off Mauritius in 1836. Although he did not visit that "Jewel in the Seychelles Crown," Aldabra, which is one of the largest atolls in the world, he was sufficiently concerned about the conservation of its rapidly disappearing giant tortoise population to join T. H. Huxley, Joseph Hooker, and a number of other distinguished naturalists in sending a memorandum on this subject to the governor of Mauritius in 1874.

One of the predominant mechanisms of speciation is isolation, whether that be through geographical, behavioral, or genetic mechanisms. Islands provide ideal places to study these phenomena, whether these are oceanic islands or habitat patches perched on the top of high mountains, which are equally effectively isolated from similar environments on other elevated landmasses. If we are to understand how the modern flora and fauna of these islands evolved, it is necessary for us to understand the geological origins of these isolated landmasses.

GEOLOGICAL AND BIOGEOGRAPHIC PERSPECTIVES

The modern Seychelles republic is spread over a huge area of almost 600,000 km² in the western Indian Ocean, with the capital, Port Victoria on Mahé, lying 1,600 km northeast of Aldabra, which is only 150 km northwest of Madagascar. These islands, or microcontinents, differ markedly in their geological origins. The granitic Seychelles in the north are derived from a detached fragment of ancient African basement rock; the Mascarenes and the Comoros, which lie to the east and west of Madagascar, are volcanic islands that erupted along fracture lines; coral atolls are scattered widely over the southern and eastern Indian Ocean; and the massive Malagasy block and many of its offshore islands are derived from crystalline basement rocks, which are estimated to have originated from an ancient orogenic event 2,420 million years ago.

For many years biologists believed that all the continental landmasses had more or less permanently occupied their present position, although very simple observations of animal and plant species distribution made it clear that many of them had close taxonomic affinities in spite of being separated geographically by either inhospitable terrain or the oceans. Some of the strongest evidence came from the study of plant fossils (and later fossil reptiles), which indicated that the floras of the southern continents during the Permian (245–290 million years ago) differed strikingly from those found in the north. The distribution of the similar species could be traced in Antarctica, Australia, India, South and Central Africa, and South America, suggesting that these landmasses had either been connected or at least adjacent at some time in the past. The inclusion of India in this list was especially surprising, since its current geographical position is predominantly above latitude 10° N, thus leading one to believe that it had not always occupied this position.

Glacial studies indicated that all of the above continents and subcontinents had been subjected to similar glaciations, which also suggested that they might have at one time been joined. Yet despite the frequent observation of the similar outlines of the west coast of Africa and the east coast of South America and the work of geologists who were forming the view that the major mountain ranges of the world may have originated through continental movement and collision, these biogeographical anomalies remained a mystery.

In 1915, Alfred Wegener, a German meteorologist and astronomer, published a paper that proposed his theory of continental drift. His evidence was based upon the similarity of continental geological features on either side of the oceans and on a wealth of biological data. Sadly, intellectual arrogance was no less common then than it is today, so his theory was quite quickly relegated to the archives of history, largely because Wegener was not a geologist and so could not possibly be expected to understand the complexities of then current geological dogma. This dismissal raised big biogeographic problems, for there was no denying the biological evidence that could be explained only by proposing that if the continents had not moved, then land bridges must have formerly connected these landmasses. Interestingly, although such bridges could not possibly explain the geological, paleontological, and biological evidence, the more recent discovery of the importance of frequent, dramatic changes in sea level as a result of worldwide glaciations does account for many local levels of biological similarity.

The supposed great southern continental landmass is called Gondwanaland, whereas the northern land mass, comprising Eurasia, Greenland, and North America, is known as Laurasia. The problem with reconciling Wegener's convincing biological evi-

dence with that of continental drift was that nobody could think of a mechanism that would allow these huge landmasses to drift across the surface of the earth. The situation remained unproven until the early 1950s, when a number of different lines of investigation coincided to bring the proof that was needed for Wegener's very original and important ideas. The most important of these were in the study of paleomagnetism, the magnetism that is induced in a rock at its deposition or formation when paramagnetic atoms in the rocks align themselves in the direction of the prevailing magnetic field. One would expect that the induced magnetic field in these rocks would point to (or close to) the present magnetic poles, but in many cases they are aligned in completely different directions. This observation leads to two possibilities: that the magnetic poles have wandered over the earth's surface or that the continents have moved relative to one another. Indeed, at last here was proof that the continents could have moved, though a mechanism had yet to be identified. Finally, in 1960, Harry Hess, a geophysicist, postulated that new ocean floors are spreading from great central mountain chains, where the youngest rocks are found, while on either side, much older rocks are located in deep trenches where the ocean floor disappears back into the earth. The observable result of this hypothesis suggests that the ocean beds are less than 150 million years old, compared with the 3.5-billion-year-old continental rocks. In the Indian Ocean we may observe mountains (the granitic Seychelles) perched on mid-oceanic ridges which very rapidly disappear into trenches that are between 4 and 5 km deep. Hence the spreading ridges in the oceans provide the mechanism whereby the continents move apart. These moving masses, which may be on the land or on the seafloor, are called plates, so that the old term *continental drift* has become known as the more accurate *plate tectonics*.

Modern studies have concluded that the Seychelles microcontinent and India separated about 75 million years ago at about 30° S, the current position of Durban. Such relative changes in position are in part related to the fact that Gondwanaland itself drifted from a position over the south pole northward as it began to break up, so that Madagascar and the Seychelles Islands finally came to occupy their current positions closer to the equator. During this time, the movement of the different segments changed so that the position of Madagascar varied from being further north off the Kenya-Tanzania coast or as far south as Durban. Between 75 and 45 million years ago, India progressively drifted northward and possibly made a temporary regressive drift southward during the same period. Over this 70-million-year interval, the granitic islands of the Seychelles were left isolated on their perches, which

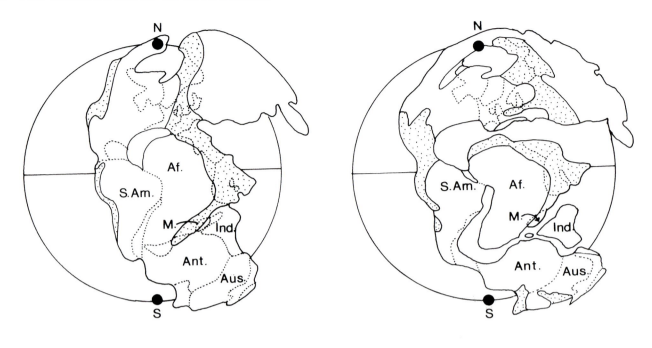

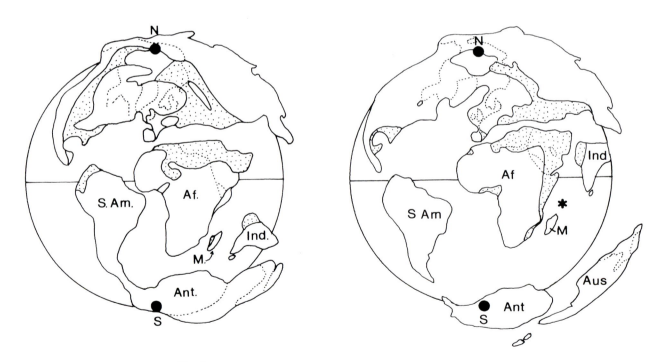

Movement of landmasses through time. *Upper left*, middle Jurassic (192 million years ago);
upper right, early Cretaceous (130 million years ago); *lower left*, late Cretaceous (70 million years ago);
lower right, early Cenozoic (60 million years ago). The star indicates the position of the Seychelles.

descend to a depth of at least 13 km and are surmounted by 500 m of sediment. The eventual collision of the Indian subcontinent with Eurasia led to the uplifting of the mighty (yet comparatively young) Himalayas, which still continue to rise today.

THE SEYCHELLES FLORA AND FAUNA

The Seychelles Islands comprise two strikingly different physical groups, the 40 or so granitic islands distributed between 4–5° S and 55–56° E and the sand cays or reef limestone islands and atolls. The difference between them is that the granitic group may rise at a comparatively great height above mean sea level (a.m.s.l.) while the latter are no more than 5 m a.m.s.l. in the case of sand cays and 8–9 m on the limestone atolls, though these slightly elevated areas often represent no more than a small percentage of the total island or atoll area. The low-lying islands of the Indian Ocean are truly desert islands with the large 145 km^2 (land area) Aldabra Atoll receiving 966 mm of rain, and nearby Assumption 867 mm. By contrast the elevated granitic islands of Mahé, Praslin, and Silhouette rise to 914, 427, and 867 m above sea level respectively, which results in the elevated and surrounding sections of these islands receiving between 2,000 and 3,000 mm of rain, whereas the highest points of Mahé (which interestingly has almost the same land area as Aldabra) may receive up to 4,000–5,000 mm of rain per year. Some of the islands in the Amirantes also receive rather more rain (D'Arros receives 1,497 mm) than their counterparts to the southeast, which demonstrates that while altitude is a predominant factor, geographical position and ocean currents probably also play an important role.

The ameliorating effect of altitude on the climate is a major factor in explaining the high levels of endemism and diversity in the flora and fauna of the granitic islands. It is also the major factor that must have determined which of the Indian Ocean islands would be colonized by man and thus would subsequently experience the greatest extent of environmental degradation. The different elevations of the high and low islands above the sea has also had a profound effect on the establishment, evolution, and survival of their biota. During periods of the major worldwide glaciations, sea level has fallen by over 100 m during the coldest periods, exposing the whole Seychelles Bank or replacing the Aldabra Atoll with an island. During periods of glacial melt, the seas have risen but never more than 10 m a.m.s.l., as is evidenced by the fragments of coral limestone that are still attached to granite boulders close to the shore on both Mahé and Praslin.

When we visit any of these islands today it is difficult to appreciate what they must have been like before the arrival of the first

seafarers. Without doubt these islands must have been visited by travelers sailing between the Far East, Arabia, and the east coast of Africa, but they left little sign of their visits. The first record we have is of John Jourdain, who visited Mahé in 1609 and wrote: "It is a very good refreshing place for wood, water and coker nutts, fish and fowle, without any feare or danger, except allargartes; for you cannot discern ever any people had been here before us" (Proctor 1984, 195). The crocodiles very soon disappeared, though the presence of the Nile crocodile on Mahé and Aldabra in the distant past and the few surviving animals on Madagascar make us wonder how these large reptiles succeeded in colonizing these isolated landmasses. It might be tempting to imagine that they represent animals which survived from Gondwanaland, as the amphibians almost certainly did, but the answer to this question is provided by studies on Aldabra. Fossil studies on this large atoll show that over the last 175,000 years or so the atoll has been inundated and its animals and plants destroyed five (or as many as nine) times. Subsequently it had been recolonized from other islands or mainland sources that remained above the rising sea. Crocodiles might have arrived periodically on the atoll, but they are only likely to have survived during a period of great sea depression, when the land area was larger, the habitats more diverse and, above all, areas of standing fresh water widely distributed.

The best-known example of such animal dispersal is probably that of another reptile, the giant tortoise of the Indian Ocean, the Caribbean, the Galapagos, and the Mediterranean, which seems to have been characteristic of these oceanic areas. It was in fact their bony armor (the dorsal carapace joined to a ventral plastron) that preadapted them to such a mode of dispersal, for they could not only float well for long periods, but being cold-blooded they could survive for very long periods without food or water. The fact that the islands had populations of giant tortoises was probably because large species or individuals were more likely to survive long periods floating in the sea at the mercy of the currents. Similarly upon arrival on a distant beach they could survive in dry environments that would be quite impossible for other terrestrial vertebrates.

That giant tortoises disappeared from all the islands that had sufficient freshwater for human settlement clearly demonstrates what a devastating effect people have had on these biota. Indeed if we look at records for the Indian Ocean, it is clear that within little more than a hundred years human settlers had exterminated these reptiles on all the islands except Aldabra, where the bush was too thick (and the atoll too remote) for the hunters to locate the tortoises once their numbers were drastically reduced (but not low enough to prevent them continuing to breed in the seclusion of the *Pemphis acidula* scrub). The large terrestrial lemurs on Madagascar and the large flightless birds of both Madagascar and the Mascarenes also disappeared over a similarly short time interval.

By the late eighteenth century, Malavois reported that the forests of Mahé were already "greatly depleted" and the "once prodigiously abundant tortoises are now rare." As a result of these observations he began a program of land reform and conservation when he became commandant in 1788. Throughout this early period the human population was quite low, rising from 250 in 1788 to 7,300 (largely slaves) in 1818. By the late 1800s the island's economy was largely based on coconuts, which had led to the destruction and replacement of most of the fringing bush. At this time Alfred Russell Wallace, another great traveler and evolutionary theorist, visited the Seychelles and reported in 1880 that "Geoffrey Neville tells us that at Mahé it was only in a few spots near the summits of the hills that he could perceive any remains of the ancient flora. Pine-apples, cinnamon, bamboos and other (alien) plants have obtained a firm footing, covering large tracts of country and killing the more delicate native flowers and ferns" (Proctor 1984, 197)

Biologists have long recognized that the number of species of animals or plants found on an island is a function of its land area. Studies of insects demonstrate this observation in relation to the Seychelles. On the islands in order of decreasing area, we find 2,090 species on the granitic Seychelles, 307 on Aldabra, 93 in the Amirantes, 92 on Bird and Denis, and 27 on Astove. Such island-area relationships are over-simplistic generalizations, for they do not take into account the effects of elevation on increasing land area, but more importantly, the effect that this has on increasing precipitation. John Peake demonstrated this clearly in 1971 when he showed that although there was a reasonable linear correlation between land area and the number of terrestrial molluscs on Indian Ocean islands, if this data were separated into that obtained for low islands and that for high islands, it was possible to derive two significant linear correlations between species numbers and land area. In other words, the greater number of species observed on high islands was closely related to such factors as the more mesic climate found on these islands and the greater geomorphological and physiographic diversity available in consequence of their greater elevation.

When we look at the plants and animals of the granitic Seychelles compared with those of the low atolls or sand cays, it is evident that we are observing ancient elements along with others that are of much more recent origin or arrival. The geographic relationships of these biota are not all that it might seem, for al-

though the plate tectonic events of up to 75 million years past may seem a long time ago, many of the organisms we encounter are themselves of very ancient origin. It is not in the least surprising that the more primitive the organism is, the more likely it is to be related to one of these ancient Gondwanaland groups. An additional factor is the question of dispersal, for if the organism is of more recent origin, then it will have been carried to the Seychelles either by sea, air, or some other mobile agency whether that be a floating "island," a plant (a tree trunk), or on or in an animal's body. Plants and animals that live in or close to the sea are adapted to the extremes of that environment, but most terrestrial (non-strand) species cannot withstand even short-term immersion in seawater. Plants of the seashore or their fringing environments (including mangrove swamps) produce seeds that are capable of floating in the sea and that will remain dormant until they are washed ashore. Perhaps the best known of these are the coconuts (*Cocos nucifera*) and the mangrove, whose fruits begin to germinate before they drop into the water and are thus capable of immediately producing anchoring roots as soon as the tide goes down and they settle into the mud of some remote creek. For any plant that does not live on the strand, it must be carried beyond that alien environment, and because its seeds cannot withstand immersion in seawater, they must be deposited by some other agency, for which the only obvious candidate is the air (for very small seeds) or via some animal agency (most probably a bird).

A feature that is of the utmost importance to plants when colonizing land is the presence of freshwater for their growth and survival. On small islands, it is usually absent, so we may observe that such places are colonized only by strand plants. On slightly larger islands (of a few hectares), freshwater may be present either in rocky pools or, more commonly, below the surface as a lens of freshwater, derived from evaporation of seawater and subsequent condensation, riding on the subterranean seawater. With larger surface areas, there is enough freshwater for plants but not enough to support human settlers. Where the amount of available water is enough to support humans, the number of plant species rises sharply and consists almost entirely of introduced plants that have been transported there either deliberately or accidentally. Many of these are, not surprisingly, weeds that often pose serious threats to many members of the indigenous flora.

The biota of the granitic Seychelles must be viewed in the context of the organisms that have evolved or have become established on other islands or microcontinents in the region. The largest of these is Madagascar (587,042 km²) which, due to its large size, age, and physiographic diversity has a rich vertebrate fauna of which all but 2 of the 159 species of amphibians are endemic, and 18 of 22 genera. As many as 257 species of the 280 species of reptiles are endemic. Five families of birds are almost entirely restricted to Madagascar, but the indigenous avifauna comprises only about 189 species (excluding the migrants and sea birds). The native mammals include 76 species, of which 73 are endemic. An important feature of the evolution of the fauna of Madagascar is that although we may find endemic families among these ancient biota, the number of species is spread through a comparatively small number of genera. Their biogeographic affinities are largely with Africa but also demonstrate a strong Asian element. This is perhaps most easily illustrated by the large fruit bats, or flying foxes (*Pteropus* spp.), which are found in Madagascar, on the islands of the Indian Ocean, including Zanzibar, and from there across Asia and through the Southeast Asia archipelago to Australia, although surprisingly they never established themselves on the African mainland, which has a rich fruit bat fauna of its own. An equally interesting pattern is demonstrated by the attractive green geckos of the genus *Phelsuma*, which occurs in Madagascar (one species is claimed to occur in Namibia) and along the islands of the Indian Ocean to the Andaman Islands off the coast of Burma but never in India or eastern Asia. These biogeographic connections may seem remote today, but as recently as the last major glaciation, from about 30,000 to 9,000 years ago, the lowering of sea level was such that the chain of islands exposed in the Indian Ocean allowed a movement of individuals that would today be impossible.

Similar levels of endemism are observed in the fauna of the granitic Seychelles, whose land area is only 0.01% of that of Madagascar. Among the vertebrate fauna, the amphibians, which are characteristically poorly represented on islands, comprise 7 genera and 11 species, of which 5 or 6 genera, 10 (9?) species, and 1 family are endemic. The legless caecilians have radiated to a remarkable degree in the Seychelles, with 5 species of the genus *Grandisonia* recorded on 8 islands (2 species on 1 island, 1 on 3, 1 on 4, and 1 on 5). The reptiles are potentially more mobile than the amphibians, especially lizards such as the geckos, several of which have been introduced on boats, although others probably could have been carried on floating islands that became detached from other continental or microcontinental landmasses. This latter occurrence is very well exemplified by the lizards, which have mainly Madagascan affinities and to a lesser degree, African (e.g., *Chamaeleo*). What is very clear is that the majority may be only specifically or subspecifically distinct, which relationship almost certainly reflects their relative dispersability. This phenomenon is also illustrated by the birds, which except for the flightless birds (formerly not uncommon in this region, though today only the

Aldabra Flightless White-Throated Rail, *Dryolimnas cuvieri*, survives), are extremely mobile. So as a consequence, most of the 40 species listed for Seychelles are at most subspecifically distinct, and 55% have strong Madagascan affinities. The Seychelles can boast few discrete species, but those that are distinct are probably specialists that have been isolated on these islands for a long time. Mammals are poor dispersers, so not surpisingly the only endemic species are bats, which probably traveled widely between islands during glacial periods as the sea level fell.

Plants, by contrast, must be dispersed by physical or animal agency so it is to be expected that on remote islands, and especially those with favorable climates, radiation will be common, giving rise to a very rich flora. Even so, the astonishing variety of the Madagascan flora is staggering: 180 families (6 or 7 endemic), 1,600 genera (about 25% endemic), and 10,000–12,000 species (85% endemic). These figures can only really be fully appreciated when one observes the flora of the African mainland, where only about 8,000 species occur in the Guineo-Congolian regional center of endemism, an area of 2.8 million km², though it contains a similar level of endemics (approximately 80%), whereas the arid northeastern Somalian-Masai regional center of endemism only carries about 2,500 species (about 50% endemic) in 1.9 million km². The wealth of the Madagascan flora is illustrated amply by the fact that in the last four years, botanists from the Royal Botanic Gardens, Kew, have found 27 new species of palm in the greatly depleted forests.

If we compare the Seychelles flora with that of Madagascar we find that the total number of flowering plants, ferns, and fern allies comprise more than 850 species, of which there is 1 endemic family (0.077%), 9 endemic genera (2.01%), and 69 endemic species (8%). The indigenous species of flowering plants comprise 19.9% of the total, but they are outnumbered by the cultivated and naturalized species, which represent about 54% of the flora; however, if we include those species whose status is unknown, this proportion could be as high as 70%. These figures contrast strikingly with those for Madagascar, where greater size, longer-term relative stability, and geomorphological and climatic diversity have all played an important role in generating an astonishing floral richness. Perhaps the most interesting and not unexpected feature of the endemic flora illustrated here is the observation that within the granitic archipelago, there is very little sign of evolutionary species radiation. The 76 endemic species are spread across 41 families and 65 genera, within which 31 families are represented only by a single species. The low islands of Aldabra and its neighbors are represented by a total flora of 274 species, of which 42 (15.3%) are endemic, 134 (48.9%) are indigenous and widespread, and 87 (31.7%) have been introduced as alien weeds or cultivated plants. Not surprisingly the pteridophytes are only represented by 2 species in these intensely seasonal and arid environments.

The natural vegetation of the granitic Seychelles inhabits the lowland and coastal habitats of the seashore, the mangroves, and the dry forest habitats, especially of the smaller islands and the drier sections of Mahé, which are largely dominated by palms. On the main mountain slopes and especially in areas of elevated rainfall, the forests are divided into the lowland forests, the intermediate forests on the slopes, and the mountain moss forests, which are subjected to frequent cloud cover and mist. The lowland forests formerly were dense habitats that came almost down to the strand, but it is the intermediate forests that are much richer in endemic species. The summit moss forests also contain endemics, but these tend to be the more specialized species.

The endemic plants of the Seychelles, which have been so brilliantly portrayed by Rosemary Wise in this book, are one of the great biological highlights of these glorious islands, where General Gordon was quite convinced that he had found the Garden of Eden on Praslin among the bizarre coco de mer (*Lodoicea maldivica*) of the Vallée de Mai. We can only guess at what the moist tropical forests must have looked like during periods of low sea level, when up to 50,000 km² of land would have been exposed. Although the flora must have been much richer at the time(s) of maximum terrestrial extension, we have no idea how many species would have failed to survive the return of high sea levels. Today, on the highest granitic island of Mahé, small remnants of the original upland forest still survive in minute pockets, where human settlement has so far, fortunately, been impossible.

Long gone from the lower slopes of Mahé, having been consumed for boat-building and fuel, are the large stands of the magnificent bois de fer (*Vateriopsis seychellarum*), which could reach heights of 30 m.[1] This tree is of special interest, for in addition to being large, it is also a representative of the family Dipterocarpaceae and is the only member in the Seychelles of this essentially Asian (and particularly Southeast Asian) family, which dominates the forests of those areas. In terms of their phytogeography, the plants possess strong indications of the very ancient origins of several species and it is perhaps those, whose dispersal mechanisms are not designed for long-distance movement that dominate the endemic plants, just as we have observed above with the rela-

tively nonmobile amphibians. In addition to *Lodoicea maldivica* and *Vateriopsis seychellarum*, we may also add the incredibly rare and endangered *Medusagyne oppositifolia*, the bois meduse, which represents a single species in one genus and is placed in an endemic family of its own, the Medusagynaceae, which are now found only as a few small specimens on rocky slopes of Mahé. It is a little difficult to single out particular plants for mention but one obvious candidate is *Nepenthes pervillei*, the pitcher plant, or liane pot à eau, which can still be found on the higher levels of Mahé and Silhouette.[2]

The most impressive and memorable feature of the Seychelles flora has to be the palms, for the occurrence of 6 monospecific genera on landmasses covering less than 300 km² in the Indian Ocean immediately brings to mind the processes of isolation and evolution that are so evident on tropical oceanic islands. The drier islands and environments, where most of these palms occur, are magical places, and the Vallée de Mai the finest of them all. These palms comprise the chou palmiste (*Deckenia nobilis*), coco de mer (*Lodoicea maldivica*), latanier millepatte (*Nephrosperma vanhoutteanum*), latanier feuille (*Phoenicophorium borsigianum*), latanier hauban (*Roscheria melanochaetes*), and latanier latte (*Verschaffeltia splendida*), whose leaves crackle in the wind as we breathe in the mysterious atmosphere of these places. In spite of the great interest that has been generated by the endemic plants of these islands, this is the first time that many of them have been illustrated in this manner. Perhaps most surprising of all is to learn how little we still know about their ecology and biology; for example, more than one recent publication suggests that the coco de mer is wind pollinated (presumably because it has a catkin-like inflorescence), yet the primeval magic of the Vallée de Mai is permeated by odor of mouse droppings, which is being generated by the male inflorescence to attract carrion-seeking dipterans, bees, and wasps.[3] The larger gecko (*Aeluronyx seychellensis*), chameleons (*Chamaeleo tigris*), and endemic snails (*Stylodonta studeriana*) will also all be found gathering around these flowers.

The extensive biological interest in and vulnerability of these riches were recognized when the Vallée de Mai and Aldabra were declared World Heritage sites in 1982 and 1983. They are now administered by the Seychelles Islands Foundation, which needs the support of all of us if this small country is to be able to preserve and treasure its fragile living wonders.

---

[1] The genus *Vateria* contains three species: one in India, one in Sri Lanka, and one in the Seychelles. Some authors place the Seychelles species in a separate genus—*Vateriopsis*.

[2] *Nepenthes* (Nepenthaceae) has a distribution which mirrors that of the fruit bats, being found on Madagascar, in the Seychelles, and on Sri Lanka, through India to Southeast Asia, north Queensland, and New Caledonia.

[3] The flies (dipterans) are after carrion or dung; the bees and wasps after nectar.

REFERENCES AND FURTHER READING

Beaver, K., and Chong Seng, L. 1992. *Vallée de Mai*. Mahé, Seychelles: SPACE Publishing Division.

Benson, C. W. 1984. Origins of Seychelles land birds. In *Biogeography and ecology of the Seychelles Islands*, edited by D. R. Stoddart. The Hague: Junk.

Bulpin, T. V. n.d. *Islands in a forgotten sea*. Howard Timmins.

Cheke, A. S. 1984. Lizards of the Seychelles. In *Biogeography and ecology of the Seychelles Islands*, edited by D. R. Stoddart. The Hague: Junk.

Coe, M., and Swingland, I. R. 1984. Giant tortoises of the Seychelles. In *Biogeography and ecology of the Seychelles Islands*, edited by D. R. Stoddart. The Hague: Junk.

Cox, C. B., and Moore, P. D. 1980. *Biogeography: An ecological and evolutionary approach*. 3d ed. Oxford: Blackwell Scientific Publications.

Diamond, A. W. 1984. Biogeography of Seychelles land birds. In *Biogeography and ecology of the Seychelles Islands*, edited by D. R. Stoddart. The Hague: Junk.

Fosberg, F. R., and Renvoize, S. A. 1980. *The Flora of Aldabra and neighbouring islands*. Kew Bulletin (Additional Series), vol. 7. London: HMSO.

High, J. n.d. *The natural history of the Seychelles*. London: Phillips.

IUCN Directory of Afrotropical protected areas. 1987. Gland, Switzerland: IUCN.

Jolly, A., Oberl, P., and Albignac, R., eds. 1984. *Key environments: Madagascar*. Oxford: Pergamon Press.

Lionnet, G. n.d. *Striking plants of Seychelles*. London: Phillips.

———. 1986. *The romance of the palm: Coco de mer*. Mauritius: L'île aux Images.

Mabberley, D. J. 1990. *The plant book*. Cambridge: Cambridge University Press.

Nussbaum, R. A. 1984. Amphibians of the Seychelles. In *Biogeography and ecology of the Seychelles Islands*, edited by D. R. Stoddart. The Hague: Junk.

Procter, J. 1984. Floristics of the granitic islands of the Seychelles. In *Biogeography and ecology of the Seychelles Islands*, edited by D. R. Stoddart. The Hague: Junk.

———. 1984. Vegetation of the granitic islands of the Seychelles. In *Biogeography and ecology of the Seychelles Islands*, edited by D. R. Stoddart. The Hague: Junk.

Robertson, S. A. 1989. *Flowering plants of the Seychelles*. Kew: Royal Botanic Gardens.

Stoddart, D. R. 1984. Scientific studies in the Seychelles. In *Biogeography and ecology of the Seychelles Islands*, edited by D. R. Stoddart. The Hague: Junk.

Walsh, R. P. D. 1984. Climate of the Seychelles. In *Biogeography and ecology of the Seychelles Islands*, edited by D. R. Stoddart. The Hague: Junk.

White, F. 1983. *The vegetation of Africa*. Natural Resources Research 20. Paris: UNESCO.

A BRIEF ACCOUNT OF
THE HISTORY OF SEYCHELLES
*(INCLUDING BOTANICAL
EXPLORATION)*

915. Ancient Arab manuscripts allude to "High islands beyond the Maldives." A series of typically Arab graves at Anse Lascars on Silhouette Island indicate that traders certainly visited the islands in the past.

1498. The Portuguese established trade routes across the Indian Ocean. Vasco da Gama (1460–1524) sailed from Malindi to India. The spices solely obtainable from the Far East were an important commodity.

1502. On da Gama's second such voyage, the coral island group now known as the Amirantes was sighted and named Ilhas do Almirante, commemorating his appointment to Admiral.

1503. The Portuguese João da Nova named an island group after himself, Jean de Nove. This was renamed Farquhar after the governor of Mauritius, Sir Robert Farquhar.

1505. The Portuguese mariner Pedro de Mascarenhas explored the area and named three islands, the Mascarenes, after himself, the present-day Mauritius, Réunion and Rodriguez.

1553. A Portuguese sailor, João de Baros, wrote in his *Decadas de Asia*, "a fruit larger than the ordinary coconut grows beneath the sea and its health-giving properties are far greater than the precious Bezoar stone."

1577–1580. Sir Francis Drake (1504–1596) circumnavigated the world and set up the first English colony in the Moluccas, a location renowned for the spices that were grown there..

1559. Elizabeth I of England granted a charter to the East India Company. Their first three voyages were to the Moluccas to import pepper and other spices. But the Dutch-ruled spice monopoly there soon prohibited this.

1606. Seychelles were recorded on Portuguese charts as either Seven Brothers or Seven Sisters, following Fernão Soares' voyage.

1609. The *Ascension* of the English East India Company, accompanied by two other ships commanded by Alexander Sharpeigh, was the fourth expedition to sail from England on a spice mission, but this time destined for India. During a storm after rounding the Cape of Good Hope, all the ships were separated and Sharpeigh sailed on alone, eventually anchoring off Mahé on January 21. John Jordaine, a company factor, wrote, "Noe signe of any people that ever had bene there." He added, "We found many coker nutts, both ripe and green, of all sorts, and much fishe and fowle and tortells, but our men would not eate any of them, they did look so ugly before they were boiled. . . . A good refreshing place without any feare or danger, except the allagartes. . ." Another wrote of the quality of the timber and called Seychelles

"An earthly paradise." (These quotations are taken from journals written by several of the crew members. Quoted in McAteer, 1991.) Sharpeigh did not make any claim for the islands on behalf of Great Britain.

In the intervening years these isolated islands were visited mainly by traders and certainly by pirates who sailed between Madagascar and the Red Sea wreaking havoc with the ships sailing from Europe to India and the Far East. Many stories abound today in Seychelles of untold wealth buried on the islands. Olivier de Vasseur, commonly called La Buse (the Buzzard), was reputed to have thrown a cryptic message, "Find my treasure who can," to the crowds before being hanged on Bourbon. (Excavations started in the 1940s at Bel Ombre on Mahé and are ongoing.)

1662. After attempts to establish settlements on Madagascar were unsuccessful, the French moved to one of the Mascarene Islands and named it Isle de Bourbon (now Réunion).

1710. The French took over Mauritius from the departing Dutch and renamed it Isle de France (now Mauritius). These two Mascarene islands were administered for the crown by the Compagnie Français des Indes Orientales.

1735. Bertrand-François Mahé de La Bourdonnais (1699–1753) was appointed governor-general of both islands and was based at Port Louis, the capital of Isle de France. One of his aims was to expand the French settlements at Pondichéry (Pondicherry) in India. Voyages between the Mascarenes and India were then dependent on the monsoon currents, following the old Portuguese trading route via Madagascar and then proceeding north of the Maldives.

1740–1748. The war of Austrian succession followed the death of Emperor Charles and the succession of his eldest daughter as queen. England alone supported her and faced hostility from the European countries that advanced counterclaims for rulership, including France. Maria Theresa was acclaimed the rightful monarch of Austria in 1748. England and France were also fighting for supremacy in India.

1742. Lazare Picault (?–1747), captain of the *Elizabeth*, was sent on an expedition by La Bordonnais in August. The objective was to chart the unmarked hazards of the islands and reefs northeast of Madagascar with a view to a shorter journey to India. Picault landed on Jean de Nove and found larger and tastier tortoises than the ones on Rodriguez. (Tortoises were taken alive from the islands and shipped back as a beef substitute.) On November 20, Picault was joined by Jean Grossin, commanding the *Charles*, and landed at Anse Boileau (Mahé). Picault wrote, "No mauvais bette," although there

were at that time hordes of crocodiles. He also saw many birds, bats, tortoises, and fish and referred to the island as Isle Abundance. Grossin noted large trees with straight trunks, ideal for ships' masts. Anse Lazare in the south of Mahé was named after him.

1744. Picault returned in May and anchored off present-day Victoria. He named the harbor Port Royal and islands Isles de Labourdonnais with the largest one, Isle Mahé. In June, en route to India, Picault visited the second largest island and gave it the name Isle de Palme. (This was later renamed Praslin, after César Gabriel de Choiseul Chevigny, Duc de Praslin, first lord of the Admiralty under Louis XV.)

1755. To try to break the Dutch monopoly of the spice trade, Pierre Poivre (1719–1786), the intendant (second in command) to the new governor-general, Colonel Jean-Daniel Dumas, made an unsuccessful attempt to establish a spice garden on Isle de France. Poivre was a keen botanist and had formerly learned about spice growing during time spent in Indonesia. He was the founder of Pamplemousses Gardens on Mauritius.

1756. France and England were engaged in the Seven Years' War when all the French colonial empire, including Canada, was lost to the English. The settlements in India were also lost but later given back. The Compagnie Français des Indes Orientales relinquished its affairs in the Indian Ocean islands and India, and control henceforth came under the minister of marine in Versailles, France, who at that time was the Duc de Praslin.

Le Cerf and *St. Benoit*, under the command of the half-Irish Corneille Nicholas Morphey, anchored off Isle Mahé on the feast of Saint Anne, September 9. On November 1, he claimed the islands for France and laid the Stone of Possession (which can be seen in the National Museum). Carved onto this are the arms of France and the inscription Isle de Séchelles in honor of the French finance minister, Vicomte Jean Moreau de Séchelles. The largest of the offshore islands was named Sainte Anne, commemorating the day of their arrival. Between this and the islands he named Longue and Ronde is Moyenne, meaning "middle." Cerf was named after his ship. Morphey's men explored the interior of Isle Mahé, and he wrote the first description of it, suggesting that the rugged terrain would be unsuitable for general habitation but the large, accessible harbor of the main island and the possibilities of exporting timber made it an excellent and strategic base. He wrote, "The various valuable trees that grew everywhere on the island astonished us." Although he was not able to visit Isle de Palme, he renamed it Isle Moras. A small island off Praslin, with exposed reddish soil, he named Isle Rouge.

1763. The Treaty of Paris ended the Seven Years' War. Although the Seychelles Islands were not at the time considered to be of great strategic importance, ministers in Isle de France realized that they did not want them to fall into English hands. Isle Mahé had an excellent harbor that was capable of accommodating two hundred ships. On land there was the plentiful supply of timber.

1768. Nicolas Marion Dufresne (1746–1772) was sent on an expedition to Isle de Séchelles to cut timber and collect tortoises, a valuable source of protein, as by now the populations on Rodriguez were almost exterminated. *La Digue*, under the command of Jean Duchemin, and *Curieuse*, under Lieutenant Lampériare, anchored off Mahé in October and the crew camped ashore, reporting much trouble from the crocodiles. They also reported problems with the slaves who were reluctant to work. Five escaped and were left behind, but there are no records of them after this; whether they survived or fell prey to the crocodiles is unknown. Duchemin described many aspects of the flora and fauna. The *Curieuse* left Isle Mahé in November to explore Isle Moras. Lampériaire acquired the island for France and renamed it Isle Praslin after the minister of marine. One of his officers returned from a trip ashore saying that he had seen "some sort of palmiste which covered the mountains; not a single tree suitable for anything but firewood." This was the legendary coco de mer (*Lodoicea maldivica*). The entrepreneurial expedition surveyor, Brayer du Barré, took thirty of their fruits with him to sell in India.

The extreme value of the coco de mer fruits plummeted with the solution of their mysterious origin. Prior to this, they had changed hands for colossal sums of money because of their extreme rarity, the mystery of their origin, and their reputed aphrodisiacal properties.

Lampériaire also named Aride, Cousin, Cousine, Felicité, Isle aux Fous (the small island between Praslin and Aride, now more commonly known as Booby), La Digue (after the ship), Marianne, Ronde, and the Three Sisters (which is puzzling because there are only two islands there, not three).

On Christmas Day, Duchemin proclaimed that all the islands that comprised the Seychelles archipelago were annexed to France.

1769. Alexis-Marie Rochon (1741–1817), a French naval astronomer, visited Isle Mahé and recorded its correct position. He sailed on the *Heure de Berger*, commanded by Lt. Jacques Grenier, who was the one to prove that a shorter sea route was indeed possible from Isle de France to India via Seychelles, as opposed to the old Portuguese routes. On Praslin, the two men collected living plants of coco de mer to take back to France. The forward-thinking Rochon was critical of slavery.

1770. Poivre, still determined to set up a spice garden, returned from retirement in France. Nutmeg and clove plants were obtained somehow from the Moluccas and unloaded at Port Louis. Within a year it became obvious that the soil and climatic conditions on Isle de France were not suitable and, as before, the plants perished.

The first twenty-eight settlers sailed from Port Louis on the *Thélémaque* and arrived on August 27. Major Delauney, the officer in charge, decided that Ste. Anne would be preferable to Isle Mahé. He remained in Seychelles as an unofficial commandant of the colony. A person of dubious character, Barré planned this settlement as a half-way point for the slave trade between Africa and Isle de France. He envisaged coconut and fish-oil factories, a spice garden, and fortification of the island and obtained financial support from many private sponsors.

1771. Duroslan, having taken over command of the *Heures de Berger*, explored an uncharted island to the south of Isle Mahé and named it Isle Berger. Between there and Isle Mahé he also named Etoile, Marie Louise, and Isle des Noeufs, and a sand cay Bondeuse. He visited the settlement on Sainte Anne. Formal possession of both Silhouette and La Digue was taken for France by Oger, an officer under Duroslan.

The *Etoile du Matin*, under the command of Captain Labiolliere, sailed to the Amirantes. Labiolliere named D'Arros, Desroche, Poivre, Remire, and St. Joseph Islands. The shorter sea route from Isle de France to India via Seychelles was now fully charted.

The English were informed of the French possession of the islands, and the Bombay Council sent ships to ascertain the possible threats to English settlements in the Indian Ocean.

Antoine Gillot was sent to Isle Mahé by Poivre and selected Anse Royale, in the southwest, as a suitable site for the Jardin du Roi spice garden, independent of the one set up on Ste. Anne by Brayer du Barré and Delauney.

1772. Gillot and an ex-soldier, Pierre Hangard, returned to Seychelles with clove, nutmeg, pepper, and cinnamon plants from the Pamplemousses garden and established the spice garden.

The enthusiasm of the first settlers was dampened by constant disagreements and the failure of their food crops. The majority were taken off, leaving a skeleton crew to maintain the French possession. Hangard eventually left Gillot and initially lived on Ste. Anne in the abandoned settlement and grew vegetables for the colonists. He remained in Seychelles for the rest of his life, having at one time vast areas of land on Isle Mahé and ninety slaves.

1773. Denis de Trobriand, commander of the *Etoile*, sighted and landed on two coral islands north of Isle Mahé, named them Denis and Isle aux Vaches (now Bird Island), and claimed them for France.

1777. Brayer du Barré left Isle de France after being proclaimed a fraud and a troublemaker by the Bourbon ordonnater De Crémont. His false claim of a prosperous silver mine in Seychelles, used as a means of extracting yet more money from sponsors, was exposed.

1778. A military detachment under Lt. Charles de Romainville, arrived on the *Hélène* to restore discipline and to build a commandant's house, barracks, prison, hospital, and slave accommodation on Isle Mahé. This area was called L'Etablissement, later to become Victoria.

1780. Romainville ordered the spice garden to be burned when ships sighted off Anse Royale were mistakenly thought to be British. All was destroyed except the cinnamon, which ironically proved itself to be a highly successful introduction—to the cost of the native vegetation.

1785. Many from the garrison had died or deserted and the replacements from the Pondichéry Regiment fared no better. Records reveal that 13,000 tortoises were exported over a five-year period.

1787. The first constitution was drafted by the governor-general, with strict control over collecting tortoises, turtles, and coco de mer and over general bartering of goods. The ownership of more than one area of land was to be reduced to a single plot and granted only to those who were prepared to cultivate it. The first administrator, Jean-Baptiste de Malavois, arrived at the same time as a new detachment of sepoy troops.

1793–1810. Privateering in the Indian Ocean was at its height. The notorious French-born pirate Jean-François Hodoul used Seychelles as his base and eventually retired there, becoming a justice of the peace under the British regime. A small island in the harbor of Victoria is named after him, and his grave can be seen in Bel Aire Cemetery.

1794. Chevalier Jean-Baptiste Quéau De Quinssy (1748–1827) took over as commandant, a position he held for eigh-

teen years and in which he acheived great respect. Records show there were 500 slaves, 70 white, and 30 free black inhabitants.

Five British ships anchored off L'Etablissement and Commodore Henry Newcome requested medical help, fresh water, and provisions. Vastly outnumbered, De Quinssy had little option but to capitulate to the enemy and to raise the Union Jack. This was to become the pattern. Each time British ships appeared, the astute De Quinssy lowered the tricolor and hoisted the British flag, so maintaining peace.

1798. The population reached 591 inhabitants; 487 of these were slaves.

1800. Following an unsuccessful assassination attempt on the life of Napoleon, the instigators and other Republican sympathizers were detained, and the minister of marine decided on Seychelles as the destination of 132 deportees. Thirty-eight prisoners were incarcerated on the *Flêche*. A further thirty-two sailed a month later on the *Chiffonne*. The latter reached Mahé first, landing its unwelcome passengers on July 14, Bastille Day.

On August 19, a battle with heavy losses to the French took place in the bay between the British *Sybille* (which had arrived flying the tricolor) and the *Chiffonne*, under repair in the harbor. The customary capitulation followed. After repairs were carried out, the *Sybille* left on September 2. The next day, nearing her destination after a seven-month voyage, the *Flêche* encountered the British *Victor*, and they fought near Frégate. The *Flêche* reached Mahé the following day, landed the prisoners, and carried on with the battle, eventually being holed and sunk. De Quinssy boarded the *Victor* with capitulation papers yet again.

Half of the Jacobin prisoners were eventually deported to the Comoros, only to be poisoned by the sultan. The remainder integrated successfully.

1804–1806. De Quinssy capitulated to the British repeatedly.

1809. The number of slaves had by now risen to 3,200.

1810. The British invade and capture Isle de France and, under the terms, claim all its dependencies.

Captain Philip Beaver, commanding the *Nisus*, sailed for Mahé, arrived on April 23, and informed De Quinssy that he was taking possession of the archipelago in the name of King George. De Quinssy capitulated for the seventh and final time. The Union Jack was to fly here for the next 165 years.

1814. The Treaty of Paris ended the Napoleonic Wars and Mauritius, Rodriguez, and Seychelles were ceded to Britain. Réunion remained French. De Quinssy anglicized his name to

Quincy and he remained in office. The Bourbons were restored in France, under Louis XVIII.

1818. Mahé, Praslin, La Digue, and Silhouette were reported to have been mostly stripped of their native vegetation.

1825. The population of Seychelles reached 7,000. The slaves, who had come mainly from Madagascar and Mozambique, outnumbered the white colonists thirteen to one. Far fewer were of Indian or Malay ancestry.

Around this time, Pierre Louis Poiret arrived on Mahé as the estate manager for the civil agent, Captain Edward Madge. Little was known about him but toward the end of his life he started to claim that he was the French dauphin who had been smuggled out of France following the death of his mother, Marie Antoinette. Miniatures of his supposed parents were found among his possessions after his death in 1856.

1835. Laws abolishing slavery were passed and within three years, 6,000 individuals were liberated in Seychelles. The lack of enforced labor necessitated a change in agriculture. Crops previously grown that needed more attention, such as coffee, cotton, sugarcane, and vegetables, were replaced by coconuts, cinnamon, and vanilla.

1841. L'Etablissement was renamed Victoria and the harbor, Port Victoria, after the queen of England.

Auguste Pervillé, head gardener at the Muséum d'Histoire Naturelle de Paris, made the first plant collection of any size. The endemic pitcher plant, *Nepenthes pervillei*, commemorates his name.

1861. The plantation owners were relieved when a ship arrived in Mahé with the first of the liberated slaves from Africa. Because the liberated local population refused to work, a poll tax was levied and they were allowed only plots of land for housing in return for three days paid work each week.

1862. On the night of October 12, after a long period of heavy rain, a landslide engulfed parts of Victoria and killed seventy-four inhabitants. This area is maintained as a sports field.

1862–1866. Sir John Kirk made several collecting trips to Seychelles.

1867. Dr. Edward Percival Wright, an Irish naturalist and lecturer in zoology at Trinity College, Dublin, visited Mahé. He collected and described new plant species. The endemic species *Pittosporum senacia* subsp. *wrightii*, *Syzygium wrightii*, and *Paragenipa wrightii* were all named after him.

1869. The Suez Canal was opened establishing a shorter trade route between Asia and Europe and Seychelles.

1871 and 1874. John Horne, who was first employed at the Royal Botanic Gardens, Kew, and later, from 1865–1891, was the director of the Pamplemousses Botanic Gardens, Mauritius, collected 700 herbarium specimens of Seychelles plants for the Royal Botanic Gardens. This was the first thorough investigation of the flora. The endemic sedge *Lophoschoenus hornei* and the frequently named *Northia hornei* (in this publication referred to as *Northia seychellana*) commemorate him.

1872. The explorer of Africa and contemporary of Livingstone, Sir Henry Morton Stanley, visited Seychelles for a month.

The islands were granted financial autonomy.

1875. The sultan of Perak, Abdullah Khan, was exiled from Malaysia and spent five years on Félicité.

1877. Baker's *Flora of Mauritius and the Seychelles* was published.

1881. General Charles Gordon of Khartoum visited Seychelles, exploring the possibilities of fortification in event of trouble with the French over Madagascar. He is perhaps better known in Seychelles for his theories on the Vallée de Mai being the site of the Garden of Eden and for designing a coat of arms for Seychelles, the basic design of which is still used.

1883. The intrepid Victorian traveler and painter Marianne North spent three months visiting Mahé, Praslin, Curieuse, and La Digue. Her many paintings of Seychelles are permanently exhibited in the gallery that she designed in the grounds of the Royal Botanic Gardens at Kew. The monotypic Seychelles genus *Northia* was named after her.

1887 and 1895. Smallpox epidemics drastically reduced the population.

1890. King Prempeh of Ashanti was exiled from West Africa to Seychelles and remained until 1924. He arrived in a leopard skin and left in morning coat, striped trousers, spats, and top hat!

The British government researched the possibility of setting up large prisoner-of-war camps to house captives of the Boer War but abandoned the idea.

1893. The first cable, operated by the Eastern Telegraph Company, linked Seychelles with the rest of the world.

1897. The administrator was given the power of a governor.

1899. Andrea Franz Wilhelm Schimper collected 140 plant specimens as part of the German expedition on the *Valdiva*.

H. P. Thomasset, a keen naturalist and the owner of Cascade Estate, west Mahé, and P. R. Dupont, the director of the botanic gardens in Victoria, made large collections of plants, which are now housed in the herbarium of the Royal Botanic Gardens, Kew. The endemic species *Grisollea thomassetii* and *Seychellaria thomassetii* were named after the former, and the synonym of *Psychotria pervillei*, *P. dupontii*, after the latter.

1903. Seychelles became a British Crown Colony under the first governor, Sir Ernest Bickham Sweet-Escott. The clock tower in the center of Victoria, which is a replica of one on Vauxhall Bridge, London, was erected to celebrate this new status.

1905 and 1908. Prof. J. S. Gardiner made large plant collections on Mahé and Silhouette during an expedition financed by the Percy Sladen Trustees.

1914–1918. The copra trade flourished during the First World War since nitroglycerin was manufactured from a copra derivative. The population of the islands had risen to 24,000 by the end of the war.

1922. Winston Churchill investigated the possibility of Seychelles being a potential location for detaining Irish political prisoners. The governor's suggestion that Cote d'Or on Praslin could be suitable was not accepted.

1923. Electricity was introduced to Mahé.

1924. State education started with classes in English as well as the native French.

1931. The Kew botanist, Victor Samuel Summerhayes, an authority on orchids, published a plant list containing 480 species, summarizing the lists of Baker, Hemsley, and the *Valdiva* expedition.

1936–1939. D. Vesey-Fitzgerald collected plants for the British Museum and Kew and reported on the vegetation.

1937. The League of Coloured People was created and laborers' wages and health care were prominent items on the agenda.

1939. The forerunner of the first political party was formed, The Taxpayers Association.

1939–1945. Approximately 2,000 Seychellois fought alongside the Allies in the Second World War. A seaplane depot was set up on Ste. Anne to protect the harbor if the need arose. The postwar governor, Sir Selwyn Clarke, realized that self-rule was inevitable.

1956. Archbishop Makarios of Cyprus spent one year in exile on Mahé.

1960. The population was now over 41,000. Christopher Swabey, visiting from Oxford University, suggested that more nature reserves should be established in Seychelles.

1960–1961. Dr. Charles Jeffrey, a botanist from Kew, spent six months studying the vegetation and made recommendations on the conservation and protection of certain localities.

1964. The first two political parties were formed: The Seychelles People's United Party, led by France-Albert René, advocated independence from Britain and James Mancham's Seychelles Democratic Party campaigned for closer links with Britain.

1967. Britain purchased the Amirante Islands of Farquhar and Des Roches from Seychelles and the Chagos Islands from Mauritius for communication and fueling purposes. Collectively they are known as the British Indian Ocean Territory, or BIOT, and by agreement are used jointly by the United States.

1970, 1972, and 1973. The Edinburgh-based botanist John Proctor visited Seychelles as a conservation advisor, made many collections, and rediscovered the monotypic *Medusagyne oppositifolia*, previously thought to be extinct.

1970. F. R. Fosberg collected plants for the Smithsonian Institution.

1971. The international airport was opened and tourism became the premier industry.

1975–1981. The botanist Mrs. S. A. Robertson lived in Seychelles, made large collections, and wrote *The Flowering Plants of Seychelles*.

1976. Seychelles gained independence from Britain on June 29. James Mancham became the first elected president of Seychelles with France-Albert René as prime minister.

1977. While James Mancham was attending a conference in London, a coup was organized and René assumed control. This date, June 5, is now celebrated as Liberation Day.

President René's party, was renamed the Seychelles People's Progressive Front and a new constitution was drafted.

1979, 1984, and 1989. President René was reelected.

1980. *The Flora of Aldabra and Neighbouring Islands* by F. R. Fosberg and S. A. Renvoise was published.

1981. An attempted coup, led by South African mercenaries, failed.

1981–1986. The botanist Dr. Francis Friedmann, from the Muséum National d'Histoire Naturelle in Paris, studied and made extensive collections of the plants of Seychelles.

1986. *Flowers and Trees of Seychelles* by Francis Friedmann was published.

1991. President René declared that Seychelles was to have a "pluralist democratic system," or multiparty state, so ending single-party rule.

1992. The exiled Sir James Mancham returned to the islands and reestablished his party.

1993. President René was reelected.

1994. The first volume of Dr. F. Friedmann's *Flore de Seychelles: Dicotylédons*, was published.

1994–1996. The Swedish botanist Dr. Annette Carlström studied and reported on the threats to the flora and habitats.

The population was estimated to be 72,800.

SELECTED
COLLECTING SITES

Although I have explored many areas of Seychelles for the purposes of this book, I have centered my collections, observations, sketching, and paintings on ten sites on five islands. Of the six on Mahé, Copolia, La Reserve, and Morne Blanc have well-maintained and clearly marked paths, permitting interested visitors the chance to observe the flora and fauna. Congo Rouge, Mont Sébért, and Bernica would be extremely difficult, if not impossible, to negotiate without a guide.

MAHÉ

Congo Rouge

This route, in the Morne Seychellois National Park, rises from 400 m at the start of the walk to 750 m at the highest point. (The recommended starting point is on the Sans Souci Road, 0.5 km west of the Mission viewpoint. The last part of this route, from the mist forest down to Le Niol, is extremely steep with little shade and is, for most people, considered to be too tiring an ascent at the beginning of a fairly long walk.) Allow five to six hours. A guide is essential because the route is little used and unmarked, and some scrambling over rocks is required. As with all forest walks, the ground can be slippery in wet weather, so suitable shoes must be worn. Habitats include open grassland, bamboo, cinnamon woodland, mist forest, and open rocky slopes. On clear days there are wonderful views from the highest point of the west coast and Thérèse and Conception Islands. (It is also spectacular on wet days to see great masses of clouds sweeping in and obliterating the landscape.) The panorama during the descent to Le Niol takes in Beau Vallon and the northwest peninsula and on out to Silhouette and North Islands. On exceptionally clear days, it is possible to see as far as the coralline Denis and Bird Islands, distances of 95 and 105 km north of Mahé. It is ideal to have two vehicles for this walk; one to drive to and leave at the start and another parked near the reservoir at Le Niol for transport back.

Endemic plants on Congo Rouge include *Dillenia ferruginea, Pittosporum senacia* subsp. *wrightii, Syzygium wrightii, Begonia seychellensis, Canthium sechellense, Craterispermum microdon, Psathura sechellarum, Glionnetia sericea, Rapanea seychellarum, Northia seychellana, Colea seychellarum, Nepenthes pervillei, Agrostophyllum occidentale, Hederorkis seychellensis, Malaxis seychellarum, Hypoxidia rhizophylla* and *H. maheensis, Curculigo sechellensis, Roscheria melanochaetes, Verschaffeltia splendida, Pandanus sechellarum, Protarum sechellarum, Seychellaria thomassetii, Mapania floribundum,* and *Garnotia sechellensis.*

Copolia

The walk starts from Bel Aire, on the Sans Souci inter-island road, Mahé, at 360 m, where there is a signpost at the roadside. The path is well maintained and marked. Some rocks are slightly difficult to negotiate near the summit (497 m), but markers indicate the best routes to follow. Allow at least three hours. There is a spectacular panoramic view of Victoria, the northwest peninsula and, to the east, the land reclamation down to the airport. Looking to the north, one sees the cluster of offshore islands (Ste. Anne, Beacon, Moyenne, Round, Long, and Cerf), and further out, the Praslin group. On clear days Frégate is visible to the northeast.

Habitats include woodland and an extensive glacis (area of exposed bedrock) at the top, with large numbers of the pitcher plant *Nepenthes pervillei*. This is possibly the most accessible location in which to see these fascinating carnivorous plants. Other endemic plants include *Dillenia ferruginea*, including some extremely dwarfed ones on the summit, *Erythroxylum sechellarum*, *Soulamea terminaliodes*, *Memecylon eleagni*, *Ixora pudica*, *Mimusops sechellarum*, *Hypoxidia rhizophylla*, *Deckenia nobilis*, *Pandanus sechellarum*, *P. multispicata*, *Protarum sechellarum*, and the sedge *Lophoschoenus hornei*.

Morne Blanc

The route starts at the west end of the Sans Souci inter-island road, near the Tea Tavern above Port Glaud. (Vehicles may be parked in the small car park opposite the restaurant.) The beginning of the route, at 420 m, is a short distance up the road from the car park and is indicated by a signboard. It is advisable to set out as early as possible because the first part of the walk, although taking only a matter of five or ten minutes, is in full sunlight, which can be tiring. From then on, until the summit (667 m), there is continuous shade from the trees. The path is well marked and maintained, steep in places but not difficult. At least three hours should be allowed to explore this area. Habitats include the rather exposed starting point, which has much citronella (lemon grass), mixed woodland, and a small area of mist forest at the summit. The view from the summit is again spectacular, with the deeply scalloped bays of western Mahé and, offshore, Thérèse and Conception Islands. Graceful tropical birds wheel around on the thermals above and alongside the cliff face, with its dramatic sheer drop of 250 m from the summit.

Endemic plants include *Dillenia ferruginea*, *Aphloia theiformis* subsp. *madagascariensis* var. *seychellensis*, *Syzygium wrightii*, *Meme-*

cylon eleagni, *Begonia seychellensis*, *Gastonia crassa*, *Psychotria pervillei*, *Timonius sechellensis*, *Northia seychellana*, *Procris insularis*, *Malaxis seychellarum*, *Deckenia nobilis*, *Roscheria melanochaetes*, and *Pandanus sechellarum*.

Bernica (Montagne Palmiste)

The route starts from Grand Anse River valley, western Mahé. It is possible to drive part way up the forestry track and to park near to the most suitable river crossing. Allow three hours. The path is not often used and is not marked, and the route is impossible to follow without a guide. Near the summit (270 m) there is a very steep rock face to negotiate. The "prize" of Bernica is the jellyfish tree, *Medusagyne oppositifolia*. The most approachable one is below the summit on the seaward side. To reach it, one has to pass through a small area of scrubby woodland on the summit and to descend a fairly steep glacis. (It is not recommended to attempt this in wet conditions because the smooth rock can be extremely slippery.) Good field characters of *Medusagyne* to be alert for are the scarlet senescent leaves and the rounded crown.

Habitats on Bernica include riverside, woodland, and glacis. Other endemic plants here include *Aphloia theiformis* subsp. *madagascariensis* var. *seychellensis*, *Memecylon eleagni*, *Psycotria pervillei*, *Paragenipa wrightii*, *Timonius sechellensis*, *Diospyros seychellarum*, *Deckenia nobilis*, and *Pandanus multispicatus*. Other plants of special interest are the tall trees of *Barringtonia racemosa* growing along the river, which often have beautiful pendulous inflorescences; the enormous bamboo thickets; and *Rhipsalis baccifera*, which can be seen soon after crossing the river. The latter is the only indigenous species of Cactaceae, the cactus family, found in Seychelles and is seen scrambling over the vertical rock face to the right of the path at the beginning of the ascent.

Mont Sébért

The route starts from Cascade, Mahé. Cars can be parked near the water treatment works, at 120 m. Allow at least four hours. The path is indistinct and not marked, and a guide is essential. Again, this walk is not recommended in wet conditions. Beside the rather steep climb at the beginning, alongside a watercourse, which can be muddy and slippery, there is an extensive, very smooth, very steep area of glacis to scale near the top. (This is rather daunting as there are very few footholds and it is not recommended for the faint-hearted.) An interesting excursion off the main path is a visit to an abandoned cinnamon distillery. It is difficult to believe that this overgrown ruin was in use until the 1950s and to conceive how the great chunks of metal were transported to the site along such steep and narrow paths for its construction.

From the summit of Mont Sébért at 550 m, one looks down onto the international airport and along the coast to the left to Victoria and the northwest peninsula. The nearby cluster of offshore islands is a picturesque sight, and on clear days it is possible to see the distant Praslin group to the north and Frégate to the west.

Habitats include grassland, woodland, glacis, and boulder field. Endemic plants include a single tree of *Medusagyne oppositifolia* (probably the same tree from which the species was described by Baker in 1877), *Glionnetia sericea*, *Timonius sechellensis*, *Mimusops sechellarum*, *Excoecaria benthamiana*, and various orchids, palms, and pandans.

La Reserve

The beginning of this walk is from the summit of the Montagne Posé Road, southern Mahé, at the entrance to Bon Espoir radio station at 240 m. Again, a signboard indicates the start. The paths are well marked and maintained and zig-zag up the shaded hillside to three viewpoints—the first at 340 m, the second at 400 m, and the third at 460 m. This is the easiest of all the sites, with no very difficult areas to negotiate. Allow at least four hours to reach all the viewpoints. All the endemic palms, except *Lodoicea maldivica*, are represented here, an area of Mahé most similar to Praslin's Vallée de Mai. The minute saprophytic *Seychellaria thomassetii* grows in several locations near to viewpoints 1 and 2. The third viewpoint is an area in which *Angraecum eburneum* subsp. *brongniartianum*, the tropic bird orchid and the national flower of Seychelles, can be found. A guide is necessary for those wanting to climb beyond these three viewpoints to the summit of Mt. Brulée because the route is not marked. This takes approximately twenty minutes to reach from viewpoint 3 but involves negotiating a ladder between massive rocks and climbing a very steep, often muddy bank. Looking toward the sea from Brulée, one can see a solitary tree of *Vateriopsis seychellarum* in the rocky area below the summit.

Some other endemic plants on La Reserve include *Dillenia ferruginea*, *Memecylon eleagni*, *Canthium carinatum*, *Paragenipa wrightii*, *Tarenna sechellensis*, *Gynura sechellensis*, *Colea seychellarum*, *Procris insularis*, *Malaxis seychellarum*, *Hypoxidia rhizophylla*, *Curculigo sechellensis*, *Pandanus sechellarum*, and *Mapania floribundum*.

Praslin (Vallée de Mai)

Praslin, 45 km from Mahé, is reached by about twenty regular flights per day from the domestic terminal at the international airport on Mahé. Flights take approximately fifteen minutes and give wonderful views of the offshore islands. Praslin can also be reached by schooner, but the departure times at either end are such that an overnight stay is necessary. This is the second largest island of the granitic group and measures 11 km by 5.5 km at its widest. The highest point is 367 m. The Vallée de Mai is a World Heritage Site and is open to visitors from 8 A.M. until 4:30 P.M. daily with the exception of Christmas Day. The most famous feature of this 30-hectare forest is the legendary *Lodoicea maldivica*, or coco de mer. Around 5,000 trees grow here, with approximately equal numbers of male and females. Endemic slugs, snails, and geckos visit the fetid-smelling flowers of the pendulous male inflorescenses. Visitors to Praslin can take advantage of guided tours around the Vallée de Mai, during which flora and fauna of special interest will be pointed out. A more leisurely wander around afterward is recommended because such a magnificent area deserves more than the fairly brisk, guided walk! On many occasions I have stood quietly and watched shy tenrec, small mammals introduced from Madagascar, ambling through the leaf litter. Sharp eyes can spot well-camouflaged chameleons and tree frogs on the foliage.

This area is the location thought by General Charles Gordon of Khartoum to be the original Garden of Eden as described in Genesis. During his visit in 1881, on a military mission from his base on Mauritius, he decided that the breadfruit tree, *Artocarpus altilis*, albeit an introduced species, was the tree of life. Coco de mer was the tree of the knowledge of good and evil, and the suggestive shape of the fruits "caused the plague of our forefathers in the Garden of Eden." The writer H. W. Estridge apparently pointed out to Gordon at a dinner party that the ten-centimeter thick husk would have been impossible for Eve to have bitten through. Gordon's reply was, "I had not thought of that."

The site has well-maintained paths, which are swept almost daily, and an information leaflet is supplied with the entrance ticket. All six endemic palms, the four endemic pandans or screw pines, and a wide range of other "specialities" are found here. The policy for many years has been to eradicate the exotic introductions, but pineapples, coffee, and ornamental palms are still very much in evidence. This is the only home of the Seychelles Black Parrot, *Coracopsis nigra barklyi*, one of the rarest birds in the world, with a total population below 100. One is more likely to hear the clear, high-pitched whistles in the canopy than to see the birds. It is well worth taking binoculars to look at fig trees where these birds and the Seychelles Blue Pigeon, *Alectroenas pulcherrima*, feed. Good close views of the parrots are often possible from the roadside below the entrance to the Vallée de Mai, where they feed on the small gherkin-like fruits of *Averrhoa bilimbi*. Allow at least three hours here, more if possible. The reserve must be treated with great respect. Collecting is strictly forbidden without prior permission from World Heritage, and visitors are requested not to leave the paths. The covering of fallen leaves often hides very deep chasms between boulders, as we unfortunately found in 1985 during our vegetation survey!

Curieuse

This small island, of 3 km², with its highest point, Curieuse Peak, at 172 m, lies 52 km northeast of Mahé and 1 km north of Praslin in the Curieuse Marine National Park. It is reached by boat from Côte d'Or (Anse Volbert), Praslin. Day trips to Curieuse can be arranged through the Praslin hotels or the travel services on Mahé.

The only plant that is not common elsewhere is *Secamone schimperianus*. Although the main population here grows on the higher parts of the island, the few isolated but more accessible plants in the Vallée de Mai could possibly be pointed out on request. Until the 1950s the leper colony established in 1833 was still in use. The doctor's house is at present (1996) being renovated and will soon become a visitors' center. The island has one of the best remaining mangrove areas in Seychelles, featuring *Rhizophora mucronata*, *Ceriops tagal*, *Bruguiera gymnorhiza*, and *Avicennia marina*. There is a boardwalk through the area that allows excellent views of these salt-tolerant trees. Some of the mangrove-related plants can also be seen: the fern *Acrostichum aureum*, *Hibiscus tiliaceus*, *Thespesia populnea*, *Xylocarpus granatum*, and *X. moluccensis*. The fruits of *Xylocarpus* are called jeu de patience or puzzle fruit in Seychelles. The large round fruits contain odd-shaped woody seeds that fit together closely. The object is to mix them up and to reassemble them.

The island has a large population of giant tortoises, brought from Aldabra as part of a controlled experiment—the monitoring of growth and reproduction rates on an island where the vegetation is more abundant and the habitat far less rugged than on their native island. Coco de mer grows naturally on the rocky slopes of Curieuse, with the large, fan-shaped leaves clearly seen from the sea. Early explorers named this island Isle Rouge because of the expanses of exposed red earth. In 1768, Marion Dufresne led an expedition to Seychelles and renamed the island Curieuse, after one of the expedition schooners. (La Digue was named after the second schooner.) Curieuse has had many fires, the most recent being in 1967 on the eastern peninsula. These have resulted in widespread erosion, a decrease in the fertility of the soil, and an intensification of the adverse effects of drought. (In tropical areas of high humidity the humus oxidizes rapidly, and unless nutrients are added to the soil, the fertility levels are reduced.) The drainage gullies constructed on the slopes should help to reduce further erosion, and the planted trees will eventually provide humus. There are various nature trails to follow, but it is requested that one does not leave the paths.

Aride

First discovered in 1756, Aride is the most northerly of the granitic islands—50 km northeast of Mahé and 16 km north of Praslin. After Aldabra, it is the second most important bird sanctuary of the Indian Ocean, with ten species of nesting seabirds. It was bought by Mr. Christopher Cadbury in 1973 and is a Seychelles Special Reserve, administered by the Royal Society for Nature Conservation. Guided tours are offered on the day excursions organized to Aride from Mahé and Praslin. Because of the possibilities of disturbing nesting seabirds on the hillside, exploration is at times confined to the plateau area only. Both of the endemic plants that are exclusive to Aride are found on this fertile coastal strip, growing just a few meters above sea level, although the main populations are higher up. When it is permissible, the relatively easy trail up through the wooded hillside to the highest point, Gros la Tête (134 m), is recommended. From the cliff top it is often possible to watch dolphins in the clear water below. This is also the best vantage point to see the Lesser and Greater Frigate birds, *Fregata ariel* and *F. minor*, gliding on the thermals or attacking returning seabirds. The latter are eventually forced to regurgitate their catch, which the acrobatic frigates swoop to retrieve. Often over 100 of these magnificent, almost prehistoric-looking birds are visible at a time, dominating the skies. They only roost on Aride and return to Aldabra to breed, but a hundred years ago they bred here, too, and it is hoped that they may do so again.

The visitor's landing fee goes toward the upkeep of this reserve. There are no facilities for overnight stays. One of the most beautiful of the endemic plants, Wright's gardenia, *Rothmannia annae*, grows naturally only on this 1.5 km by 0.5 km island. There is still some doubt about the status of the newly described *Peponium*. It is similar to and at present has the same name as an African species, but further research may possibly prove it to be a new endemic subspecies because there are several small but significant differences.

Aride has over a million resident nesting seabirds. Because of this, leaving the paths is strictly prohibited, for various reasons. The sooty terns, *Sterna fuscata*, lay their eggs and raise well-camouflaged chicks all over the hillside. The shearwaters, *Puffinus l'herminieri* and *P. pacificus*, excavate long underground burrows in the relatively looser soil off the path. If one steps on the roof of a burrow, it will collapse, causing possible injury to both intruder and bird. Also, some plants of *Peponium vogelii* climb over rocks and soil very close to the paths and could easily be damaged.

SILHOUETTE

This is the third largest of the granitics, 5 by 5 km, and it supports the only remaining area of primary forest in Seychelles. Mt. Dauban, named after the first family to settle here, rises to 780 m, second highest point to Mahé's Morne Seychellois at 905 m. Silhouette lies 19 km northwest of Mahé and was named after the French minister Etienne de Silhouette. Arab graves alongside the beach at Anse Lascars, indicate visitors, if not inhabitants, long before the arrival of the first Europeans in the eighteenth century. Silhouette is a government-owned island, and official permission to stay has to be sought from the Island Development Company (I.D.C.) unless one has booked to stay at the Silhouette Lodge Hotel. At present there are no organized facilities for exploration.

The island has a narrow coastal plateau on the eastern side, which supports the village of La Passe, with a jetty, hotel, and farm. The only other settlement is Grande Barbe on the southwest coast. A well-used path over the mountains connects the two settlements, and the higher reaches are botanically extremely rich. The path from La Passe to Anse Mondon on the north coast is regularly used, but botanically it is not particularly interesting. Other paths are not marked nor maintained, and it is not advisable to explore without a guide.

The terrain is very steep in places and, like all such sites, only to be attempted in dry conditions. Silhouette has its own endemic plants: *Psychotria silhouettae*, *Carissa edulis* var. *sechellensis*, *Achyrospermum seychellarum*, and *Pisonia sechellarum*, as well as most of the other endemic species. The plant currently called *Pseuderanthemum tunicatum*, which has its only location here, is slightly different from its counterparts, which are widespread throughout tropical Africa. It may prove to be a new subspecies with more critical research. Two other nonendemic plants of special interest that occur only on Silhouette are *Amaracarpus pubescens* and *Trilepisium madagascariensis*.

For all walks one needs to be reasonably fit and sensitive to the conservation of both flora and fauna. It is advisable to start walking as early as possible in the mornings, so as to get well on one's way before the heat of the sun becomes too great. Plenty of water should be carried, as well as protection against the sun. Keep to the paths. Footsteps very soon destroy the vegetation. Some of the mountain slopes have what appears to be solid earth between the boulders. This peaty soil is often only a veneer covering a network of fragile roots. Below these can be deep, empty cavities. On Aride and Cousin especially it is essential not to leave the paths as the Audubon and Wedgetailed Shearwaters breed in long, often shallow, underground burrows. Ensure that no litter is left behind and that no plants are damaged. Please do not forget to inform others where you will be walking and at what time you expect to return.

THE THREE MAIN HABITATS
OF THE GRANITIC ISLANDS

Throughout this book I have referred to three categories of terrain: coastal or lowland (from sea level to 150 m), midaltitude (from 150 m to 400 m), and high altitude (from 400 m to 900 m).

LOWLANDS

The coastal belt, from sea level to 150 m, has obviously been the area to suffer most in the 225 years that the islands have been inhabited. A large percentage of the population live and work in the coastal zone. The quality of the soil here is affected by the treatment of the forests in the past. In the forests, leaf fall replenishes the humus. But in steep upland areas where the trees have been cleared, where there is no longer a protective canopy and the evaporation rate is greatly increased, the high rainfall leeches out the nutrient. The result is twofold. The water is not as plentiful as in the past, and what does seep down from the hills lacks nutrients.

Unfortunately, early expeditions and settlers all failed to collect or describe the local plants here before the ground was cleared of vegetation for building and furnishing houses and providing cooking fuel. We know from records that there were many large, straight-trunked trees at low altitude and can only surmise which species they were. An unknown number of boatloads of timber were exported to Mauritius and Réunion. The rich, well-drained alkaline soil, particularly in the south of Mahé and on other less hilly islands, was found to be ideal for establishing coconut plantations, and as a result, more large areas of natural vegetation were cleared. Copra, the dried kernel of the nut that yields coconut oil, was at one time one of the major exports. (Visitors can still see the various processes in the production of copra at the factory on La Digue.)

There are few large tree species left in these lower regions. The glossy-leaved *Calophyllum inophyllum* (takamaka) is common, typically fringing most beaches, although at present an increasing number of trees on Mahé and some on Praslin, Silhouette, and La Digue are suffering from a vascular wilt disease. *Terminalia catappa* (badamier) is also widespread, recognizable from its tiers of branches and senescent red leaves. Isolated individuals or small communities of other species have survived and give an indication of the former vegetation at this level. The row of *Heritiera littoralis*, (bois de table) growing alongside the car park in Francis Rachel Street, Victoria, was on the seafront before the reclamation started twenty-five years ago. The solitary *Mimusops sechellarum* (bois de natte) and *Intsia bijuga* (gayak) between Danzille and Anse Major, Mahé, and *Northia seychellana* (capucin) on Curieuse are all near sea level. *Cordia subcordata* (porcher), with attractive orange flowers, is found on many of the granitic islands. A more natural woodland exists on Aride, a relatively undisturbed island, where over 70 percent of the trees are *Pisonia grandis* (Warman and Todd 1984; Baum et al. 1985).

The narrow, flat coastal strips, often referred to as plateaux, examples of which are found on Aride, Cousin, and Cousine, were formed around 6,000 years ago from beach sand, from soil washed down from the hills and, on the islands supporting bird colonies, from guano.

Two endemic plants with no economic value and a natural preference for these lowland areas, *Pandanus balfourii* and *Allophylus sechellensis*, have survived and can still be found, although the latter is very rare.

One exceptionally fascinating habitat is the mangrove area. These originally fringed much of the coastline, but now only a few locations still remain. Mangrove swamps arise where mud and peat are deposited along shorelines that are protected from heavy wave activity, often by an offshore coral reef. They in turn protect the land by taking the force of heavy seas during storms. All mangrove species are salt-tolerant and adapted to fluctuations in tidal levels. Trees are zoned according to the degree of toleration. The six species in Seychelles, all of which can be found at Port Launay and Baie Ternay on Mahé, are, from the seafront to landward, *Avicennia marina*, *Sonneratia caseolaris*, *Rhizophora mucronata*, *Ceriops tagal*, *Bruguiera gymnorhiza*, and *Lumnitzera racemosa*. The stilt roots of *Rhizophora* and *Ceriops* help to stabilize the plants in the shifting sediment. *Sonneratia*, *Avicennia*, and *Lumnitzera* have pneumatophores, erect lenticular pinnacles rising above the mud from the spreading underground root systems. Air diffuses through these structures down to the roots. *Bruguiera*, *Ceriops*, and *Rhizophora* have fruits that germinate on the parent tree. These break off and fall into the water or sediment, differing slightly in habit according to family, but all soon take root. The fruits of *Avicennia* and *Sonneratia* fall and float, and the seeds germinate away from the parents. Large trees of *Xylocarpus granatum*, with their wide-spreading flanged butresses, have a lower tolerance to saltwater and are often found at the back of this habitat with other mangrove-related plants, the fern *Acrostichum aureum* and *Hibiscus tiliaceus*. Mangrove areas provide habitats for various animals. The stilt roots give protection to young fish, mollusks, and crustaceans. Crabs aerate the soil by burrowing, and the mounds so formed provide a drier base for the fern to colonize. Birds and insects recycle decomposing organic matter, adding nutrients to both the soil and water. They also pollinate the mangrove trees.

MIDALTITUDES

Midaltitude terrain ranges from 150 to 400 m and naturally supports the largest numbers of the endemic plants, but these are mainly now on ground that is not suitable for cultivation or building. Many of these species are endangered. Inselbergs, the steep-sided rocky eminences rising abruptly from their surroundings, occur throughout the tropics. The isolated sites of Copolia, Bernica, and Mt. Sébért are typical examples, with severe exposure, great areas of bare rock, and pockets of poorly drained soil in crevasses. The vegetation is mainly native with only occasional aliens or annuals. On Mt. Sébért, sampling has indicated 85 percent of species to be endemic, whereas from the surrounding areas the average falls to 5 percent.

No original forest exists anywhere in Seychelles at this level, and on Mahé, large areas have been cleared for the tea plantations. Housing in these higher altitudes, with their cooler conditions, especially at night, is popular and much sought after. Praslin and Curieuse have both lost vegetation owing to periodic fires. Silhouette has the most unexploited areas of midaltitude forest, albeit secondary, with many areas still to be explored.

HIGH ALTITUDES

Mist, or cloud, forests occur in the high-altitude areas of Mahé and Silhouette at 600–900 m and in some valleys at 400 m. A cooler, damper atmosphere than the humid heat of the lower areas gives rise to a change in the vegetation and plant requirements. These high-altitude species are all dependent on more moisture than their lowland counterparts and many show typical xeromorphic features. A higher percentage of the plants have coriaceous (leathery) leaves, hairs, or waxy surfaces, features designed to minimize desiccation. Buttress roots, the wide-spreading flanges radiating from the tree trunks at ground level, are more common at lower altitudes, and rarely seen here. Stilt roots, however, are more commonly seen. Those of *Pandanus sechellarum* and the palm, *Verschaffeltia splendida*, provide extra stability in the loose soil. These adventitious roots can grow downward and outward, forming a conelike base around the main trunk near ground level, as in the latter, or from crown level, as in the former. The main trunk of the pandan usually disappears, and the tree is supported by the stilt roots.

Epiphytes flourish in the mosses that festoon all the trees. The canopy is lower, rarely above 15 m, and trees frequently have a stunted appearance. Compared to the number of recorded species of midaltitude, the mist forest areas have far fewer. Single species dominate in places. At the highest point of Congo Rouge, Mahé, *Glionnetia sericea*, with its clusters of tubular sweet-scented flowers, spreads over a large area, while much reduced trees of *Northia seychellana*, with their tomentose, rusty-backed leaves, cover the slopes. The latter occurs on Morne Seychellois, up to the summit at 905 m, and it is also the dominant species on many of the higher parts of Silhouette.

Many of the plants on the high ridges, which live in shallower soil, are exposed daily to full sunlight. The typically damp, cloudy night conditions prevent their desiccation. The forest is refreshed by the water vapor of the night being returned to the trees, but their daily nourishment, photosynthesis, comes from the sun.

It is in the shady areas of the lower mist forest and the ravines above 600 m that the tree ferns *Cyathea sechellarum* and *Angiopteris erecta* and many terrestrial ferns can be seen. *Begonia seychellensis* is characteristic of these damp, shady habitats. Throughout the "backbone" of Mahé and in the moist areas of Silhouette, above 200 m, three species of sooglossid frogs can be found. These minute amphibians are possibly the world's smallest frogs and, although rarely seen, make their presence known by frequent high-pitched calls. Possible affinities with both African and Oriental species suggest that they have Gondwanan origins. Stick insects also prefer the damp atmosphere of these higher regions and can be found mainly on the ferns that appear to be their favorite food plants.

CLIMATE

The daily range of temperature on oceanic islands fluctuates less than continental equatorial areas. In the western Indian Ocean the two seasons are determined by the monsoon winds. From May until early October, the southeast monsoon or trade wind blows, and pressure is low over southern Asia and high over southern Africa. The stronger winds result in rougher seas (but never exceeding force 6) and temperatures remaining between 24 and 30° C. Rainfall is lower and humidity averages 80 percent. From November until April the northwest monsoon takes over, and high pressure develops over northern Africa and southern Asia and low over southern Africa. With less strong and more variable winds, in Seychelles the temperatures are higher, between 30 and 32° C. Humidity can be up to 100 percent and the sea is calmer. The transition periods between these two monsoons are hotter, since there is very little breeze. The relative humidity is, on average, higher, and the sea is as flat as glass.

In December and January the rainy season occurs. Victoria can experience between 339 and 398 mm of rain during these months, in comparison with an average of 74 mm in August (calculated from manuscript data, R. P. D. Walsh, *Biogeography and Ecology of the Seychelles Islands*, edited by D. R. Stoddart). The amount of rainfall varies not only from island to island but in different areas of the same island. In Victoria, at sea level, the mean is 2,378 mm per annum, whereas at Cascade, at an altitude of 180 m, it rises to 3,124 mm. It is estimated that on the summits of the central massif, rainfall probably measures as much as 5,000 mm. Mahé, with higher mountains, experiences a higher rainfall than Praslin, which in turn receives more than the lower islands, such as Aride.

The granitic Seychelles escape the cyclone belt because they are so close to the equator. Cyclones, however, are recorded in the Aldabra region, although infrequently, which result in periods of heavier rain in the granitic islands.

THE NATIONAL PARKS

The National Parks and Nature Conservancy Ordinance of 1969 and various subsequent amendments were instrumental in designating certain areas of the islands as national parks or special reserves. Although complete protection is given to both flora and fauna, the general public is able to visit and enjoy the variety of the sites.

A land area covering 30 km^2 of the central massif of western Mahé was designated as Morne Seychellois National Park in 1979. Rising from sea level to the summit of Morne Seychellois, various habitats are encountered. Mahé's best examples of mist forest are located in this park.

On Praslin, 50 km northeast of Mahé, the Vallée de Mai Nature Reserve lies within the Praslin National Park. This was first decreed a reserve in 1966, under the Wild Birds Protection Regulation. In 1983 the Vallée de Mai attained the status of a World Heritage Site, a year later than Aldabra Atoll. *Lodoicea maldivica* (coco de mer) grows here in great numbers with all five of the other endemic palms. Beside supporting approximately thirty species of endemic plants, many of the avian counterparts live in this 18-hectare woodland, including *Coracopsis nigra barklyi*, the Seychelles Black Parrot. Other interesting species found in the Vallée are the three species of harmless snakes, geckos, snails, chameleons, caecilians, bats, and freshwater crabs, shrimps and fish, many of which are endemic.

Some of the small, uninhabited and mainly unvisited islands, Beacon (north of Moyenne), Booby (between Praslin and Aride), Île Vache Marine (off western Mahé), and Les Mamelles (north of Ste. Anne), along with Cousin and the Vallée de Mai, were created nature reserves by the Wild Bird Protection Regulation of 1966. Cousin has been owned and administered by the International Council for Bird Preservation since 1975. Aride is privately owned but has been administered by the Royal Society for Nature Conservation since 1973. Both islands are managed as strict nature reserves, meaning that visitors can enjoy the beauty and see the special features by way of a series of trails in the company of a guide. On La Digue, the area in which the small population of *Tchitrea corvina*, Black Paradise Flycatchers, nest was declared a managed nature reserve in 1982. The Forestry and Conservation Division of the Ministry of National Development holds responsibility for the management. Visitors are requested to remain in groups and not to leave the well-maintained paths. As with all bird reserves, one should be as quiet as possible.

The marine parks were established to safeguard certain areas, and fishing, shell-collecting, or interfering with any aspect of the diverse marine life is strictly prohibited. Curieuse Island is surrounded by a marine national park, declared as such in 1979. This island is listed as a protected breeding site for turtles.

Baie Ternay Marine National Park, at the northwest point of Mahé and established in 1979, has a very good fringing reef. The soft corals in the bay are said to be the best on Mahé (Salm, pers. comm. 1995). The sheltered bay is particularly rich in both large and small reef fish.

Port Launay Marine National Park, so designated in 1979, protects a coral reef and, on the shoreline, one of the best areas of mangrove vegetation in Seychelles. At present however, the general public is excluded from the marine park because of the nearby National Youth Service camp. The mangrove area lies before the camp and can be visited.

Sainte Anne Marine National Park, so designated in 1973, encloses the six islands in the bay to the north of Victoria. The area has good reefs, corals, sea grasses, sandflats, and beaches. Round Island and the privately owned Moyenne and Cerf can be visited by arrangement with the travel services on Mahé. Round Island has an information center. Glass-bottom and semi-submersible boats give excellent panoramas of reefs and marine life, almost comparable to scuba diving without getting wet!

The sea around Silhouette is classified as a marine park, but the island itself as yet has no official national park status.

COLLECTING AND PAINTING THE ENDEMIC FLOWERING PLANTS

This book is a rather unusual account of a flora. Botanical illustrators almost always work from dried herbarium sheets to produce detailed line drawings in ink and rarely have the chance to see the plants in the field and in three dimensions. It becomes easy for a desk-bound illustrator to imagine that all plants are in varying shades of brown and dried! So, apart from being a lot of hard work in the planning and financing stages and in the arduous climbing and searching for plants, this project has been totally enjoyable and has reassured me that leaves come in a multitude of different greens and are succulent, while flowers are anything but brown!

Painting in the tropics, especially in the open air, takes some getting used to. On very hot days the paint tends to dry too quickly, while during times of high humidity it hardly dries at all. One is frequently readjusting to new climatic conditions. Keeping hands cool and dry is difficult. Damp flannels, towels, and talcum powder help. So near to the equator the hours of daylight are regular and limited. It is light by 6.30 A.M. and by five o'clock every afternoon, the light starts to go; by 6:30 in the evening it is completely dark, and painting by electric light is not recommended if colors are to be portrayed correctly.

The paintings of the endemic flowering plants are on a high quality, pure-rag, acid-free paper, with a "not" surface, purchased in A3 block form, which eliminates the need for any preliminary stretching. The rigidity of the cardboard backing also facilitates sketching in the field. I have used artist-quality watercolors, mainly from the permanent color range. For leaf veins and hairs, designer's gouache in zinc white was mixed with watercolor to give a more opaque appearance. From experience I know which paints not to take to the tropics. On my first visit, I opened my paint box to find everything coated with a semiliquid orange mess!

My list of endemic plants was based on the publications of J. Proctor (1974), S. A. Robertson (1989), and F. Friedmann (1986, 1994), and from discussions with many botanists. At the start of each trip I have visited the appropriate ministries, renewed acquaintances, and obtained permission to collect plants. Pencil sketches were made from herbarium specimens prior to my departure in the cases where good published photographs and illustrations were not available. (These were to facilitate identification in the field.)

On finding the plants that I needed, I cut selected parts, choosing typical growth forms with as little insect damage as possible. I took the bare minimum of each. These were then put into polyethylene bags and sealed to prevent desiccation. Back at my accommodation, when the specimens were not in use, they were stored in these sealed bags and kept under refrigeration. I found it sensible never to collect more than four or five species at a time. Plants do not last indefinitely, even in a refrigerator, and it would be an impossibility to produce a botanically accurate portrayal of a plant that has shriveled. Usually it has been a race against time for me to produce a plate in a day, knowing that there were other plants waiting in the refrigerator! When the collections have been from the higher reaches of the islands, it is hardly possible to repeat what may well have been a six-hour trek to get another piece if the first wilts. I knew that there would be no shortcuts when painting the enormous, faceted fruit of *Pandanus sechellarum* and ensured that this was the only subject I had for the three days it took to paint! It would have been an interesting exercise to ascertain exactly how much paint was used in the many washes of color laid down in portraying such a sculptured subject.

When a specimen had many leaves, some were cut off, leaving the bases of the petioles. This gives a clearer and less confused view of the plant in both a painting and a pressed specimen while still indicating where leaves arose. On the paintings, damaged leaves have been replaced by perfect ones because a botanical illustration should be characteristic of the species it portrays, not of one particular plant. But in the cases of *Dillenia ferruginea* and *Pisonia sechellarum*, where insect damage is constant and characteristic, I have painted what I have seen. I spent several hours collecting insects from *Dillenia* and the most common by far was the green weevil depicted on the painting. Observations of the wild busy lizzie, *Impatiens gordonii*, showed that the main pest happily eating the leaves was a hawk moth caterpillar, which was also added.

In most cases all parts have been painted life size. The exceptions are the complete palms and pandans shown in monochrome, which were important to include for identification purposes on the relevant plates, and the gigantic male and female inflorescences and fruit of *Lodoicea maldivica* (coco de mer). With so many of the endemic trees having large leathery leaves, I have lost count of the number of tubes of various shades of yellow paint I have used. One cannot treat such leaves with any degree of delicacy, and I applied coat after coat of washes to build up the colors to portray these thick textures, leaving areas of white, or lightly washed paper, for highlights.

On the plates I have endeavored to show both flowering and fruiting habits. Often there has been a gap of several years between finding and painting one and adding the other. Therefore, planning the composition of a plate from the start was impossible. The leaves, fruits, and seeds of *Northia seychellana*, for example, were painted five years before I found any flowers. Marianne North was unable to find them, either, during her three-month visit in 1883. She wrote, "I could make out nothing certain of the flowers, and

was told 'it had no flower,' or, 'a red flower,' or, 'a white one,' each statement most positive, from those who lived actually under the trees!" Eventually flowers were found and sent to the Royal Botanic Gardens, Kew, where Sir Joseph Dalton Hooker described it as a new genus, which he named after the intrepid lady.

As the paintings were completed and if the plant material was still in reasonable condition, specimens were pressed and dried for incorporation as reference material for the illustrations in the Fielding Herbarium, Oxford. The plants were placed between sheets of absorbent newspaper, and great care was taken to ensure that the leaves, fruits, and flowers were arranged as flat and as naturally as possible before being put into a plant press. I am still not sure what the employees of Barclays Bank in Victoria thought on the occasions when this English woman asked if there were any old copies of *The Times* available. "Madame, you can read yesterday's paper if you wish," was the frequent answer. At least once a day all the sheets of newspaper were changed for fresh, dry ones. This not only extracted moisture from the plants but helped to prevent the formation of molds, which are very quick to develop in such humid conditions. In good weather the press was left out-of-doors with the straps left fairly loose to allow the air to circulate. Overnight, the straps were buckled tightly to keep the specimens flat. Because it is important to get the specimens dried and flattened as quickly as possible if elite herbarium sheets are to be achieved, the press and its contents frequently acted as a rather hard cushion to my chair while I painted. A few flowers of each collected plant and some of the smaller fruits were put into alcohol. (I took with me on collecting trips small vials filled with gin for this purpose and have to admit than any not used gave me extra energy for the homeward trek!) More exact measurements for descriptions may be taken from these at a later date, obviously immersed in a more suitable fluid, either with a hand lens or a microscope. (Dried material can be rehydrated for the purposes of dissection by briefly boiling the parts needed in water. These can also then be pickled.)

Back at Oxford, the pressed specimens, in fresh newspaper, were parceled in plastic wrap and placed in the deep freeze for several days. This is done to kill any insects or insect eggs or larvae that may be present on the plants. Using field notes, labels were written, denoting the Latin name, when and where each one was collected, details of the whole plant and its habitat, including names of other plants in the vicinity, the collector's name, and a number. The dried plants were then mounted onto stiff cards, the labels attached, and a herbarium accession number added. A standard-size photocopy of the finished painting will accompany each specimen in this reference collection.

ARRANGEMENT OF
THE PLATES

The families are alphabetically arranged with genera and species following alphabetically. I have followed nomenclature for the dicotyledons from Friedmann (1994). One exception is the genus *Northia*, for which I have followed Pennington (1991) and used the specific epithet *seychellana*. For the monocotyledons I have followed Robertson (1989).

As more research needs to be undertaken on the Orchidae before stating categorically which species are definite endemics, I have omitted those which are most doubtful, following discussions with Dr. P. Crib at the Royal Botanic Gardens, Kew.

All the plants were drawn to scale at the sizes indicated in the "Illustration" information facing each plate. As reproduced in this book, each plate has been reduced to 60 percent of its original size, with the exceptions of numbers 5, 15, 32, 34, 45, 51, 57, 58, 59, 60, 61, 63, 68, 70, 71, 74, and 77, which are at 53 percent.

ILLUSTRATIONS AND DESCRIPTIONS OF THE ENDEMIC PLANTS

THE DICOTYLEDONS

ACANTHACEAE Jussieu

This family is composed of 357 genera and 4,350 species of mainly tropical herbs, climbers, shrubs, and a few trees. The distribution is cosmopolitan but primarily tropical. Many genera are cultivated as ornamentals including *Acanthus, Crossandra,* and *Thunbergia.* The ancient Greeks recognized the design possibilities of the deeply dissected leaves of the temperate *Acanthus* and carved them on the capitals of Corinthian pillars. The granitic Seychelles have five indigenous genera and many cultivated introductions.

Pseuderanthemum Radlkofer

This genus comprises 60 tropical species, which are often cultivated as ornamentals or greenhouse plants.

PLATE 1. *Pseuderanthemum* sp. (related to *P. tunicatum* [Afzelius] Milne-Redhead) (E. W. Milne-Redhead, 1936, *Bull. Misc. Info.,* Kew 1936:264)

HABIT. This plant is a perennial herb that roots at the nodes and grows as high as 60 cm. It is mainly glabrous but is puberulous at the nodes and at the top of floral axis. The stems are angular and lack stipules.

LEAVES. The leaves, which may reach 18 cm in length, are opposite and decussate with acuminate apices and truncate bases. The margins are crenulate, and the petioles are up to 1.5 cm long.

INFLORESCENCES. The inflorescences are terminal racemes, up to 25 cm long, with pairs of pointed bracteoles, which are up to 2.5 mm long, at the bases of the 3 mm long pedicels.

FLOWERS. The flowers are bisexual. The calyx, which may reach 3 mm in length, has five pointed lobes, is glabrous on the outer surface, and has glandular hairs on the inner. The corolla is tubular, pale bluish-mauve, and up to 1.5 cm long. It has five lobes, the upper two of which are fused for half their length; the lateral pair and lower one are free. The two stamens are fused to the tube at the throat. The anthers are puberulent. The style is up to 11 mm in length and has a bilobed stigma.

FRUITS. The fruits are green, glabrous obovoid capsules, up to 2 cm in length and dehisce into two valves.

DISTRIBUTION. Silhouette

This is a very rare plant known from one location in the remaining area of primary forest on Silhouette. Originally it grew on Mahé. H. P. Thomasset collected plants at 300 m from Rivière Chauve Souris at the turn of the century. More critical research needs to be undertaken before this attractive herb can be permanently added to the list of endemic plants. There are several small characters that differentiate it from the African species, *P. tunicatum.* The staminodes are different in length, and the disk is fused in the Seychelles species. Because of the possible relationship, I have included it in this publication. Five members of the de Jussieu family became distinguished botanists in France: Antoine (1686–1758), Bernard (c. 1699–1777), Joseph (1704–1779), Antoine Laurent (1748–1836), and Adrien Laurent Henri (1797–1853). Bernard became a demonstrator at the Jardin des Plantes in Paris in 1722 and revised and completed the system of Linnaeus, which laid the foundation of the modern system of classification. His nephew Antoine Laurent published this is *Genera Plantarum Secundum Ordines Naturel.* More than half the plant families established at this time are still recognized.

Other members of this family in the granitic islands are *Asystasia gangetica, Barleria cristata, B. prionitis, Crossandra infundibuliformis, Graptophyllum pictum, Hemigraphis alternata, Justicia brasiliana, J. gardineri, J. gendarussa, Pseuderanthemum carruthersii* (an ornamental shrub with variegated leaves and white flowers with mauve guide lines into throats, on short terminal spikes), *P. malabaricum* (an ornamental shrub with opposite pairs of ovate leaves to 15 cm and long, terminal spikes having clusters of pale mauve flowers), *Thunbergia alata, T. erecta, T. fragrans,* and *T. grandiflora.*

ILLUSTRATION. Flowering habit collected and painted on October 20, 1992, at 1×. Fruiting habit collected and painted on October 20, 1992, at 1×. Herbarium sheet: Rosemary Wise 183 (The Fielding Druce Herbarium, University of Oxford: hereafter, OXF).

ANACARDIACEAE Lindley

This family comprises 73 genera and 850 species of trees, shrubs, and lianas and has a tropical and subtropical distribution. There are a few native genera in temperate regions of North America and Eurasia. The plants often have allergenic resins that are exuded from the leaves or bark during rainstorms. Some people are extrasensitive to these and can also react to certain edible fruits in the family, for example, mangos (*Mangifera indica*), pistachios (*Pistacia vera*), and cashews (*Anacardium occidentale*). Tannins for the production of leather are obtained from *Cotinus*, *Rhus*, and *Schinopis*. The granitic Seychelles have two indigenous genera and some cultivated introductions, including *Spondias cytherea*, the widely grown "golden apples."

Campnosperma Thwaites

This genus consists of 10 species, which are found in Madagascar, Seychelles, Southeast Asia, Malaysia, and the western Pacific.

PLATE 2. *Campnosperma seychellarum* Marchand
(N. L. Marchand, 1869, *Révision du groupe des Anacardiacées*, p. 173)

Vernacular name: bois de montagne

HABIT. This species is a tree that grows to a height of 20 m and has gray bark. It is dioecious and lacks stipules.

LEAVES. The leaves are alternate, lanceolate, glabrous, and coriaceous. They can be as long as 30 cm. The apices are obtuse and the bases cuneiform. The margins are entire. The 12–14 pairs of secondary veins are camptodromous, and the tertiary veins are distinctly reticulate. The petioles are caniculate and up to 1.5 cm long.

INFLORESCENCES. The inflorescences are dense, almost sessile panicles with minute deltoid bracts.

FLOWERS. The flowers are 2 mm wide. In the male flower the three sepals are 1 mm long, and the three creamy-white, imbricate petals 2 mm long. The six stamens are 1.5 mm long. In the female flower, a circular disk surrounds the pistil, which is 0.8 mm long. The six staminodes are 1.2 mm long, and the stigma is bilobed.

FRUITS. The single-seeded fruits are dark-red drupes, 1 cm in length.

DISTRIBUTION. Mahé and Praslin

According to John Horne, possibly quoting Baker, *Campnosperma* was "common on all islands," which seems highly unlikely. The remaining trees are confined to just a few areas on inaccessible slopes between 300 and 700 m on Mahé. It has probably become scarce for the same reason as have many other of the hardwood trees, which were felled for timber. Pirogues were often made of this wood. One tree grows just below the Mission viewing lodge. Many fine examples grow on the large glacis below Morne Blanc, behind the Tea Tavern. On Praslin, the only known tree grows in the Vallée de Mai, in the vicinity of the pandanus grove.

Other members of this family in the granitic islands are *Anacardium occidentale*, *Mangifera indica*, *Spondias cytherea*, and *Schinus terebinthifolius*.

ILLUSTRATION. Flowering habit collected and painted on September 20, 1989, at 1×. Fruiting habit collected and painted on September 27, 1989, at 1×. Herbarium sheets: Rosemary Wise 102, 104, 108, 210 (OXF).

APOCYNACEAE Jussieu

This family consists of 215 genera and 2,100 species, mostly of lianas, but some trees, shrubs, herbs, and succulents are also represented. Most occur in the tropics, although there are a few temperate genera. The economic uses of the Apocynaceae include drugs and poisons, rubber, and timber. Many species, with their characteristic imbricate five-petaled flowers, are cultivated as ornamentals, including *Allamanda*, *Plumeria* (frangipani), *Nerium* (oleander), and *Vinca* (periwinkles). The Madagascar periwinkle, *Catharanthus roseus*, which is grown ornamentally in many Seychelles gardens, contains alkaloids that are beneficial for the treatment of some blood cancers. In the granitic Seychelles there are four indigenous genera and many cultivated introductions.

Carissa Linnaeus

This genus comprises 37 species with a distribution from the Old World to Australia. In many areas the thorny species are grown for hedging. Some have edible fruits that are frequently eaten by baboons in West Africa.

PLATE 3.   *Carissa edulis* (Forsskaol) Vahl var. *sechellensis* (Baker)   (M. Pichon, 1949, *Memoires de l'Institute scientifique de Madagascar*, series B, vol. 2, p. 3)

Carissa sechellensis Baker   (Baker, 1877, *Flora of Mauritius*, p. 222)

Vernacular name: bois sandal

HABIT. The plant is a tree with slender branches and branched spines, is glabrous in all parts, and contains latex. It may grow as high as 12 m. Stipules are absent.

LEAVES. The opposite, ovate leaves have acuminate apices and cuneate bases, are glossy, have entire, repand margins, and are 7 cm long. The venation is fine and faint, with five pairs of immersed brochidodromous secondary veins. The petioles are up to 3 mm long.

INFLORESCENCES. The inflorescences are terminal or axillary cymes, each having four to eight flowers on peduncles that are as long as 6 mm.

FLOWERS. The flowers are white. The calyx is up to 1 mm with five deltoid lobes also as long as 1 mm. The corolla tube is up to 1.2 cm in length, with five imbricate, spreading lanceolate lobes that are up to 1 cm long. The stamens and pistil are inserted in the tube.

FRUITS. The fruits are subglobose red berries up to 1.5 cm long.

DISTRIBUTION. Silhouette

On Silhouette the practice of burning the aromatic wood of this tree as a means of deterring mosquitoes or for inducing restful sleep has resulted in its extreme rarity. The remaining trees favor rocky habitats, often in exposed areas. One seedling was taken from Silhouette in the 1980s and is growing in the botanic garden in Victoria, where it flowers and fruits frequently. The wood of *Carissa edulis* var. *sechellensis* is fine-grained and extremely hard, and fallen trees can remain for many years on the forest floor without rotting.

The genus *Carissa* was named by the Swedish botanist Carolus Linnaeus (1770–1778), who was appointed as a lecturer in botany at the University of Uppsala in 1730. He published *Systema Naturae* (1735), *Genera Plantarum* (1737), and *Species Plantarum* (1753). These pioneering editions introduced a new system of plant classification that was based on sexual morphology. He used the binomial system of nomenclature, which was universally adopted for both plants and animals.

Other members of this family in the granitic islands are *Allamanda cathartica*, *A. violacea*, *Alstonia macrophylla*, *Beaumontia grandiflora*, *Catharanthus roseus*, *Cerbera manghas*, *C. venenifera*, *Kopsia arborea*, *K. fruticosa*, *Mascarenhasia arborescens*, *Nerium oleander*, *Ochrosia oppositifolia*, *Plumeria obtusa*, *P. rubra*, *Tabernaemontana coffeoides*, *T. divaricata*, and *Thevetia peruviana*.

ILLUSTRATION. Flowering habit collected and painted on May 21, 1991, at 1×. Enlargement of flower, 3×. Fruiting habit collected and painted on May 21, 1991, at 1×. Leaves collected and painted on July 20, 1990. Herbarium sheets: Rosemary Wise 130, 139 (OXF).

ARALIACEAE Jussieu

This family consists of 57 genera and 800 species of trees, shrubs, lianas, epiphytes, and a few herbs with a distribution mainly in Indomalesia and America. Probably the most well known member of the family is *Panax quinquefolia*. The stimulant and alleged aphrodisiac, ginseng, is extracted from the roots. *Hedera* and *Fatsia* species are grown as attractive pot or outdoor plants. The granitic Seychelles have two indigenous genera and one cultivated introduction.

Gastonia Commerson ex Lamarck

This genus is distributed throughout East Africa, Madagascar, Seychelles, Mascarenes, Malesia, and Papuasia.

PLATE 4.   *Gastonia crassa* (Hemsley) F. Friedmann
  (F. Friedmann, 1987 [1986], *Adansonia* 8:45–256)

Indokinga crassa Hemsley   (W. B. Hemsley, 1906, *Hooker's Icones plantarum*, t. 2805)

Vernacular name: bois banane

HABIT. The plant is a shrub or small tree, glabrous in all parts, with lightly fissured grayish brown bark. It grows as high as 10 m. The bracts are caducous.

LEAVES. The imparipinnate leaves are crowded at ends of the branches and have rachises up to 1.25 m long. There are from five to nine leaflets, which are oblong and coriaceous, having asymmetric bases and entire margins. The petiolules are up to 1 cm long. There are 10 pairs of brochidodromous secondary veins.

INFLORESCENCES. The inflorescences are obconical umbels and are either terminal or secondary, near the ends of the branches.

FLOWERS. The flowers are up to 1 cm across. The calyx is 5 mm long with irregular margins and is lobed to 7.5 mm. The petals are coherent to a caducous calyptra. There as many as 100 stamens, in three whorls, with cream or pink anthers and 12–21, 3 mm long stigmas.

FRUITS. The fruits are globular and dark purplish-black when mature, with a persistent style that is up to 12 mm long.

DISTRIBUTION. Mahé, Praslin, Silhouette, La Digue, and Félicité

The distribution of *G. crassa* is from mid- to high altitude, (400–700 m) on Mahé, but lower on Praslin. The shady ridge at the summit of Congo Rouge has many of these understory shrubs, which are mostly vegetative, growing along with *Northia seychellana*, *Colea seychellarum*, *Roscheria melanochaetes*, *Aphloia theiformis* subsp. *madagascariensis* var. *sechellensis*, *Pandanus sechellarum*, *Protarum sechellarum*, *Aframomum angustifolia* (cardamom), and *Hypoxidia mahéensis*. On the higher reaches of Morne Blanc, *G. crassa* grows in full sunlight, flowering and fruiting regularly. At anthesis, the flowers are very attractive to pollinating bees, and swarms of them are good indicators to the location of the plants. Other visitors to the flowers are green skinks (*Phelsuma* spp.) and sun birds. Although the indehiscent anthers are usually yellow, a pink form exists. This coloration is not so obvious when the anthers have dehisced.

Other members of this family in the granitic islands are *Gastonia lionnetii*, *G. sechellarum* var. *sechellarum*, *G. sechellarum* var. *contracta*, *G. sechellarum* var. *curiosae*, *Polyscias fruticosa*, *P. guilfoylei*, *P. cumingiana*, *P. scutellaria*, and *Schefflera procumbens*.

ILLUSTRATION. Habit with leaf and immature infructescence; mature fruits; inflorescence with cream anthers; and inflorescence with pink anthers; all painted at 1×. Leaf with five leaflets; painted at 0.25×. Flowering habit collected and painted on June 3, 1991. Pink anthered flowers painted on October 13, 1992. Fruiting habit collected and painted on September 12, 1989. No specimens pressed.

ARALIACEAE Jussieu

Gastonia Commerson ex Lamarck

PLATE 5. *Gastonia lionnetii* F. Friedmann   (F. Friedmann, 1987 [1986], *Adansonia* 8:253)

HABIT. The plant is a tree with grayish brown, lightly fissured bark. It grows as high as 5 m.

LEAVES. The leaves are imparipinnate on a rachis up to 25 cm long. The leaflets number from seven to nine, are glabrous and elliptic with asymmetric bases, and reach 25 cm in length. The 9 or 10 secondary veins are brochidodromous, and the upper surface of the leaf is bullate.

INFLORESCENCES. The inflorescences are erect and branched, up to 40 cm long, and have umbels of six to nine flowers. The bracts are caducous.

FLOWERS. The creamy yellow flowers are as wide as 15 mm. The calyx is cup-shaped and up to 5 mm long, and the four or five 5 mm long lobes, each having an apical hood, are spreading. Petals are absent. The 30 stamens are arranged in one or two whorls and are attached to a disk at the base of the calyx lobes. There are 8–13 stigmas.

FRUITS. The fruits are purplish-black berries that are up to 9 mm long.

DISTRIBUTION. Mahé

Gastonia lionnetii is known from two sites: at 400 m, in the vicinity of the Mission and at Casse Dent, both off the Sans Souci Road. Its characters show it to be a fully fertile intermediate between *G. crassa* and *G. sechellarum*. The somewhat overgrown site near the Mission was carefully cleared in 1994, and selected endemic trees were left. A seedling nearby may prove to be from the parent plant (author pers. obs., 1995), but the ongoing clearing of the site could be detrimental to its survival. The specific name commemorates Mr. Guy Lionnet, the former head of the Department of Agriculture, a well-known naturalist and writer, who lives in Seychelles.

ILLUSTRATION. Habit with both young fruits and flowers; painted at 1×. Monochrome enlargement of flower; drawn at 5×. No record of when specimen was collected or painted. Herbarium sheet: Rosemary Wise 194 (OXF).

ARALIACEAE Jussieu

Gastonia Commerson ex Lamarck

   Gastonia sechellarum has been subdivided into three distinct varieties by Friedmann (1987 [1986], *Adansonia* 8:45–256): *Gastonia sechellarum* var. *sechellarum*; *Gastonia sechellarum* var. *contracta*; and *Gastonia sechellarum* var. *curiosae*.

PLATE 6.   *Gastonia sechellarum* (Baker) Harms var. *contracta* F. Friedmann and *Gastonia sechellarum* (Baker) Harms var. *curiosae* F. Friedmann   (F. Friedmann, 1987 [1986], *Adansonia* 8:251)

   Gastonia sechellarum Harms   (H.G.A. Engler and K.A.E. Prantl, 1894, *Naturl. Pflanzenfam.*, part 3, vol. 8, p. 43)

   Polyscias sechellarum Baker   (Baker, 1877, *Flora of Mauritius*, p. 128)

G. sechellarum (Baker) Harms var. *contracta* F. Friedmann

LEAVES. The leaflets of this variety are far more "sculptured" than those of other varieties, with the leaf blade being rounded (bullate) between the secondary veins.

INFLORESCENCES. The inflorescences are erect and branched.

DISTRIBUTION. Mahé

   Several fairly small trees grow in dense vegetation in the Casse Dent area, off the Sans Souci Road. This is one of several endemic species that has an extremely limited distribution and is critically endangered.

G. sechellarum (Baker) Harms var. *curiosae* F. Friedmann

LEAVES. The leaflets of this variety have undulate margins and are again sufficiently different from those of the other varieties to be recognizable from this character alone. The eight or nine pairs of secondary veins are brochidodromous.

FLOWERS. The flowers, which were not collected, are considerably smaller than in the other varieties.

DISTRIBUTION. Curieuse. There are only two or three surviving specimens of this tree, all confined to a small area of Curieuse Island.

ILLUSTRATION.
G. sechellarum var. *contracta*. Leaf painted on October 2, 1993, at 1×. Herbarium sheet: Rosemary Wise 201 (OXF).
G. sechellarum. var. *curiosae*. Leaf painted on October 16, 1994, at 1×. Herbarium sheet: Rosemary Wise 205 (OXF).

ARALIACEAE Jussieu

Gastonia Commerson ex Lamarck

PLATE 7. *Gastonia sechellarum* (Baker) Harms var. *sechellarum*
F. Friedmann (F. Friedmann, 1987 [1986], *Adansonia* 8:251)

Gastonia sechellarum Harms (H.G.A. Engler and K.A.E. Prantl, 1894,
Naturl. Pflanzenfam, part 3, vol. 8, p. 43)

Polyscias sechellarum Baker (Baker, 1877, *Flora of Mauritius*, p. 128)

HABIT. The plant is a tree, glabrous in all parts, with light gray, slightly fissured bark. It grows as high as 12 m.

LEAVES. The leaves are imparipinnate, with a pendulous rachis as long as 1 m. The 9–17 leaflets are elliptic with entire margins and are up to 24 cm long. The 10–12 secondary veins are brochidodromous, and the midribs are often pink on lower surface. The upper surfaces are bullate.

INFLORESCENCES. The inflorescences are pendulous umbels, branched to two orders, and up to 1.2 m long.

FLOWERS. The flowers are up to 8 mm wide, and there are from three to nine per umbel on pedicels that are up to 1.7 cm long. The calyx is up to 3.5 mm long and has no or as many as five minute teeth. There are four or five cream, spreading petals, 5 mm long. The 10–17 stamens are attached to a disk at the bases of the petals.

FRUITS. The globose, dark purple fruits are up to 7 mm wide and have persistent styles.

DISTRIBUTION. Mahé, Praslin, Silhouette, and Félicité

One mature tree in the Victoria Botanic Garden was originally brought as a seedling from Félicité. With no near competition for light, it has grown to a height of approximately 6 m. The leaves are less coriaceous than all the other Seychelles' *Gastonias*, and young leaflets often have a conspicuous deep pink midrib. This tree flowers and fruits frequently. In the wild, there are a very few isolated individuals surviving in small populations.

ILLUSTRATION. Leaves and young fruits; painted at 0.33×. Rachis showing one full-size leaflet; inflorescence with young and mature fruits painted at 1 ×. Flowering habit collected and painted on June 31, 1991. Fruiting habit collected and painted on June 2, 1991. Herbarium sheet: Rosemary Wise 148 (OXF).

ARALIACEAE Jussieu

Schefflera Forster and Forster

This genus has 200 species in the tropics and subtropics and includes trees, shrubs, and epiphytes. Many are grown as ornamental trees and pot plants.

PLATE 8.   *Schefflera procumbens* (Hemsley) F. Friedmann
(F. Friedmann, 1987 [1986], *Adansonia* 8:254)

Geopanax procumbens Hemsley   (W. B. Hemsley, 1906, *Hooker's Icones plantarum*, t. 2821)

HABIT. The plant is a climbing epiphytic and has gray, lenticellate bark.

LEAVES. The leaves are palmate on petioles up to 20 cm long. There are as many as 10 coriaceous leaflets, which are elliptic and have acuminate apices and cuneate bases. The margins are entire. The 10 pairs of secondary veins are brochididromous. The petiolules are up to 4 cm long.

INFLORESCENCES. The inflorescences were not seen.

FRUITS. The fruits are cream, clustered, globose, and succulent. They are up to 8 mm wide.

DISTRIBUTION. Silhouette and formerly on Mahé

This threatened creeper is now confined to a few small areas of Silhouette located between 400 and 700 m. (Mt. Dauban and Gratte Fesse) and in the Pisonia forest in the upper reaches of the Anse Mondon Valley. Thomasset collected specimens from Cascade Estate, Mahé (Hebarium sheet: Thomasset 192). Collecting is far from easy in terrain such as that of Silhouette—the boulders present almost impossible obstacles, and *Schefflera* prefers to flower and fruit in the canopy. Some fruits fell to the ground in front of one of the members of the Oxford University Expedition in 1990 and were given to me to paint. As yet I have not seen flowers and the chances of doing so seem extremely remote; however, for identification purposes, the leaves, stems, and fruits are all sufficiently characteristic.

ILLUSTRATION. Leaves and fruiting habit collected and painted on July 28–29, 1990, at 1×. Stem with buds collected and painted on October 20, 1990, at 1×. Herbarium sheets: Rosemary Wise 132, 166 (OXF).

ASCLEPIADACEAE R. Brown

This family comprises 348 genera and 2,900 species of lianas, scramblers, and herbs, as well as a few trees and shrubs. The distribution range is in the tropics and subtropics, especially Africa, although there are a few temperate species. The family contains two subfamilies, Periocoideae and Asclepoideae, which are sometimes treated as separate families. All species contain milky juices, giving rise to the common family name of milkweed. Asclepiads are grown mainly for their attractive flowers, which include *Asclepias*, *Hoya*, and *Stephanotis*. Many species are poisonous and are used locally as sources of fish poisons. The granitic Seychelles have four indigenous genera and a few cultivated introductions.

Secamone R. Brown

This genus comprises 100 species from the Old World tropics.

PLATE 9. *Secamone schimperianus* (Hemsley) Klackenberg
(J. Klackenberg, 1992, *Opera Botanica*, 112, p. 48)

Toxocarpus schimperianus Hemsley (W. B. Hemsley, 1906, *Hooker's Icones plantarum*, t. 2807)

HABIT. The plant is a liana up to 5 m long with slender, twining stems and minute stipules.

LEAVES. The leaves are opposite, lanceolate, glabrous, and coriaceous. They may be as long as 15 cm. The midribs are red, and there are numerous pairs of extremely faint secondary veins.

INFLORESCENCES. The inflorescences are puberulent, axillary cymes that arise singly and alternately at the nodes. The flowers are clustered on pedicels that are up to 3.5 mm long.

FLOWERS. The flowers are tubular, white to pale pink, and up to 3 mm wide. The five sepals are 1.2 mm long and pilose at their apices. The 3.5 mm long corolla has five contorted lobes, each of which is 1.5 mm long.

FRUITS. The fruits consist of two diverging spindle-shaped follicles that are up to 9 cm long. The seeds are flattened, 1 cm long, and have long silky hairs (2.5 cm).

DISTRIBUTION. Mahé, Praslin, and Curieuse

The main population of this endangered creeper is on Curieuse Island, where as many as 100 plants survive on the high ridges at 50–150 m (Clive Hambler, pers. comm., 1996). Curieuse has experienced several severe fires, the latest being in 1967, which have caused erosion and decreased the soil fertility. Some parts of the island are almost desertlike in appearance, even though the annual rainfall is 250 cm per year. *Secamone* survives in pockets of the remnant vegetation that formerly covered the island. Isolated plants have been sighted from the ledges of Mont Sébért (where it was collected last century by Horne), and there are a few plants in the Vallée de Mai and elsewhere on Praslin. Other related species contain pharmacologically active substances but at present this particular plant has not been studied sufficiently to evaluate its medicinal possibilities. The specific name commemorates Dr. Andre Franz Wilhelm Schimper, the botanist on the German Deep Sea Expedition, 1898–1899. He visited Seychelles in 1898 on board the *Valdivia* and died of malaria contracted in Africa the following year.

Other members of this family in the granitic islands are *Asclepias curassavica*, *Calotropis gigantea* (cultivated), *Cryptostegia madagascariensis*, *Cynanchum callialata*, *Gomphocarpus physocarpus*, *G. fruticosus*, *Sarcostemma viminale*, and *Tylophora coriacea*.

ILLUSTRATION. Flowering habit collected and painted on July 13, 1990, at 1×. Fruiting habit collected and painted on July 14, 1990, at 1×. Herbarium sheet: Rosemary Wise 126 (OXF).

BALSAMINACEAE Richard

This family consists of 2 genera and 850 species of herbs and subsucculents distributed throughout temperate and tropical Eurasia, Africa, Madagascar, and Central and North America. All have toothed leaves that are alternate or opposite and watery, and almost translucent stems. Many are grown as ornamentals.

Impatiens Linnaeus

The 850 species that comprise this genus are distributed in the tropics and northern temperate regions, especially in India. Many cultivated species are grown ornamentally or as pot plants. There is one species in the granitic Seychelles.

PLATE 10. *Impatiens gordonii* Horne ex Baker   (Baker, 1877, *Flora of Mauritius*, p. 38)

Impatiens thomassetii J. D. Hooker   (W. B. Hemsley, 1916, *Journal of Botany* 54, suppl. 2, p. 5)

Vernacular name: balsamine sauvage

HABIT. The plant is a succulent perennial herb, glabrous in all parts, and up to 1 m in height. Stipules are absent.

LEAVES. The alternate and elliptic leaves have acuminate apices and cuneiform bases. They are up to 15 cm long, with crenate margins and petioles as long as 13 cm. The eight or nine pairs of secondary veins are semi-craspedodromous. There are two 4 mm long bracts at the bases of the 8 cm peduncles.

FLOWERS. The flowers are up to 5 cm wide and occur in pairs. The two upper sepals are deltoid, while a third lower one is contracted into an 8 cm long spur. The three petals are white, shading to pink at the bases. The emarginate standard is up to 2.5 cm long and keeled at the back. The two wing petals are deltoid, 2.5 cm long, and lobed almost to the base.

FRUITS. The fruits are 2 cm long dehiscent capsules that are glandular and fusiform.

DISTRIBUTION. Mahé and formerly on Silhouette

This species is now very uncommon and endangered, occurring at only two sites on Mahé—Trois Frères and Morne Seychellois, both of which are at approximately 600 m. Thomasset collected it from Cascade Estate (Herbarium sheet: Thomasset 5) and from Morne Blanc. The number of plants at the sites on Mahé is possibly decreasing, but further exploration of Silhouette could yield more than the one population of approximately 100 plants that was discovered in June 1995 by P. Matyot and M. Kirkpatrick. The species is easily propagated and could be reintroduced to sites where collections have been made in the past. The Latin generic name *Impatiens*, meaning "impatience," refers to the explosive release of the seeds, which occurs however lightly the ripe capsule is touched.

Other members of this family in the granitic Seychelles are *Impatiens balsamina*, a cultivated herb with colorful, often double, flowers and *I. walleriana*, a cultivated herb with pink or white flowers that are up to 4 cm wide.

ILLUSTRATION. Flowering habit collected and painted on April 13, 1992, at 1×. Fruiting habit collected and painted on April 14, 1992, at 1×. Herbarium sheet: Rosemary Wise 177 (OXF).

BEGONIACEAE   Agardh

This family of 2 genera, *Hillebrandia* and *Begonia*, has 920 species of succulent herbs and shrubs, some of which are climbers, from the tropics and subtropics. The granitic Seychelles has one genus.

Begonia Linnaeus

The 900 species of herbs in this genus are found in the tropics and subtropics, especially of America. Some species have edible leaves. Most have characteristically asymmetrical leaves. There are over 10,000 recorded hybrids and cultivars, which are grown for their attractive flowers and foliage.

PLATE 11.   *Begonia seychellensis* Hemsley   (W. B. Hemsley, 1916, *Journal of Botany* 54, suppl. 2, p. 15)

Begonia aptera sensu Baker   (Baker, 1877, *Flora of Mauritius*, p. 129)

Vernacular name: begonia sauvage, oseille marron

HABIT. The plant is a dioecious, perennial herb, glabrous in all parts, that reaches 1.5 m in height. The stems are succulent, are often tinged red, and have fleshy caducous stipules that are up to 4 cm long and glabrous in all parts.

LEAVES. The leaves are up to 25 cm long, alternate, simple, asymmetric, and three-lobed with cordate bases. The upper surfaces are green to brownish-green, and the lower surfaces are either green or purplish-red. The margins are dentate. The venation is actinodromous. The petioles reach 15 cm in length.

INFLORESCENCES. The inflorescences are lax, axillary, branched cymes.

FLOWERS. The flowers are white or pale pink. Male flowers are on pedicels that are up to 2.5 cm long and have two elliptic tepals that are 14 mm long and enclose 25–30 stamens. Female flowers have pedicels up to 1.2 cm long that end in two 1 cm long foliar bracts.

FRUITS. The fruits are laterally compressed capsules that reach 2.5 cm in length.

DISTRIBUTION. Mahé and Silhouette

Begonia seychellensis is another species that Horne reported as being "common on all islands," which, again, seems very unlikely. Most of these threatened plants are found at high altitudes (between 500 m and 850 m) in shady, damp habitats, often alongside streams—conditions that are certainly not found on all islands. When less light is available, the undersides of the leaves become deep pink to purplish-red in color. The limited light that diffuses through the leaves is reflected back by this coloration. One of the best areas to see these plants is at the eastern part of the Congo Rouge path. Beyond the bamboo area, then the slightly unimpressive, mainly cinnamon woodland, the start of the mist forest is proclaimed with the tree ferns, *Cyathea sechellarum*, luxuriant mosses, and the begonias. It is in areas such as these that the six species of rare stick insects are found, usually feeding on ferns.

Other members of this family in the granitic islands are *Begonia coccinea*, a cultivated small shrub with dense pendulous clusters of pink flowers; *B. hirtella*, an herb with asymmetric pleated leaves and sparse clusters of pale green or pink flowers; *B. humulis*, a small roadside herb with hairy asymmetric leaves and clusters of white flowers; and *B. ulmifolia*, a fleshy herb with glabrous asymmetric leaves and dense clusters of greenish pink flowers.

ILLUSTRATION. Habit with white flowers and green leaves and habit from a shadier area with pink flowers and leaves with pinkish-mauve undersurfaces. Flowering habit collected and painted on July 24, and August 2, 1990, at 1×. Fruiting habit collected and painted on July 27, 1990, at 1×. Herbarium sheet: Rosemary Wise 133 (OXF).

BIGNONIACEAE Jussieu

This family of 112 genera and 725 species comprises trees, shrubs, lianas, and a few herbs. They are mainly tropical and come principally from South America. Valuable timbers are obtained from some species, including *Tabebuia* in Seychelles. Other species are grown as attractive street trees, for example the scarlet-flowered *Spathodea* and the purple-flowered *Jacaranda*. The granitic Seychelles has one indigenous genus and many cultivated introductions.

Colea Bojer ex Meissner

This genus comprises 20 cauliflorous species from Madagascar and the Mascarenes and 1 from Seychelles.

PLATE 12. *Colea seychellarum* Seemann (B. C. Seemann, 1860, *Trans. Linnean Society* 23:8)

Colea pedunculata Baker (Baker, 1877, *Flora of Mauritius*, p. 244)

Vernacular name: bilimbi marron

HABIT. The plant is a tree, glabrous in all parts and with smooth grayish-brown bark. It grows as high as 10 m. Stipules are absent.

LEAVES. The opposite, imparipinnate leaves have a glandular rachis that is up to 55 cm long. The leaflets are opposite, ovate, with obtuse apices and cuneate bases, asymmetric, subcoriaceous. The margins are entire. The leaflets are up to 12 cm long, and there are three to four pairs per rachis. The six or seven pairs of secondary veins are brochidodromous. The petiolules are up to 1.5 cm long.

INFLORESCENCES. The inflorescences are cauliflorus panicles bearing from 10 to 20 flowers. The inflorescences are up to 30 cm long, arising from trunks and older branches.

FLOWERS. The calyx is campanulate with five minute lobes. The corolla is tubular and curved, shading in color from cream to pink and purple, and is up to 3.5 cm long. It has five obtuse, reflexed lobes that are cream-colored but deepening to bright yellow in the throat. The four stamens are inserted in the tube.

FRUITS. The fruits are green, cauliflorus, succulent, cylindrical berries with persistent styles and reach 15 cm in length.

DISTRIBUTION. Mahé, Praslin, and Silhouette

The vernacular name, bilimbi marron, or wild bilimbi, likens the shape of fruit of *Colea* to that of the sharp-tasting *Averrhoa bilimbi*, a common ingredient of Creole cookery. The endemic fruits are rarely seen however because they are eaten by birds and possibly also by fruit bats. *Colea seychellarum* Seeman grows from mid- to high altitude. There are several large trees alongside the path at La Reserve that flower frequently, and at the place where one has to cross the stream on the top ridge of Congo Rouge, smaller trees border the water. Flowers and fruits are cauliflorus, arising directly from the trunk or main branches of the trees. In the past, *Colea* was mainly collected for firewood and for charcoal-making. The authority, Berthold Carl Seemann (1838–1907), was trained at the Royal Botanic Gardens, Kew, in techniques of plant collecting.

Other members of this family in the granitic islands are *Crescentia cujete*, *Jacaranda mimosifolia* (cultivated), *Macfadyena unguis-cati*, *Millingtonia hortensis* (cultivated), *Saritaea magnifica*, *Spathodea campanulata*, *Tabebuia pallida*, *T. rosea*, and *Tecoma stans*.

ILLUSTRATION. Shoot with both young and mature leaves; cauliflorus flowers and fruits; all painted at 1×. Flowering habit collected and painted on August 16, 1989. Fruiting habit collected and painted on August 16, 1989. Herbarium sheet: Rosemary Wise 90 (OXF).

COMPOSITAE Giseke

This is an enormous cosmopolitan family of 900 genera and 21,000 species of trees, shrubs, climbers, and herbs. Many are grown as ornamentals including *Senecio, Aster, Centurea, Doronicum, Dahlia, Bellis* and, *Helianthus*. The Compositae also contain some noxious weeds, including dandelions (*Taraxicum*) and thistles (*Carduus, Circium,* and *Sonchus*). One of the greatest killers of grazing livestock is the poisonous *Senecio*. Some genera are edible: *Cichorium* (chicory), *Lactuca* (lettuce), *Cynara* (globe artichoke), and *Helianthus tuberosus* (Jerusalem artichoke). *Arnica* is used as a medicine. In the granitic Seychelles there are four indigenous genera and many introductions.

Gynura Cassini

This genus comprises 50 species from the Old World tropics.

PLATE 13. *Gynura sechellensis* Hemsley (W. B. Hemsley, 1916, *Journal of Botany* 54, suppl. 2, p. 2)

Senecio sechellensis Baker (Baker, 1877, *Flora of Mauritius*, p. 178)

Vernacular name: jacobe

HABIT. The plant is a perennial herb or woody small shrub, glabrous in all parts, with slightly angular stems, lacking stipules, and up to 2 m high.

LEAVES. The leaves are obovate or elliptic, with acute or rounded apices and attenuate bases, bullate and slightly succulent. They have dentate margins and are up to 15 cm long. The venation is faint, and there are six pairs of craspidodromous secondary veins. The petioles may be as long as 4 cm.

INFLORESCENCES. The inflorescences are lax corymbs at the ends of the branches. They may reach to 10 cm in length and have from 10 to 20 heads. The peduncles are up to 2 cm long and have an involucre of seven or eight oblong bracts that are up to 8 mm long.

FLOWERS. The flowers are yellowish-orange, and there are approximately 30 in each head. The corolla tube is up to 12 mm long and has five valvate lobes. The anthers are 2 mm long, and the style, which extends beyond the corolla, has a bilobed stigma.

FRUITS. The fruits are one-seeded, longitudinally striate achenes. They are 3 mm long and have a terminal, white, 7 mm long pappus.

DISTRIBUTION. Mahé and Silhouette

Gynura sechellensis represents one of the few remaining endemic herbs. Although it is found at various altitudes, it is most common in the mid- to higher areas above 400 m. Patches of this orange-flowered composite grow at the high stretches of the San Souci roadside along with *Begonia humulis, Cynorkis fastigiata, Malaxis sechellarum,* and *Lophoschoenus hornei.* The more open areas of the high-altitude forests, for example, the view points in La Reserve and the summit of Morne Blanc, also have populations of these plants. In shady woodland *Gynura* is frequently found growing with *Procris insularis* and the orchid, *M. seychellarum* in the loam on the tops of rocks.

The vernacular name, jacobe, refers to an initial likeness of this plant to the European *Senecio jacobaea.* Infusions made from this plant are given to sooth rashes, especially on young children. Some plants are grown in the Palm House in Kew Gardens, London.

Other members of this family in the granitic islands are *Ageratum conyzoides, Ayapana triplinervis* (cultivated), *Bidens pilosa, Chrysanthemum indicum, Coreopsis lanceolata* (cultivated), *Cosmos caudatus* (cultivated), *Elephantopus mollis, Emilia sonchifolia, Erigeron karvinskianus, Gaillardia pulchella* (cultivated), *Gerbera jamesonii* (cultivated), *Helianthus annuus* (sunflower, cultivated), *H. tuberosus* (Jerusalem artichoke, cultivated), *Lactuca indica, L. sativa* (lettuce, cultivated), *Melampodium divaricatum, Melanthera biflora, Parthenium hysterophorus, Pterocypsela indica, Sigesbeckia orientalis, Synedrella nodiflora, Tithonia diversifolia, Tridax procumbens, Vernonia cinerea, Wedelia trilobata* (cultivated), *Youngia japonica.*

Vernonia sechellensis, with a single collection in 1874 from Fôret Noire, Mahé (Herbarium sheet: Horne 497), is almost certainly extinct.

ILLUSTRATION. Habit with buds and flowers and detail of mature fruits; painted at 1×. Enlargements of flowers; painted at 7×. Flowering habit collected and painted on August 16, 1989. Fruiting habit collected and painted on August 17, 1989. Herbarium sheets: Rosemary Wise 87, 195 (OXF).

CUCURBITACEAE Jussieu

This family consists of 120 genera and 766 species of climbers. Most of these are succulent but a few are woody. The distribution is primarily through the tropics and subtropics with a few temperate species. Many important food crops are in the cucurbita, including gourds, marrows, pumpkins, and squash. The genus *Cucumis* includes cucumbers and melons. Loofahs are produced from the dry skeletons of the fruits of *Luffa cylindrica*.

Peponium Engler

This genus comprises approximately 20 species of climbers that are mainly succulent but occasionally woody. They are restricted to Africa, Madagascar, and the one taxon in the granitic Seychelles.

PLATE 14. *Peponium vogelii* (Hooker f.) Engler (C. Jeffrey, 1967, *Flora of tropical East Africa. Cucurbitaceae*, p. 81)

Bryonopsis laciniosa auct. non (L.) Naud (Baker, 1877, *Flora of Mauritius*, p. 130)

Vernacular name: calebasse marron

HABIT. This plant is a climber, scrambling over ground and vegetation. It is up to 8 m long, with grayish-green stems. At each node there are two spiraling tendrils that reach 20 cm in length.

LEAVES. The leaves, which may be up to 16 cm long, are alternate and palmately lobed. They have obtuse or attenuate apices, cordate leaf bases, and dentate margins. The upper surfaces are glabrous and bullate, and the lower surfaces are pubescent. The venation is actinodromous.

FLOWERS. There is generally one male flower, sometimes two, in each leaf axil. These have 8 cm long pedicels. The calyx, which is tubular and up to 2.5 cm long, has five narrow 7 mm long lobes. The corolla is yellow, up to 3 cm long, and conspicuously veined and has five obovate, fibrillate lobes. There are three stamens. The female flowers are solitary, and the pedicels may reach 10 cm in length. The calyx tube is up to 3 cm long and swollen at the base. It has five narrow 7 mm long lobes. The corolla is 3 cm long and yellow, with five lobes, two of which are slightly larger than the others. There are three staminodes and a 12 mm long style with a three-lobed stigma.

FRUITS. The fruits are obovate, glabrous berries up to 6 cm long. They are light green at first, becoming light brown when mature. They dehisce into three valves. The peduncles are up to 16 cm long.

DISTRIBUTION. Aride

The earliest record of this climbing plant was from the forests of the Cascade area of Mahé (Herbarium sheet: Horne 460). It is found now only on Aride and was first looked at in detail by two previous wardens of the island, Gill Lewis and Ian Bullock (1987–89). Although it presently shares a name with an African species, there are significant morphological differences. The African plants have either white or yellow flowers, whereas those of the Aride population are exclusively yellow. The fruits on Aride ripen to light brown, whereas their African counterparts are bright red. In East Africa, the plants are found from 80 to 240 m in altitude. On Aride they are locally common at all altitudes from a few meters above sea level, on the plateau, to the summit at 134 m. More research is necessary to determine the status of this plant but it seems highly likely that it will eventually be described as an endemic subspecies. For this reason I include it.

I paid my second visit to Aride in 1989 especially to paint this newly described plant, possibly a fellow endemic to *Rothmannia annae*. I arrived late one afternoon. On this occasion the journey over from Praslin was in an inflatable boat. Thousands of seabirds were wheeling and calling overhead in the failing light as I searched the plateau area and located the plant, which was straggling over everything in the banana plantation. At 7 A.M. the following morning I hurried along to collect a piece of the night-flowering creeper to paint, but I was too late for flowers—they had all withered. That day was spent painting the leaves. I set out an hour earlier the next morning and collected open flowers by flashlight. On a small island with over a million seabirds present, painting has to be undercover. Indoors, I did not consider the problem of geckos on the ceiling, and my finished work became indelibly marked. Fortunately, the damage occurred on the white background.

Other members of this family in the granitic islands, all of which are cultivated, are *Benincasa hispida*, *Citrullus lanatus*, *Cucumis anguria*, *C. melo* (melon), *C. metuliferus*, *C. sativus* (cucumber), *Cucurbita moschata* (squash), *Lagenaria siceraria* (bottle gourd), *Luffa cylindrica*, *Momordica charantia*, *Sechium edule* (chouchoute), and *Trichosanthes cucumerina* (snake gourd).

ILLUSTRATION. Habit with female flower, leaves, and tendrils; male flower; fruit; all painted at 1×. Flowering habit collected and painted on July 7, 1990. Fruiting habit collected and painted on July 8, 1990. Herbarium sheet: Rosemary Wise 125 (OXF).

DILLENIACEAE Salis

This is a large family containing 12 genera and 300 species of trees, shrubs, herbs, and lianas, many of which have large white or yellow flowers. The leaves are usually alternate and deciduous and have very prominent venation on the undersurface. Some species have leaves with surfaces that are exceptionally rough and used as sandpaper in rural communities. The distribution of the family is almost pantropical.

Dillenia Linnaeus

This genus consists of 60 species in the Indian Ocean, Indomalasia, and Australia. Only three occur in the granitic Seychelles.

PLATE 15. *Dillenia ferruginea* (Baillon) Gilg   (H.G.A. Engler and K.A.E. Prantl, 1894, *Naturl. Pflanzenfam.* part 3, vol. 8, p. 125)

Wormia ferruginea (Baillon) J. Hutchinson and V. Summerhayes (V. S. Summerhayes, 1928, *Bull. Misc. Info.*, Kew 1928:388)

Vernacular name: bois rouge

HABIT. The plant is a tree up to 20 m in height with a rounded crown and reddish brown bark.

LEAVES. The leaves are alternate. Seedling leaves have margins that are either serrate or entire with small points formed by extensions of the secondary veins. Sapling leaves are glabrous, shiny, and usually flushed from crimson to purple and can be as long as 1 m in length. Their bases are amplexicaul, forming water-holding pockets. The young leaves on mature trees have rust-colored silky hairs. Older leaves are glabrous on the upper surface and lightly tomentose below, coriaceous, and characteristically holed by weevils. The petioles are 5 cm long with 5 mm long silky hairs. There are from 36 to 42 parallel secondary veins and scalariform tertiary veins. The venation is very pronounced on the undersurface.

INFLORESCENCES. The inflorescences are terminal and lateral racemes that are up to 30 cm long and bear many flowers.

FLOWERS. The flowers are regular and perfect. They reach 4 cm in width. The two outer sepals are pubescent and the three inner ones glabrous. There are five free, crumpled white petals, which are twice as long as the sepals. There are many stamens and from 7 to 10 carpels.

FRUITS. The fruits are syncarpous and fleshy with axile placentation and persistent sepals. They are up to 1.5 cm wide. The seeds are covered with orange, convoluted arils.

DISTRIBUTION. Mahé, Praslin, Silhouette, and Curieuse

Dillenia ferruginea is a common woodland tree at mid- to high altitude (La Reserve, Mahé, Vallée de Mai, Praslin), but it is also found at sea level (Curieuse). The forest trees are usually larger than their neighbors and emergent. When trees are in the open or at the roadsides (Sans Souci, Mahé, alongside the tea plantation, for example), the characteristic insect damage to the leaves is easier to observe. Black or green weevils, probably of the same species, leave circular holes, frequently in such numbers to give the leaves a lacelike appearance. The leaves of many plants have evolved to contain toxic compounds that give protection against insect damage, but at the same time, certain insects have coevolved with an immunity to these. Often this is such a specialized relationship that the insects can eat leaves only from this species or from members of the same family.

Specimens of this species are stunted when growing on areas of exposed bedrock (locally called glacis). For example, on the summit of Copolia, Mahé, the trees are often not more than 2 m tall at maturity.

The genus *Dillenia* was named by Linnaeus (1707–1778), the Swedish botanist who formulated the binomial system of plant classification. *Ferruginea* is from the Latin *ferruginous*, meaning "rusty." When Linnaeus visited Oxford Botanic Gardens in 1736, Johann Jacob Dillenius (1687–1747), the German-born professor of botany and keeper of the botanic gardens, was hostile toward Linnaeus's new system, and their first meeting was far from successful. James Sherard (1659–1728), the benefactor of the chair of botany, accompanied them on their walk around the gardens. Linnaeus wrote, "When I visited Dillenius, I found James Sherard with him, to whom he said 'This is the man who has thrown all botany into confusion.'" Linnaeus did not speak English, but the words *botany* and *confusion* to a classical scholar were sufficient to give a clear meaning. Linnaeus then picked a flower and demonstrated his new system, which was based on sexual characters. Although Dillenius did not accept the new system at the time, he appreciated Linnaeus's intelligence and forthwith held him in high esteem.

Other members of this family in the granitic islands are *Dillenia indica*, a cultivated tree with white flowers, and *Dillenia suffruticosa*, a cultivated shrub with yellow flowers that are up to 10 cm wide.

ILLUSTRATION. Flowering habit, fruits, young flush leaves, and young leaf showing water-holding pocket; painted at 1×. Dead leaf painted at 0.5×. Flowering habit collected and painted on August 10, 1989. Fruiting habit collected and painted on August 10, 1989. Herbarium sheets: Rosemary Wise 82, 100 (OXF).

Rosemary Wise.

DIPTEROCARPACEAE   Blume

This family consists of 16 genera and 530 species of small to very tall trees. They are distributed in tropical Asia and Indomalaysia, and two genera occur in tropical Africa. Concentrated in Malaysia, they are often the dominant species of the rain forest and provide the world's main source of hardwood.

Vateriopsis Heim
This monotypic genus occurs only on Mahé.

PLATE 16.   *Vateriopsis seychellarum* (Dyer) Heim

Vateria seychellarum   (Dyer in Baker, 1877, *Flora of Mauritius*, p. 526)

Vernacular name: bois de fer

HABIT. The plant is a tree with resinous bark and can reach a height of 30 m. The stipules are up to 3 cm long and caducous and leave semicircular scars below the leaves.

LEAVES. The leaves are alternate, obovate, coriaceous, and glabrous, with acuminate or rounded apices and truncate bases. They reach 25 cm in length. Immature leaves are frequently a flushed apricot color. The 20–22 pairs of secondary veins are parallel, craspedodromous, and prominent on the undersurface. The tertiary venation is scalariform. The petioles are up to 8 cm long and swollen at the base of the leaf blade.

INFLORESCENCES. The inflorescences are axillary spikes, from 5–10 cm long, and have few flowers.

FLOWERS. The flowers are up to 2 cm wide. The calyx has five persistent 8 mm long sepals. The five petals are yellowish-white tinged with pink at the tips. Numerous stamens are fused at the base to form a 0.8 mm long staminal tube. The ovary is large and conical and has a 2 mm long style.

FRUITS. The fruits, which are up to 4 cm long, are globose, woody, indehiscent, rough-textured, and light brown in color. A fruit contains a single seed.

DISTRIBUTION. Mahé

This plant is a very rare, endangered tree growing at altitudes of 250–600 m and is the only member of the subfamily *Dipterocarpoideae* found outside of Asia and Australia. Most related genera are highly gregarious and tend to dominate the forests, especially in Southeast Asia. *Vateriopsis* once was certainly more widespread in Seychelles and may have dominated, but the indiscriminate felling of trees for the high-quality timber by early settlers almost resulted in its extinction. (The name, bois de fer, means "iron wood.") As well as being a valuable wood for furniture and boat-building, exudations of the sap of bois de fer were once used in the manufacture of incense. An infusion of the leaves is said to be helpful in the treatment of liver troubles. At one time there were only about 10 remaining trees on Mahé, but the seeds germinate readily, and young trees have now been planted in the Bois de Fer valley. One isolated old tree that is protected by a wire fence stands on the bank on one of the higher stretches of the Sans Souci Road, between Victoria and Port Glaud. In this location, some associated species are *Northia seychellana*, *Cinnamomum verum*, *Chrysobalanus icaco*, *Pandanus hornei*, *Protarum sechellarum*, *Drypetes riseleyi*, *Dillenia ferruginea*, and *Cynorchis fastigiata*. On September 7, 1989, Lindsay Chong Seng took me to see *Nepenthes pervillei* on a rocky outcrop at the top of La Misère, Mahé. In one of the villages there, Lindsay spotted a large tree of *Vateriopsis* previously not known to the conservation department. With so few trees remaining, this was an exciting find, and both flowers and fruits were collected to be painted.

There are no related species in the granitic Seychelles.

ILLUSTRATION. Flush leaf and flowering habit; painted at 0.5×. Habit with fruits; painted at 1×. Flowers; painted at 1×. Flowering habit collected and painted on September 30, 1989. Fruiting habit collected and painted on September 7, 1989. Herbarium sheets: Rosemary Wise 98, 176 (OXF).

EBENACEAE Guerke

This is a pantropical family of 2 genera and 485 species of trees and shrubs with a few temperate genera. Many are of importance for their timber, especially those that produce ebony. In the granitic Seychelles there is a single genus.

Diospyros Linnaeus

This genus comprises 475 species from America, Africa, Madagascar, Seychelles (1 species), and Asia. Many species of this genus produce ebony. Some species have edible fruits, including *Diospyros virginiana*, *D. kaki* (persimmons), and *D. lotus* (date plum).

PLATE 17. *Diospyros seychellarum* (Hiern) A.J.G.H. Kostermans   (A.J.G.H. Kostermans, 1977, *Blumea* 23: 496)

Maba seychellarum Hiern   (Hiern, 1873, *Ebenaceae, Trans. Cambridge Philosphical Society*, p. 130; Baker, 1877, *Flora of Mauritius*, p. 196)

Vernacular name: bois sagaye

HABIT. The plant is a tree with zig-zagging, sparsely hairy, terete branches, with no stipules, and a monopodial crown. The trees can reach 10 m in height.

LEAVES. The leaves are alternate and oblong lanceolate, with obtuse apices and cuneate bases. They are coriaceous and up to 4 cm long and have entire margins. The venation is indistinct, with 8–10 pairs of secondary veins.

FLOWERS. The flowers are white, axillary, solitary, and dioecious. The calyx is campanulate, pubescent, and up to 2.5 mm long, with three or four shallow lobes. The corolla tube is pubescent on the outside, is up to 4 mm long, and has three or four spreading lobes. The male flowers have as many as 20 stamens, and the female flowers as many as eight staminodes.

FRUITS. The fruits are ovoid, mucronate acorns that are green when young, becoming light brown at maturity.

DISTRIBUTION. Mahé, Praslin, Silhouette, Ste. Anne, and Félicité

Diospyros seychellarum is usually a narrow understory tree whose trunks rarely exceed 30 cm. in diameter, so it is of no commercial value. It grows from the lowlands (Bernica) to altitudes of 500 m. The trees found in the shady, moist habitat of La Reserve, Mahé, appear to flower and fruit infrequently, unlike those enjoying more open areas, for example, near to the summit of Bernica. *D. seychellensis* was once a popular plant used by the "bon homme du bois," or local medicine man. He used it like a wand, shaking it at any person who may have tried to put a curse on him. The vernacular name, bois sagaye, probably originates from the Swahili word *asagye*, meaning "spear." Infusions of the leaves were used as a general medicine.

Other members of this family in the granitic islands are *Diospyros digyna*, a cultivated tree with elliptic leaves to 16 cm and *D. philippensis*, a cultivated tree with ovate leaves to 20 cm, white flowers to 1 cm., and edible pink fruits 12 cm wide.

ILLUSTRATION. Habit with flower buds, detail of flowers, and detail of mature fruits; painted at 1×. Enlargement of bud; painted at 3×. Flowering habit collected and painted on August 12, 1989. Fruiting habit collected and painted on September 20, 1989. Herbarium sheets: Rosemary Wise 85, 110, 188 (OXF).

ERYTHROXYLACEAE   Kunth

This family comprises 4 genera and 260 species of shrubs or small trees. The distribution is pantropical but mainly in the New World. The economic uses include timber, cocaine, oils, and dyes. There is one species in the granitic Seychelles.

Erythroxylum P. Brown

This genus consists of 250 tropical species distributed in the Americas, Madagascar, and Seychelles. In South America, the bushes are used for hedging. *Erythroxylum coca* and *E. novagranatense* yield cocaine; the former is chewed as a stimulant in South America, and the latter cultivated for local anaesthetics in Sri Lanka and Java.

PLATE 18.   *Erythroxylum sechellarum* O. E. Schultz
(H.G.A. Engler, 1907, *Pflanzenr.*, part 4, fasc. 134, p. 158)

E. laurifolium sensu Baker   (Baker, 1877, *Flora of Mauritius*, p. 35)

Vernacular name: café marron petite feuille

HABIT. The plant is a shrub or small tree up to 8 m high that is glabrous in all parts with gray-brown, fissured bark. The stipules are lanceolate and 1.5 mm long.

LEAVES. The leaves are alternate, obovate, and coriaceous. They reach lengths up to 12 cm and have caniculate, variable petioles that are 3–8 mm long. The 9–13 pairs of secondary veins are camptodromous.

FLOWERS. The flowers are axillary. There are three to five in a cluster, and they have rigid, 5 mm long pedicels. The five-lobed calyx is up to 6 mm in length, tubular, and continuous with the pedicel. The five petals are spreading, with a 1 mm upright, central ligule. A staminal tube is formed by the stamens fusing for 2 mm at the base. The flowers differ in having three either short or long styles.

FRUITS. The fruits are erect, red, ovate, slightly asymmetrical, and up to 15 mm long.

DISTRIBUTION. Mahé, Praslin, Silhouette, La Digue, Curieuse, and Félicité

Erythroxylum sechellarum is one of the most common of the endemic plants. It is found from sea level to high altitude and is able to thrive on glacis as well as in the forest. On the more exposed areas of Copolia and Mont Sébért, *Erythroxylum* grows as a rather columnar shrub. It is only in the shaded forests that it develops into a tree, examples of which are found on La Reserve, Mahé. Infusions of the leaves are used medicinally for reducing fevers. The generic name *Erythroxylum* is derived from *eryth*, meaning "red" and *xylum*, "wood."

There are no related species in the granitic islands.

ILLUSTRATION. Flowering and fruiting habits; painted at 1×. Enlargements of whole flower; painted at 8×. Flower with one petal removed to show staminal tube; painted at 8×. Flowering habit collected and painted on June 18, 1990, and June 23, 1991. Fruiting habit collected and painted on August 8, 1989. Herbarium sheets: Rosemary Wise 91, 213 (OXF).

EUPHORBIACEAE Jussieu

The family is the second largest of the angiosperms and consists of 326 genera and 7,750 species of trees, shrubs, lianas, and herbs with a distribution that is cosmopolitan, excluding the Arctic. One of the most important commodities derived from this family is rubber, which is produced from tapping *Hevia* species. Latex is present in the Euphorbiaceae and is toxic in all species. The staple food source in many countries is cassava (*Manhiot*). Other uses from species in this large family are medicinal (castor oil comes from *Ricinus communis*), timber (*Ricinodendron* species, African oak), many cultivated ornamentals including poinsettia (*Euphorbia pulcherrima*), and some edible fruits. *Acatha* species and *Codiaeum variegatum* are commonly grown as garden hedges. The granitic Seychelles has seven indigenous genera and some cultivated introductions.

Drypetes Vahl

This genus comprises 200 tropical species from eastern Asia, South Africa, and Seychelles and is used mainly for timber.

PLATE 19. *Drypetes riseleyi* Airy Shaw (H.K.A. Shaw, 1965, *Kew Bulletin* 18:272)

Riseleya griffithii Hemsley (W. B. Hemsley, 1917, *Journal of Botany* 55:286)

Vernacular name: bois marée petite feuille

HABIT. The plant is a tree, dioecious and spreading, with gray bark. It can reach a height of 20 m. The stipules are up to 0.5 mm and caducous.

LEAVES. The leaves are alternate and elliptic, with acuminate apices and decurrent bases. They are coriaceous and glabrous, dark green on the upper surface, paler on the lower, with entire margins. They are as long as 11 cm. The eight pairs of secondary veins are brochidodromous, with randomly reticulate tertiary venation. The petioles are up to 2 cm long.

FLOWERS. The male flowers are caducous and not seen. Female flowers are in fascicles of two to five on pedicels up to 2 cm long. The four tepals are imbricate and up to 8 mm long. The style is as long as 7 mm and has two stigmas.

FRUITS. The fruits are ovoid, tomentose, greenish brown or light brown drupes, up to 4 cm long, and usually contain two pyrenes (but sometimes one or three).

DISTRIBUTION. Mahé, Praslin, and Silhouette

A very rare, endangered tree, known from a few sites only. Formerly it was more widespread, but the fine-grained, light-colored timber was in great demand, especially for oar-making. There are a very few isolated trees remaining on Mahé. One grows alongside the Sans Souci Road in the vicinity of the lone *Vateriopsis seychellarum*, with *Dillenia ferruginea* and *Northia seychellana*. On Praslin it is found in the Vallée de Mai. *Drypetes* is more widespread on Silhouette, growing at midaltitudes. The specific epithet commemorates the Hon. Risely Griffith, a government administrator.

Most euphorbs have woody dehiscent fruits. *Drypetes* is unique in having fleshy drupes.

Other members of this family in the granitic islands are *Acalypha hispida* (cultivated), *A. indica*, *A. wilkesiana* (cultivated), *Aleurites moluccana* (cultivated), *Breynia disticha* var. *disticha* f. *nivosa* (cultivated), *Codiaeum variegatum* (cultivated), *Euphorbia cyathophora*, *E. hirta*, *E. hypericifolia*, *E. lactea* (cultivated), *E. leucocephala* (cultivated), *E. millii* (cultivated), *E. prostrata*, *E. pulcherrima* (poinsettia, cultivated), *E. pyrifolia*, *E. thymifolia*, *E. tirucalli* (cultivated), *Excoecaria benthamiana* (endemic), *Hevea brasiliensis* (rubber, cultivated), *Jatropha curcas*, *J. multifida* (cultivated), *J. integerrima* (cultivated), *J. podagrica* (cultivated), *Manihot esculenta* (manioc, cultivated), *M. glaziovii* (cultivated), *Pedilanthus tithymaloides* (cultivated), *Phyllanthus acidus* (cultivated), *P. amarus*, *P. maderaspatensis*, *P. pervilleanus*, *P. tenellus*, *P. urinaria*, *Ricinus communis* (cultivated), and *Wielandia elegans*.

ILLUSTRATION. Habits with both young and mature fruits and two views of seeds; painted at 1×. Fruiting habit collected and painted on June 25, 1990 and October 26, 1992. Herbarium sheets: Rosemary Wise 84, 119, 190 (OXF).

EUPHORBIACEAE Jussieu

Excoecaria Linnaeus

This genus comprises 40 species from the Old World tropics, some of which yield excellent timbers (African sandalwood comes from East Africa).

PLATE 20. *Excoecaria benthamiana* Hemsley (W. B. Hemsley, 1906, *Hooker's Icones plantarum*, t. 2741)

Vernacular name: bois jasmin

HABIT. The plant is a shrub or small tree, is monoecious, has white latex, and can reach a height of 5 m. The stipules are deltoid, caducous, and up to 3 mm long.

LEAVES. The leaves are alternate and elliptic, with obtuse apices and obtuse bases. They are also coriaceous and glabrous with entire margins and up to 20 cm long. The venation is raised on both surfaces. The 12–14 pairs of secondary veins are brochidodromous.

INFLORESCENCES. The inflorescences are axillary cymes that are up to 6 cm long.

FLOWERS. The male flowers are in groups of three, the central ones being without bracteoles, while the laterals have three succulent, glandular bracteoles. They have three deltoid tepals with valvate tips and three stamens. The female flowers are on pedicels up to 5 mm long and have three imbricate tepals and three stigmas.

FRUITS. The fruits are three-lobed green capsules, up to 1.5 cm long.

DISTRIBUTION. Mahé and Praslin

Excoecaria benthamiana grows both on dryer glacis, where mists provide the required moisture (e.g., Mt. Sébért), or rarely in the hygrophile forests on Mahé. The sap of this tree, like most of the others in the family, contains a strong irritant and great care should be exercised when collecting the plant. The woody fruits dehisce loudly when mature, showering the seeds some distance from the parent plant.

ILLUSTRATION. Fruiting habit and detail of fruits; painted at 1×. Englargement of flowers; painted at 10×. Flowering habit collected and painted on September 11, 1989. Fruiting habit collected and painted on September 11, 1989. Herbarium sheet: Rosemary Wise 116 (OXF).

FLACOURTIACEAE   De Candolle

This is a family of 88 genera and 875 species of trees and shrubs that are widespread in the tropics and subtropics, but with some species in temperate regions. A few species are ornamental while others are cultivated for timber, fruits, or medicinal oils. There are three indigenous genera in the granitic Seychelles.

Aphloia (DC.) Bennett

This polymorphic genus is distributed in East Africa, Madagascar, the Mascarenes, Seychelles.

PLATE 21.   *Aphloia theiformis* (Vahl) Bennett subsp. *madagascariensis* (Clos) H. Perrier var. *seychellensis* (Clos) F. Friedmann, comb. nov.   (F. Friedmann, 1994, *Flore des Seychelles*, pp. 194–95)

A. madagascariensis Clos var. *seychellensis* Clos   (D. Clos, 1857, *Annales des Sciences Naturelles*, series 4, 8:273)

A. mauritiana Baker var. *theiformis* sensu Baker   (Baker, 1877, *Flora of Mauritius*, p. 12)

A. seychellensis Hemsley   (W. B. Hemsley, 1916, *Journal of Botany* 54, suppl. 2, p. 2)

Vernacular name: bois merle

HABIT. The plant is a shrub or small tree, glabrous in all parts, up to 12 m in height with smooth bark and straggling branches. The stipules are deltoid and 4 mm long.

LEAVES. The leaves are alternate, elliptic, glabrous, and up to 8 cm long with crenate margins and petioles ranging in length from 4 to 7 cm. The six pairs of secondary veins are brochidodromous.

FLOWERS. The flowers are axillary, single or clustered, with pedicels up to 18 mm long. The calyx has four or five imbricate sepals, three of which are larger than the others. There are no petals but there are numerous 3 mm long stamens and an asymmetric pistil.

FRUITS. The fruits are indehiscent globose, fleshy berries that are 1 cm wide and have many seeds. The fruits are light green when young but become white at maturity.

DISTRIBUTION. Mahé, Praslin, and Silhouette

The specific name, *theiformis*, refers to the similarity of the leaf shape to that of *Camellia sinensis*, the tea plant. In the Mascarenes the leaves of a related species are infused for a beverage. In Seychelles, *Aphloia* has several medicinal uses. An infusion is reputed to be used for the treatment of sexually transmitted diseases, especially gonorrhea. The addition of leaves to bathwater helps to reduce skin infections. A decoction of leaves, boiled in water for a considerable time, is taken as a general tonic. When the leaves of several other plants are added, the liquid gives relief to the gums of teething children.

Although mainly a low-altitude species, bois merle also grows in the higher areas and is locally common in both. The succulent berries are attractive to and dispersed by the endemic bulbul, *Ixos crassirostris*, commonly called merle. This gives rise to the vernacular name of the plant, bois merle. Several rather sparse shrubs can be seen at the furthest viewpoint at the summit of Morne Blanc, there they grow alongside *Gastonia crassa*, stunted trees of *Northia seychellana*, *Pandanus sechellarum*, and *Syzygium wrightii*.

Other members of this family in granitic islands are *Flacourtia indica*, *Flacourtia jangomas*, *Hydnocarpus pentandra*, and *Ludia mauritiana* var. *sechellensis* F. Friedmann.

ILLUSTRATION. Habit showing both flowers and fruits; painted at 1×. Monochrome detail of flowers, drawn at 8×. Flowering habit collected and painted on June 18, 1990. Fruiting habit collected and painted on August 31, 1989. Herbarium sheet: Rosemary Wise 142 (OXF).

FLACOURTIACEAE   De Candolle

Ludia Commerson ex Jussieu

This genus consists of 23 species with distribution in East Africa, Madagascar, the Mascarenes, and Seychelles.

PLATE 22.   *Ludia mauritiana* Gmelin var. *sechellensis* F. Friedmann

Ludia sessiflora sensu Baker   (Baker, 1877, *Flora of Mauritius*, p. 11)

Vernacular name: prunier marron, petite prune

HABIT. The plant is a tree or shrub, glabrous in all parts, and is up to 10 m in height, with smooth, light-brown bark and slender branches.

LEAVES. The leaves are alternate and elliptic, up to 9 cm long, slightly falcate, with entire or dentate margins and 1 cm long petioles. Juvenile leaves are shiny and have larger emarginate teeth than the mature leaves. The six pairs of secondary veins diverge at an angle of 40 degrees. The tertiary veins have random reticulation.

FLOWERS. Not seen.

FRUITS. Not seen.

DISTRIBUTION. Mahé, Praslin, Silhouette, Curieuse, and Félicité

Ludia mauritiana var. *sechellensis* is common at 350 m (La Reserve, Mahé). Many seedlings grow alongside the shady paths there, with *Dillenia ferruginea*, *Canthium carinatum*, *Curculigo seychellensis*, and all endemic palms except *Lodoicea maldivica*. It is only when seedlings grow in open spaces that they are able to develop into large trees, as can be seen on Mt. Sébért. The venation is sufficiently different from all other species (being prominent and with the secondaries arising at an acute angle to the midrib) to identify this tree easily from the leaves alone. Unfortunately, I was never able to locate flowers or fruits.

ILLUSTRATION. Leaves painted on July 23, 1995, at 1×. Herbarium sheet: Rosemary Wise 208 (OXF).

GROSSULARIACEAE De Candolle

This family comprises 22 genera and 325 species of cosmopolitan trees and shrubs. Some produce edible fruits; the genus *Ribes* produces white, red, and black currants and gooseberries. Many species are grown as ornamentals.

Brexia Nor. ex Thouars

PLATE 23.   *Brexia madagascariensis* (Lam) Ker-Gawler subsp. *microcarpa* (Tulasne) F. Friedmann

Brexia microcarpa Tulasne   (L.-R. Tulasne, 1857, *Annales des Sciences Naturelles*, series 4, 8:160)

Vernacular name: bois cateau

HABIT. The plant is a tree that is glabrous in all parts and up to 7 m high, with grayish-brown, lightly fissured bark, and caducous, 1 mm long stipules.

LEAVES. The leaves are alternate, elliptic or obovate, acute or obtuse at apices, with cuneiform bases, coriaceous, and as long as 20 cm. The margins are entire. The orange petioles are up to 2 cm long.

INFLORESCENCES. The inflorescences are axillary umbels, with peduncles up to 4.5 cm long. From four to eight flowers are borne on each, with 2 cm long bractless pedicels.

FLOWERS. The calyx is up to 3 mm long with five shallow lobes. The five petals are slightly succulent, pale green shading to pink, and 14 mm long. The five stamens are inserted below the orange disk, which has four or five pointed appendages between each filament. The style is up to 9 mm long, with a four- or five-lobed stigma.

FRUITS. The fruits are woody, cylindrical, lightly ridged, dark olive green, and up to 6 cm long.

DISTRIBUTION. Mahé, Praslin, Silhouette, and Félicité

A now threatened and very rare endemic subspecies, found at altitudes in excess of 500 m on Mahé and Silhouette, at far lower ones in the Vallée de Mai, and at an altitude of 30 m on Félicité. The vernacular name cateau suggests that the fruits provided food for the endemic Black Parrot, or, in the past for the now extinct Green Parakeet. On Mahé, *Brexia* grows on Congo Rouge, on Mt. Jasmin, and in a few other rather inaccessible locations. It has a reputation for bringing good fortune to households and for that reason seedlings used to be brought down from the mountains and planted in gardens. Fishermen often took the fruits with them in the pirogues as good-luck charms.

There are no related species in the granitic Seychelles.

I have followed Dr. D. J. Mabberley (1987) and included this species in the Grossulariaceae. Dr. F. Friedmann has put it in the Brexiaceae (1994), and Dr. R. Brummit (1992) in the Escalloniaceae.

ILLUSTRATION. Flowering and fruiting habits collected and painted on August 15, 1995, at 1×. Herbarium sheet: Rosemary Wise 209 (OXF).

ICACINACEAE Miers

This family of 60 genera and 500 species of trees, shrubs, and lianas occurs mainly in the tropical regions of Central and South America, Africa, Madagascar, Seychelles (2 indigenous genera), Indomalaysia, and Australia. The economic uses include timber (*Apodytes* and *Cantleya*), starch (*Humerianthera* and *Poraqueiba*), and *Citronella* for infusions.

Grisollea Baillon

This genus comprises two species, one in Madagascar and one in Seychelles.

PLATE 24. *Grisollea thomassetii* Hemsley (W. B. Hemsley, 1906, *Hooker's Icones plantarum*, t. 2789)

Vernacular name: bois gros la peau on Silhouette; bois marée on Mahé

HABIT. The plant is a tree that is dioecious, up to 15 m in height, and has spongy bark that can be as thick as 1.5 cm. Stipules are absent.

LEAVES. The leaves are alternate, up to 25 cm long, glabrous, oblong, and coriaceous, with 1–2 cm long petioles. The venation is rather indistinct, with the 12 pairs of brochidodromous secondary veins slightly raised on the upper surface.

INFLORESCENCES. The inflorescences are axillary branched panicles up to 6 cm long.

FLOWERS. The calyx of the male flower is fused to half its length and has five or six lobes which are pubescent on the tips. There are six minute cream petals that are up to 1 mm long, six 2.5 mm long stamens, and a tomentose pistillode. Female flowers were not seen.

FRUITS. The fruits are 2 cm long ovate, flattened, drupes that are yellow when ripe. (They were not seen.)

DISTRIBUTION. Mahé and Silhouette

The species is a very rare tree that generally grows at midaltitude. On Silhouette, there are several trees at the summit of the path crossing the island from La Passe to Grand Barbe at about 400 m. The vernacular name originates from the extreme thickness of the bark, a good field character. Other species occurring with *Grisollea* at this site are *Tarenna sechellensis*, *Dillenia ferruginea*, *Deckenia nobilis*, *Verschaffeltia splendida*, *Dracaena reflexa* var. *angustifolia*, *Northia seychellana*, *Canthium bibracteatum*, and *Colea seychellarum*. Formerly it was said to be "not uncommon in the forests of the Cascade Estate" (Hebarium sheet: Thomasset 54). Maybe a thorough search could reveal remaining trees, although much of the area is now built up. *G. thomassetii* is most similar to *G. myriantha*, which is found in Madagascar.

This was one of the last species to be painted, a tree I was beginning to think that I would not find. In October 1993 I visited Silhouette again, especially to look for *Grisollea*, when my time on the island was limited to two days. As soon as I had put my luggage into the guesthouse, I climbed up the steep path from La Passe and, fortunately, found two trees that afternoon. The remaining time was spent painting. Unfortunately there was not enough time available to search for more trees and I have depicted only male flowers.

There are no other members of this family in the granitic islands.

ILLUSTRATION. Flowering habit; painted at 1×. Enlargement of male flower and individual stamens; painted at 20×. Flowering habit collected and painted September 14–16, 1993. Herbarium sheet: Rosemary Wise 199 (OXF).

LABIATAE Jussieu

This family consists of 224 genera and 5,600 species of shrubs and herbs, rarely trees, with a cosmopolitan distribution. The leaves of many are aromatic and used as culinary or medicinal herbs: mint (*Mentha*), basil (*Ocimum*), oregano (*Origanum*), rosemary (*Rosmarinus*), sage (*Salvia*), thyme (*Thymus*). *Monarda* leaves are used to flavor teas and are best known in the brand Earl Grey. Oils are distilled from lavender (*Lavendula*). Many species are grown as ornamentals including *Coleus*, *Nepeta*, and *Plectranthus*.

Achyrospermum Blume

This genus contains 10 species in the Old World tropics.

PLATE 25. *Achyrospermum seychellarum* Baker (Baker, 1877, *Flora of Mauritius*, p. 259)

HABIT. The plant is an herb up to 2 m high. The stems are woody and square in section and lack stipules.

LEAVES. The leaves are opposite and decussate with inciso-crenate margins. The apices are acuminate and the bases decurrent. The 10 pairs of secondary veins are semi-craspedodromous, and the tertiaries are ladder-like. The leaf blade is bullate. The petioles are up to 7 cm long.

INFLORESCENCES. The inflorescences are congested, sessile, axillary racemes with up to 10 flowers. The pedicels are up to 1 mm long and have minute bracts.

FLOWERS. The flowers are bisexual. The distinctly ribbed calyx is up to 6 mm long. The 1.5 cm long arching corolla tube is white with five pink lobes. The four stamens extend beyond the uppermost two lobes.

FRUITS. The fruits consist of four woody nutlets that are up to 2.5 mm long and are enclosed in the persistent calyx.

DISTRIBUTION. Silhouette

Although this understory herb is now confined to small areas at high altitudes on Silhouette, it was previously found on Mahé (Herbarium sheets: Horne 553 and Thomasset 7). In some of the higher parts of Silhouette, especially in the Pisonia forest discovered by Dr. F. Friedmann in 1983, *Achyrosperma* is one of the most common species (Caroline Awmack, pers. comm.) Being able to reproduce asexually by means of runners, large areas of the forest can be covered by the herb. The plants are frequently parasitized by the scale insect *Icerya seychellarum*. The seeds germinate readily.

Other members of this family in the granitic islands are *Clerodendrum indicum* (cultivated), *C. calamitosum* (cultivated), *C. serratum* (cultivated), *C. speciossimum*, *C. philippinum* (cultivated), *C. wallichii* (cultivated), *C. thomsonae* (cultivated), *Coleus prostratus*, *Gmelina phillipensis*, *Leonotis nepetifolia* (cultivated), *Leucas aspera*, *L. lavandulifolia*, *Mentha arvensis*, *M. spicata*, *Ocimum basilicum* (basil, cultivated), *O. canum* (cultivated), *O. gratissimum* (cultivated), *O. tenuiflorum* (cultivated), *Plantago major*, *Plectranthus amboinicus*, *P. prostratus* (cultivated), *P. scutellariodes* (cultivated), *Pogostemon heyneanus*, *Premna obtusifolia*, *Solenostemon scutellarioides*, *Tectona grandis* (teak, cultivated), *Thymus vulgaris* (thyme, cultivated), *Vitex doniana*, and *V. trifolia*.

ILLUSTRATION. Flowering habit, mature leaf, and mature fruit; painted at 1×. Detail of flower; painted at 6×. Flowering habit collected and painted on July 27, 1990. Fruiting habit collected and painted on July 18, 1990. No specimens pressed.

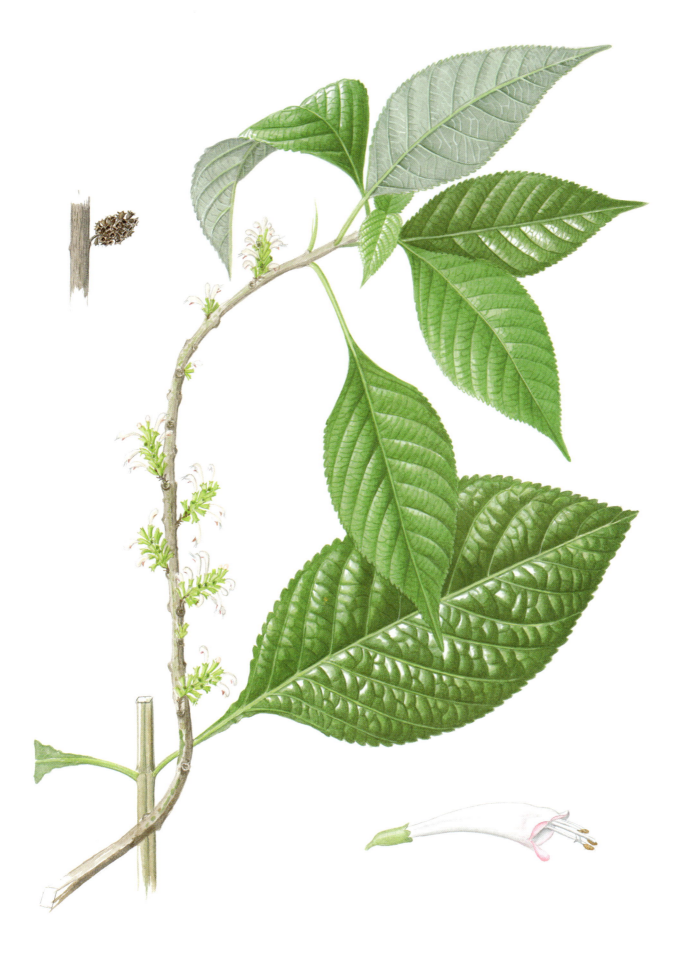

LEGUMINOSAE Jussieu

This family has a cosmopolitan distribution in tropical, subtropical, and temperate regions. It contains 657 genera and 16,400 species of trees, shrubs, lianas, and herbs, some of which are aquatic or xerophytic. These are divided into three subfamilies: the Caesalpiniodeae, the Mimosoideae, and the Papilionoideae. The Caesalpiniodeae has genera that produce timber, oils, edible fruits, and ornamentals. Many of the Papilionoideae are of immense importance as food crops, including *Pisum* (peas), *Phaseolus* (beans), *Glycine* (soy bean), *Lens culinaris* (lentils), and *Arachis hypogea* (peanuts). Many legumes have root nodules with nitrogen-fixing bacteria present, which enable them to take up atmospheric nitrogen and convert it into other nitrogenous compounds. These extra nitrates are beneficial to plants that may be growing on poor soil.

Acacia

This genus is included in the Mimosoideae and contains 1,200 species of mainly tropical and subtropical trees and shrubs. Plants from this subfamily contain important fodder crops (*Leucaena, Mimosa*, and *Prosopis*). The bark of several species of Australian wattles is used in the tanning industry. Gum arabic is obtained from *Acacia stenocarpa* and *A. senegal*. *A. seyal* provided the Shittim wood mentioned in the Bible. Most acacias are woody and armed with spines to deter predators. Glands between the pinnae and on the petioles exude nectar, which ants feed on. In return, they defend the plant from other insects. Some mimosoid species, including *Mimosa pudica*, a common roadside weed in Seychelles, have the ability to fold their leaves rapidly downward when touched. This defensive mechanism is thought to deter grazing herbivores.

PLATE 26. *Acacia pennata* (Linnaeus) Willdenow (C. Willdenow, 1806, *Species Plantarum*, 4:1090)

HABIT. This plant is a liana that is scrambling and woody and up to 10 m long, with recurved spines and 2 mm long stipules.

LEAVES. The leaves are alternate and as long as 25 cm, each with a 25 cm long canniculate rachis. Petioles are up to 4 cm with an elliptical gland below the lowest pair of pinnae. There are 13–15 pairs of pinnae, each having 40–50 pairs of glabrous leaflets up to 9 mm long.

INFLORESCENCES. The inflorescences are either axillary racemes or terminal panicles.

CAPITULUMS. The capitulums are spherical, are up to 1.7 cm wide, and each have around 25 greenish-yellow flowers.

FLOWERS. The calyx is up to 3 mm long and has five lobes. The corolla is up to 3 mm long, also with five lobes. The stamens are up to 1.7 mm long and inserted on a tubular disk.

FRUITS. The fruits have not yet been seen.

DISTRIBUTION. Silhouette

This rare plant was first collected by Dr. F. Friedmann in 1980. It is found only as an understory plant in the *Pisonia sechellarum* forest, above Anse Mondon, or scrambling over rocks at a few locations near to Jardin Marron. Initially it was thought to be *Acacia pennata* and presently named as such, but it does not exactly resemble any of the known forms of this widely spread legume. As yet, the fruits have never been seen in the wild nor from the plants in cultivation at the botanic gardens in Nancy, France, although the latter do flower occasionally. If and when fruits are obtained, the study of them, together with the fact that, unlike other flowers of *A. pennata* from Asia, the flowers of the Seychelles plants lack pedicels, may determine this plant to be a new addition to the endemics list. For this reason I have included it here.

Other mimosoid legumes in the granitic islands are *Acacia confusa, A. farnesiana, A. polystachya, Adenathera pavonina, Albizia lebbeck, A. saman, Calliandra surinamensis, Desmanthus virgatus, Leucaena leucocephala, Mimosa pudica, Paraserianthes falcataria, Parkia pedunculata, Pithecellobium dulce*, and *P. unguis-cati*.

ILLUSTRATION. Painted partly in August 1990 and finished from herbarium sheets kindly lent by Dr. F. Friedmann; all parts painted at 1×. No specimens pressed.

MEDUSAGYNACEAE Engler and Gilg
This is a monotypic genus found only on Mahé.

Medusagyne Baker

PLATE 27. *Medusagyne oppositifolia* Baker (Baker, 1877, *Flora of Mauritius*, p. 16)

Vernacular name: bois meduse (French); jellyfish tree (English)

HABIT. The plant is a small tree with rounded crown that reaches heights of 10 m and has dark, deeply fissured bark.

LEAVES. The leaves are opposite, elliptic, coriaceous, and shiny and up to 8 cm long, with crenate margins and 5 mm long petioles. The senescent leaves are characteristically bright red. The venation is faint with variable brochidodromous secondaries. The tertiary veins are finely reticulate.

INFLORESCENCES. The inflorescences are lax panicles, up to 8 cm long, and located at the ends of branches. They usually have both male and bisexual flowers, which are partially hidden by the dense foliage.

FLOWERS. The male flowers are borne at the ends of the panicles. They have a calyx consisting of five imbricate, reflexed sepals that are persistent. The five petals are up to 5 mm long, are white or white tinged with pink, occasionally pink (on Mont Sébért), and are initially spreading but becoming reflexed. The stamens are numerous and slightly longer in the male flowers than in the bisexual ones. The bisexual flowers have a superior ovary, with up to 25 fused carpels, each having a persistent capitate stigma that persists in the fruit.

FRUITS. The fruits are at first green, subglobose and pendulous, and up to 1.5 cm long. When mature, the reddish-brown carpels dehisce from the base, spreading outwards and releasing the winged seeds from the opening inner margin. The carpels remain attached to the central column, resembling the ribs of an umbrella.

DISTRIBUTION. Mahé

Medusagyne oppositifolia is an extremely rare tree that is critically endangered, grows between 150 and 500 m, and until recently was known only from two sites—Mt. Sébért and Mt. Bernica (Mt. des Palmes). In the last few years at least two other sites have been discovered. All the localities are within 2 km of the sea and are typically open, rocky glacis. Until the British botanist John Proctor found six trees in June 1970, *Medusagyne* was thought to be extinct because no specimens had been sighted since 1903. It is commonly thought that Baker named this tree bois meduse (or jellyfish tree) because of the resemblance of the mature fruits to miniature marine medusae, but his description of 1877 states "No fruits seen." In Greek mythology, Medusa was one of the three snake-locked Gorgons, to whom Baker was likening either the prominent stigmas of the bisexual flower or the mass of stamens of the male, an interesting coincidence.

Medusagyne oppositifolia was originally placed in the family Ternstroemiaceae (now Theaceae) by Baker. In 1924, after indicating that it had no close affinities to any other family, Engler and Gilg awarded it the status of a family of its own, Medusagynaceace. Recent DNA sequencing at the Royal Botanic Gardens, Kew, has revealed that its ancestors are in fact Ochnaceae and the South American family Quiinaceae, with which it has been placed in a monophyletic clade (Fay et al. 1995).

The present habitat requirements suggest that the species originally flourished in exposed areas prone to drought. No seedlings have been recorded locally, and all existing trees appear to be of a similar age. Associated species at both known sites include *Mimusops sechellarum*, *Pandanus multispicatus*, and, especially on Bernica, *Deckenia nobilis*. Generally, attempts at propagation have not been successful; however, seeds collected by Dr. F. Friedmann, of the Laboratoire de Phanerogamie in Paris, germinated, and two 3 m tall trees are now flowering regularly in the botanic gardens at Nancy, France.

ILLUSTRATION. Flowering habit, young fruits, mature fruits, detail of senescent leaf; painted at 1×. Enlargement of young fruit; painted at 3×. Enlargement of one carpel of dehisced fruit; painted at 6×. Flowering habit collected and painted on March 11, 1986. Fruiting habit collected and painted on March 12, 1986 (mature), May 5, 1992 (immature). Herbarium sheets: Rosemary Wise 18, 83, 144, 189 (OXF).

MELASTOMATACEAE Jussieu

This family consists of 215 genera and 4,750 species of shrubs and herbs, with a few trees and lianas. The distribution is tropical, especially South America. Some species from the genus *Memecylon* produce good timber and others are cultivated as ornamentals. The granitic Seychelles has one indigenous genus and two cultivated introductions.

Memecylon Linnaeus

This genus comprises 150 species from the Old World tropics. A yellow dye is produced from *Memecylon edule*.

PLATE 28. *Memecylon eleagni* Blume   (Blume, 1851, *Mus. Bot. Lugd. Bat.* 1:356)

Memecylon pervilleanum Naud   (Naud, 1852, *Annals of Sciences*, series 3, p. 18)

Vernacular name: bois calou

HABIT. The plant is a shrub or small tree with fissured grayish-brown bark, slender branches, and no stipules.

LEAVES. The leaves are opposite and decussate, glabrous, coriaceous, obovate or elliptic, with entire margins and reach a length of 6 cm. The venation is faint on both surfaces. There are from six to eight pairs of secondary veins. The petiole is up to 7 mm long.

FLOWERS. The flowers are axillary, with one or two on short cymes. The calyx is shallowly cup-shaped and up to 2.5 mm long. There are four white apicular petals that are up to 5 mm long. The eight stamens are about 4 mm long and have white filaments, yellow anthers, and pale blue connectives. The styles are simple, white or blue, up to 4 mm long.

FRUITS. The fruits are up to 8 mm across, globose, green at first, but ripening to dark blue or black.

DISTRIBUTION. Mahé, Praslin, Silhouette, La Digue, Curieuse, and Félicité

This shrub or small tree is one of the most frequently seen endemics, occurring at all altitudes. On the rocky outcrops that provide spectacular view points at La Reserve, Mahé, *Memecylon eleagni* is one of the dominant species, growing with *Erythroxylum sechellarum*, *Diospyros seychellarum*, *Ludia mauritiania* var. *sechellensis*, and *Deckenia nobilis*. The shrubs are always compact in shape, 1–2 m high and, along with *Paragenipa wrightii*, look as though they would be equally at home in a garden. When *Memecylon* is found in forest habitats, it attains tree status and can reach a height of 8 m, with a spreading habit and deeply fissured, gnarled branches.

Other members of this family in the granitic islands are *Melastoma malabathricum*, *Memecylon caeruleum* (a shrub with axillary clusters of deep blue flowers and black globose fruits to 1.5 cm. long), *Memecylon umbellatum* (a cultivated tree from the botanic garden, having clusters of deep blue or purple flowers and purple fruits to 8 mm across), and *Clidemia hirta*.

ILLUSTRATION. Flowering and fruiting habits; painted at 1×. Detail of flowers; painted at 4×. Flowering habit collected and painted on June 19, 1990. Fruiting habit collected and painted on August 9, 1989. Herbarium sheet: Rosemary Wise 88 (OXF).

MORACEAE Link

This family comprises 48 genera and 1,200 species of trees, shrubs, lianas, and herbs, that are distributed throughout the tropics and subtropics, with a few in temperate areas. Many have edible fruits, including figs (*Ficus*), jackfruit (*Artocarpus heterophyllus*), and breadfruit (*A. altilis*). Hops, the dried fruits of *Humulus lupulus*, are invaluable in the brewing of beers. Both *Castilla* and *Ficus* species are tapped for the production of rubber. Narcotic drugs and hemp, used in rope-making, are obtained from *Cannabis sativa*. In the granitic Seychelles there are two indigenous and three introduced genera.

Ficus Linnaeus

This genus comprises 800 species from the tropics, subtropics, and warm temperate areas. The genus has many economical uses including timber, rubber, paper, and edible fruits. *Ficus sycamorus*, the mulberry fig, is the host plant on which silkworms feed. Some species climb up trees, sending down aerial roots. Eventually these enclose and strangle the host. Examples of *F. benghalensis* can be seen on Frigate and Aride. Each species of fig attracts a specific agaontid wasp that reproduces within the syconium.

PLATE 29.   *Ficus bojeri* Baker   (Baker, 1877, *Flora of Mauritius*, p. 286)

HABIT. The plant is a tree that is glabrous in all parts and has translucent latex and grayish-brown bark. It reaches a height of 15 m. The stipules are pointed, up to 3 mm long, and caducous.

LEAVES. The leaves are alternate and ovate, with acute apices and cordate bases. They are scabrid, have serrate margins, and are as long as 20 cm. The eight pairs of secondary veins, which are much lighter in color than the leaf blade, are distinct and brochidodromous. The petioles are up to 4 cm.

RECEPTACLES. The receptacles are globose, green syconia up to 1 cm thick, on peduncles up to 1 cm long. The figs contain both male and female flowers, which line the inner wall of the syconia.

DISTRIBUTION. Mahé, Silhouette, La Digue, and Félicité

Dr. Friedmann, in his recent publication (1994), refers to *Ficus bojeri* as indigenous and says that Berg sites specimens from Madagascar; however, since previous publications have referred to this as an endemic species, it is included in this volume for historical reasons (Procter 1974; Robertson 1989). Unlike the other figs in Seychelles, *F. bojeri* has a scabrid, or sandpaper-like, leaf surface.

The specific name commemorates Wenceslaus Bojer (1795–1858), who was a founding member of The Royal Society of Mauritius in 1850. Following his appointment as the curator of Mauritius' museum, Bojer was appointed professor of botany at the Royal College, Port Louis, in 1828 and director of the Royal Botanic Gardens, Pamplemousses.

Other members of this family in the granitic islands are *Artocarpus heterophyllus* (cultivated), *A. altilis* (cultivated), *F. lutea*, *F. reflexa* subsp. *seychellensis*, *F. rubra*, *F. pumila* (cultivated), *F. elastica*, *F. benghalensis*, *F. microcarpa*, *Milicia excelsa*, *Morus alba* var. *indica* (cultivated), and *Trilepisium madagascariensis*.

ILLUSTRATION. All parts painted at 1×. Fruiting habit collected and painted on June 21–22, 1990. Herbarium sheet: Rosemary Wise 123 (OXF).

MORACEAE Link

Ficus Linnaeus

PLATE 30.   *Ficus reflexa* Thunberg subsp. *seychellensis* (Baker)
Berg   (Berg, 1986, *Adansonia*, p. 49)

  F. rubra Vahl var. *seychellensis*   (Baker, 1877, *Flora of Mauritius*,
    p. 284)

  Vernacular name: afouche petite feuille

HABIT. The plant is a tree, shrub, or epiphytic strangler with white latex, light gray bark, and adventitious roots. It can reach as high as 15 m. The stipules are persistent, chartaceous, reddish brown, and up to 2.5 cm long.

LEAVES. The leaves are alternate and elliptic, have acuminate apices and cuneate bases, are coriaceous, and have entire margins. The are up to 15 cm long. The six to eight pairs of secondary veins are brochidodromous and have reticulate tertiaries that are very pronounced on the lower surface. The petioles are up to 3 cm long.

FRUITS. The figs were not seen.

DISTRIBUTION. Mahé, Praslin, Silhouette, Frégate, and Aride

Ficus reflexa subsp. *seychellensis* grows at elevations from sea level to 500 m. It is the only endemic species that can be found in Victoria, where shrubs grows naturally on walls around town. Several grow on the wall below the roman catholic cathedral in Oliver Maradan Street. These are easy to study and collect but appear not to fruit. The plants on other islands produce figs more frequently (Annette Carlström, pers. comm., 1995). Fruits from all species of fig in Seychelles are consumed by Blue Pigeons and fruit bats. This painting was produced on my last visit in 1995, and unfortunately I was unable to find figs to add to it.

ILLUSTRATION. Vegetative shoot showing persistent stipules; painted at 1×. Leaves collected and painted July 28, 1995. Herbarium sheet: Rosemary Wise 207 (OXF).

MYRSINACEAE R. Brown

This family is composed of 39 genera and 1,250 species of trees, shrubs, lianas, and a few herbs from the tropics, subtropics, and occasionally the temperate Old World. The family is of little economic value and is best known for ornamentals, including *Ardisia, Myrsine*, and *Suttonia*. The granitic Seychelles have two genera: one indigenous and one introduced.

Rapanea Aublet

This genus comprises 150 species found in the tropics and subtropics. Some African species are grown for timber.

PLATE 31.   *Rapanea seychellarum* Mez   (H.G.A. Engler, 1902, *Pflanzenr.*, part 4, fasc. 236, p. 376)

Myrsine capitellata Wallich   (Baker, 1877, *Flora of Mauritius*, p. 190)

HABIT. The plant is a shrub with gray bark and is up to 5 m high.

LEAVES. The leaves are alternate and obovate, with obtuse apices and attenuate bases. They are glabrous and coriaceous, with entire margins and reach a length of 12 cm. The 10 pairs of secondary veins are brochidodromous. The tertiary veins are parallel and finely reticulate. The petioles are magenta and up to 6 mm long.

INFLORESCENCES. The inflorescences are axillary, with three to five flowers on each fascicle. The pedicels are up to 3.5 mm long.

FLOWERS. The flowers are white, tinged with pink, and up to 5 mm wide on pedicels up to 3.5 cm long. The calyx is up to 0.8 mm long with five rounded lobes, each 0.5 mm long. The corolla has five free petals. In the male flowers, the petals are up to 2.5 mm long, with the stamens opposed and fused to the base of the petals. The anthers are pink and 1.2 mm long. The pistil is up to 1.5 mm long. The female flowers have five petals up to 1.5 mm long with staminodes up to 0.8.mm. The pistil is 1.8 mm long and has a large irregular pyramidal stigma.

FRUITS. The fruits are dark blue, globose drupes, up to 5 mm long. They were not seen.

DISTRIBUTION. Mahé, Praslin, and Silhouette

The main population of the endangered shrub *Rapania sechellarum* is on the upper parts of Morne Seychellois at 900 m, an area that I have not visited. Many rather impoverished shrubs grow on the knoll at the highest part of Congo Rouge and these possibly flower and fruit infrequently. The extreme bright green of the leaves and the striking magenta petioles are characteristic features. Other plants in this area include *Syzygium wrightii*, *Glionnetia sericea*, *Northia seychellana*, *Canthium sechellense*, *Psidium cattleianum*, and the rare endemic grass, *Garnotia sechellensis*. On Silhouette there are some shrubs of *Rapanea* on Mont Laurant.

Other members of this family in the granitic islands are *Ardisia crenata* and *A. elliptica* (cultivated).

ILLUSTRATION. Vegetative shoot; painted at 1×. Enlargement of inflorescence; painted at 6×. Vegetative habit collected and painted on November 2, 1992. Flowering habit painted from a photograph supplied by Dr. J. Gerlach. Herbarium sheets: Rosemary Wise 161, 186 (OXF).

MYRTACEAE Jussieu

This is a large family of 121 genera and 3,850 species of trees and shrubs with a tropical, subtropical, and temperate distribution. The leaves are mostly opposite, always entire, and have subepidermal cells that contain oils. Eucalyptus trees provide timber and oils. Many other species provide oils and flavorings, including clove (*Syzygium aromaticum*), allspice (*Pimenta dioica*), and bay rum (*Pimenta racemosa*). The edible fruit include guavas (*Psidium guajava*). Fruits of several species of *Eugenia*, or jamalac, are eaten or used for jam-making in Seychelles. The granitic Seychelles have two indigenous and five introduced genera.

Syzygium Gaertner

This genus includes 500 species of trees and shrubs, often aromatic, with a tropical and Old World distribution.

PLATE 32. *Syzygium wrightii* (Baker) A. J. Scott
(A. J. Scott, 1980, *Kew Bulletin* 34 [3]:496)

Eugenia wrightii Baker = *Eugenia sechellarum* Baker   (Baker, 1877, *Flora of Mauritius*, p. 117)

Vernacular name: bois de pomme

HABIT. The plant is a tree or scrambling shrub with gray to light brown bark and is up to 15 m high. Stipules are absent.

LEAVES. The leaves are opposite, glabrous, coriaceous, shiny, and up to 20 cm long. They vary in shape from broadly ovate to oblong. Young leaves are often flushed pink or purple. The apices are cuspidate and the bases subcordate or truncate. The margins are entire. The venation is lax, with 16–20 pairs of camptodromous secondaries. The tertiary veins are randomly reticulate. Petioles are also variable in length and can be up to 3 cm long.

INFLORESCENCES. The inflorescences are lateral and terminal cymes, either lax or tightly congested.

FLOWERS. The flowers are pedunculate or sessile. The calyx is funnel-shaped, persistent, and five-lobed, often with one lobe extended. It is green, shaded to deep pink at the lobes. The five petals are orbicular, are up to 7 mm wide, and fall at an early stage. There are numerous 2 cm long bright yellow stamens in three whorls.

FRUITS. The fruits are globose and 2.5 cm long. They are green at first, changing to deep pink, then to maroon, and finally to black. The calyx lobes are persistent.

DISTRIBUTION. Mahé, Praslin, Silhouette, Curieuse, and Félicité

Syzygium wrightii grows at altitudes of 100–700 m, often in the vicinity of streams and is far more common at the higher range. It varies in habit from a small tree, seen at the roadside on the Sans Souci Road between Port Glaud and the Tea Tavern, and a scrambling shrub, growing in the *Nepenthes pervillei* locality at Le Niol. The leaf shape is variable, depending on altitude. On scrubby areas of Curieuse, it is a very common tree and grows alongside pandans and palms (including *Lodoicea maldivica*), near to the population of *Secamone schimperianus* (formerly *Toxocarpus schimperianus*). The masses of bright yellow stamens make this one of the most conspicuous of all of the endemic species. My first flowering specimen was collected and painted on Curieuse and had a more compact inflores-

cence than those of subsequent collections on Mahé. Both types are illustrated. Crushed leaves are used medicinally as a poultice. The specific epithet commemorates Edward Percival Wright (1834–1910), an Irish naturalist and lecturer in zoology at Trinity College, Dublin, who visited Seychelles in 1867. From 1889 until 1904 he was a professor of botany at the same university.

Other members of this family in the granitic islands are *Callistemon citrinus*, *C. speciosus*, *Eucalyptus camaldulensis*, *E. citriodora*, *E. robusta*, *E. staigeriana*, *Eugenia grandis*, *E. jambos*, *E. javanica*, *E. malaccensis*, *E. uniflora*, *E. brasiliensis*, *Melaleuca quinquenervia*, *Pimenta dioica*, *P. racemosa*, *Psidium cattleyanum*, *P. guajava*, *Syzygium aromaticum* (clove, cultivated escape with opposite, glossy leaves, to 10 cm, clustered flowers, dark purple fruits to 2.5 cm), *S. jambos* (cultivated escape, with pale yellow or pink fruits), *S. malaccense* (cultivated, with red fruits up to 5 cm), *S. cumini* (cultivated, with black berries up to 2 cm), and *S. samarangense* (cultivated, with white or pink berries up to 3–5 cm).

ILLUSTRATION. Inflorescence with almost sessile habit. Inflorescence with long peduncle. Young flush leaves, fruits, and galled female flowers. All painted at 1×. Flowering habit collected and painted on July 13, 1990. Fruiting habit collected and painted on August 23, 1990. Flush leaves collected and painted on June 24, 1990. Herbarium sheets: Rosemary Wise 146, 197 (OXF).

NEPENTHACEAE Dumortier

This family contains 1 genus with 70 species of shrubby climbers. The distribution ranges from Madagascar, Seychelles, and Sri Lanka to Australia and New Caledonia, with a center in Malaysia. The pitchers of *Nepenthes rajah* in Sabah can hold up to 2 liters of fluid and can supposedly drown rats! Some species are grown ornamentally. The stems of the Malaysian *N. reinwardtiana* and *N. distillatoria* are used in basket-making.

Nepenthes Linnaeus

PLATE 33. *Nepenthes pervillei* Blume (Blume, 1853, *Mus. Bot. Lugd. Bat.* 2:10)

Nepenthes wardii Wright (E. P. Wright, 1871, *Trans. Royal Irish Academy* 24:576)

Vernacular name: pot à eau (French); pitcher plant (English)

HABIT. The plant is a prostrate or climbing liana, with woody, terete, reddish-brown stems.

LEAVES. The leaves form in rosettes and are obovate and amplexicaul, with acute apices and attenuate or decurrent bases. They are coriaceous and glabrous, have entire margins, and are up to 25 cm long. The four or five pairs of secondary veins on the lamina are parallelodromous, and the midribs extend beyond the apex, forming peduncles that terminate in pitchers or tendrils. Juvenile pitchers have peduncles up to 40 cm long, and these urn-shaped pitchers have two longitudinal, ciliate crests on the opposite face to the insertion of the peduncle. (These early pitchers are introrse—or facing inward.) The pitcher mouths are oblique with revolute, ribbed margins. Above this, the operculum is round, horizontal, and up to 3 cm across. In mature pitchers, the peduncle is up to 5 cm long and the crests are absent. These pitchers are extrorse (face outward), and according to habitat can be red, green, yellow, or orange, and are as long as 21 cm.

INFLORESCENCES. The inflorescences are erect panicles with lateral cymes and are up to 40 cm long.

FLOWERS. The male flowers have four or five tepals fused at the base with acute lobes 2 mm long. There are six anthers arising from a short staminal column. Female flowers have three or four tepals, fused at the base, with obtuse lobes 2 mm long. The obconical ovaries have three or four stigmas.

FRUITS. The fruits are tubular, coriaceous capsules that dehisce into three persistent valves. They are olive green when young, becoming light brown at maturity.

DISTRIBUTION. Mahé and Silhouette

Linnaeus named the genus *Nepenthes* in 1753, likening it to the story in Homer's *Odyssey* of Helen mixing wine with the drug nepenthe (Greek, "no mind"), which was said to free the mind of worry and grief. The shape of some of the pitchers is very similar to that of Greek drinking vessels. The first recorded reference to the carnivorous nature of the plant was in 1858, when Hooker wrote on the habit of *Nepenthes villosa* in Borneo: "a great provision of nature for decoying and the destruction of insects." Linnaeus was not prepared to accept this bizarre fact.

Germination takes place in the soil but the plants develop into climbers or epiphytes. The midvein of the leaf extends to form the tendrils and pitchers. The first pitchers always turn inward, and two horizontal frontal frills are usually present. The confusion arising from the suggestion that a second species of *Nepenthes* exists in Seychelles is due to this dimorphic nature of the young plants. Immature, frilled pitchers are often found semisubmerged in leaf litter or soil, where they appear to trap different prey than the higher, mature ones. The one collected for this painting was completely filled by an enormous dead slug. Adult pitchers are variable in size and color, the latter according to light and habitat. On the glacis at the summit of Copolia, the plants grow in full sunlight, are exposed to winds, and are considerably smaller and more colorful than plants found in more sheltered habitats (Salazie and the summit of Congo Rouge). The latter plants are frequently light green only and can be three times greater in length than the former.

The nectaries on the lid and between the teeth on the rim attract insects. This nectar flows freely so that a percentage of visitors will be trapped and digested by the plant, supplementing the plant's nutritional needs. The heavy armature of veins and thickened, spindle-shaped cells in the pitcher's walls ensure that the majority of insects are unable to bite their way out. Below the rim, the wax-secreting zone has downward projecting, smooth, waxy scales. Insects cannot climb back up because the scales are slippery, sensitive to disturbance, and easily shed. Below this area is the liquid. The surface tension is low, and the struggling prey soon becomes waterlogged and drowns. This activity stimulates glands in the plant wall to discharge a fast-acting digestive acid. Unlike other carnivorous plants, there are no moving parts in *Nepenthes*. The lid does not close, as was once suggested, but prevents rain water from entering, which would dilute the fluids. Associated plants on Copolia are *Lophoschoenus hornei*, *Pandanus multispicata*, *Memecylon eleagni*, and the pigeon orchid, *Dendrobium crumenatum*. At the Salazie site the vegetation is predominantly *Cinnamomum verum* and *Chrysobalanus icaco*.

Probably the most spectacular panorama is at the Le Niol end of the Congo Rouge path. Several hectares of the ground and all of the trees and shrubs (including *Psathura sechellarum*, *Syzygium wrightii*, *Chrysobalanus icaco*, and *Craterispermum microdon*) are festooned with the creepers. *Nepenthes* grows at ten sites on Mahé and at two on Silhouette. One pitcher collected on the ridge of Mt. Dauban, Silhouette, in 1990 by Caroline Awmack, a botanist on the Oxford University Expedition, measured 21.5 cm. Some authorities have suggested that *N. pervillei* should be placed in its own genus, *Anurosperma*. The specific epithet is after Auguste Pervillé, French gardener and explorer, who visited Seychelles in 1841.

ILLUSTRATIONS. *Overleaf, left*: Mature fruits, leaf rosette with pitchers, and male inflorescence; all painted at 1×. Pitchers habit painted in March 1986. Fruiting and flowering habits painted in October 1989. Herbarium sheets: Rosemary Wise 112, 17, 114 (OXF). *Overleaf, right*: Male inflorescence; painted at 1×. Enlargement of male flower; painted at 8×. Young pitcher with frill, leaf rosette from exposed glacis with mature fruits, leaf rosette from shaded location with female flowers, and detail of closed pitcher showing variation in shape; all painted at 1×. Flowering habits, male and female, collected and painted on September 11, 1989. Fruiting habit collected and painted on September 12, 1989. Pitchers collected and painted on April 12, 1986 and July 14, 1990. Frilled young pitcher collected and painted on September 30, 1992. Herbarium sheets: Rosemary Wise 17, 135 (OXF).

NYCTAGINACEAE Jussieu

This family comprises 34 genera and 350 species of trees, shrubs, and herbs found primarily in the tropics and subtropics, although there are also some temperate species. Bougainvillea, which has colorful bracts enclosing rather insignificant tiny flowers, is one of the most well known of the many ornamental species and is seen throughout the Mediterranean and tropics. The granitic Seychelles have four genera, two indigenous and two introduced.

Pisonia Linnaeus

The genus contains 35 species of trees and shrubs from the tropics and subtropics, especially from America. The leaves of some are edible (*P. grandis* and *P. alba*). Many species have sticky, barbed fruits that attach themselves to the feathers of birds.

PLATE 34.   *Pisonia sechellarum* F. Friedmann   (F. Friedmann, 1987 [1986], *Adansonia* 8:384)

Vernacular name: mapou de grand bois

HABIT. The plant is a tree with spongy, water-retaining, smooth bark and reaches 22 m in height.

LEAVES. The leaves are subcoriaceous, elliptic, and membranous, with acute apices and attenuate bases. They may be as long as 30 cm. The 15 pairs of secondary veins are brochidodromous. The petioles are up to 5 cm long.

INFLORESCENCES. The inflorescences are branched panicles with three or four flowers on each.

FLOWERS. The perianth is yellow, and is 5 mm in length, with five or six deltoid lobes that become reflexed.

FRUITS. The fruits are olive green, fleshy, cylindrical, indehiscent achenes that are up to 4 cm long.

DISTRIBUTION. Silhouette

All species of *Pisonia* are alike in that they have glandular, sticky, or barbed fruits that are dispersed by adhering to the fur or feathers of animals. *Pisonia grandis*, which is common on Aride, has sticky, spined fruits that get entangled in the feathers of the nesting seabirds, rendering flight impossible and so causing the birds to starve to death. The rotting carcasses form ideal "compost heaps" for germinating seeds and young plants. In other parts of the world, *P. grandis* is called the cabbage tree, and the leaves are eaten. The critically endangered species *Pisonia sechellarum* is found only on Silhouette Island, growing at an altitude of 400–550 m. The leaves are of obvious attraction as food to insects, mainly for the moth *Epicroesa* sp., and it was not possible to collect any specimens that had not been attacked. In the 1930s the low-altitude forests of Silhouette were felled and cleared. The higher parts of the island, being steep and extremely inaccessable were left untouched and now harbor the only remaining primary forest area in the granitic islands. The Oxford University Expedition of 1990 estimated that there are approximately 190 of these trees growing in this seldom-visited forest.

Other members of this family in the granitic islands are *Boerhavia coccinea*, *Bougainvillea x buttiana*, *B. glabra*, *B. spectabilis*, *Mirabilis jalapa*, and *Pisonia grandis* (which has ovate leaves up to 30 cm, clustered white flowers to 5 mm, and cylindrical, sticky, barbed fruits to 1 cm long).

ILLUSTRATION. Vegetative shoot, male inflorescence, and fruits; painted at 1×. Flowering habit and leaves collected and painted from July 24–25, 1990. Fruiting habit painted from photograph. Herbarium sheets: Rosemary Wise 131, 165, 181 (OXF).

PIPERACEAE Agardh

This is a tropical family of 15 genera and 2,000 species of small trees, shrubs, lianas, epiphytes, and herbs, most of which are from the rain forests. Spices and stimulants are extracted from *Macropiper* and *Piper*.

Piper Linnaeus

This genus comprises 1,000 species, including tropical small trees, shrubs, and lianas. Black pepper is obtained from grinding the complete unripe fruits of *Piper nigrum*. If the pericarp is removed before the grinding process takes place, white pepper is produced. Some species, especially *Saururus* and *Houttuynia*, are grown commercially. In Fiji and the west Pacific, a drink, Kava, is made from the roots of *P. methysticum*. Originally, women and children chewed the roots and spat out the pulp, which was then diluted and fermented. Nowadays machines cope with the grinding process.

PLATE 35.   *Piper* sp. Unnamed at present and only leaves have been collected (F. Friedmann, 1994, *Flore des Seychelles*, p. 73)

HABIT. The plant is a liana that grips trees with its adventitious roots.

LEAVES. The leaves are membranous and ovate, with acuminate apices and cordate bases. They reach a length of 15 cm. The petioles are up to 3 cm long.

DISTRIBUTION. Silhouette

This recently discovered creeper occurs at one locality in the primary forest area above Anse Mondon, Silhouette. At present only the leaves have been collected, but these are sufficiently different from those of other known species. Due to the low numbers and confined distribution, *Piper* sp. is categorized as critically endangered. Cultivation would be beneficial for further collections. If the flowers and fruits were available for taxonomic study, they would most probably confirm that this species is an addition to the endemics list. As such, I have included it in this collection.

Other members of Piperaceae in the granitic islands are *Peperomia dindygulensis*, *P. pellucida*, *P. portulacoides*, *Piper betle* (betel nut; sheathed petioles and cordate leaves to 15 cm. long), *P. nigrum* (black pepper), *P. radicans*, and *Pothomorphe umbellata*.

ILLUSTRATION. Vegetative habit collected and painted on July 15, 1990, at 1×. Herbarium sheets: Rosemary Wise 129, 173 (OXF).

PITTOSPORACEAE R. Brown

This family consists of 9 genera and 240 species of evergreen trees, shrubs, and lianas in the Old World tropics and Australia, where eight of the nine genera are endemic.

Pittosporum Banks ex Gaertner

The 200 species of this genus ranges from tropical South Africa to New Zealand to the Pacific. Cultivated species of trees and shrubs are grown ornamentally in the Mediterranean. Most of the economic uses of the family—timber, oils, and marquetry are from *Pittosporum*. There is one genus in the granitic Seychelles.

PLATE 36. *Pittosporum senacia* Putterlick subsp. *wrightii* (Hemsley) Cufodontis (Cufodontis, 1955, *Oesterreichische Botanische Zeitschrift* 102:365–78)

Pittosporum wrightii Hemsley (W. B. Hemsley, 1916, *Journal of Botany* 54, suppl. 2, p. 2)

Vernacular name: bois joli coeur

HABIT. The plant is a dioecious tree that reaches 5 m in height and has grayish-brown bark. Stipules are absent.

LEAVES. The leaves are alternate, spirally arranged, glabrous, obovate, with cuspidate apices and attenuate bases. They are up to 12 cm long. The petioles are up to 1.5 cm. The 8–10 pairs of secondary veins are brochidodromous with reticulate tertiaries.

INFLORESCENCES. The inflorescences are terminal panicles.

FLOWERS. The flowers are up to 7 mm across. They have five sepals that are fused for three-quarters of their length. The five cream or pale yellow petals are 7 mm long and reflexed at anthesis. The male flowers have five 6 mm long stamens and 6 mm long pistils. The female flowers have five minute staminodes and 4.5 mm long styles with bilobed stigmas.

FRUITS. The fruits are globose capsules that dehisce into two valves and expose orange-red seeds that are heavily coated with mucilage.

DISTRIBUTION. Mahé and Silhouette

One good field character of this tree, which grows at 200–500 m altitude, is the strong aroma of young carrots that is released when the leaves are crushed. Often when trees grow in full sunlight, the leaves are lime green and sufficiently different in color from other neighboring species to make them easily recognizable at a distance.

An infusion of the leaves is used locally as a cure for coughs. Other medicinal properties are said to be beneficial for reducing fevers, for indigestion, and for the treatment of cardiovascular diseases. This may well explain the vernacular name, bois jolie coeur, which literally means "good heart wood." *Pittosporum senaica* subsp. *wrightii* is an example of a xerophytic plant, one that is able to withstand dry conditions and periods of drought. Several rather isolated trees can be seen at the side of the exposed Le Niol path, below the pitcher plant area, growing with *Curculigo sechellensis*, the bracken fern *Dipcranopteris linearis*, and isolated trees of *Dillenia ferruginea* and *Calophyllum inophyllum*. But, by contrast, a few larger trees grow among dense vegetation at the highest point of Congo Rouge. Plenty of seeds are produced, which regenerate readily.

The generic name *Pittosporum* is from the Greek *pitta*, meaning "pitch" and *sporum*, "seed." The fruits open to reveal the scarlet seeds with their mucilaginous coating.

The authority, William Botting Hemsley (1843–1924), worked at the Royal Botanic Gardens, Kew, from 1860 until 1906, acting as keeper from 1899.

There are no related species in the granitic islands.

ILLUSTRATION. Habit with inflorescence and details of immature and ripe fruits; painted at 1×. Enlargement of open fruit showing sticky seeds; painted at 4×. Flowering habit collected and painted on September 24, 1990. Fruiting habit collected and painted on June 19, 1989. Herbarium sheet: Rosemary Wise 182 (OXF).

RUBIACEAE Jussieu

This family is huge and cosmopolitan, comprising 630 genera and 10,400 species of trees, shrubs, lianas, and a few herbs and extending from the Arctic to the Antarctic. Many are cultivated as ornamentals, including *Gardenia*, *Mussaenda*, and *Ixora*. A very few are of economic importance, and these are used mainly as drugs and stimulants, such as coffee (*Coffea*) and quinine (*Cinchona*).

Canthium Lamarck

This genus consists of 50 species from the Old World tropics. Some species produce edible fruit and others, good timber.

PLATE 37.   *Canthium carinatum* (Baker) Summerhayes
(V. S. Summerhayes, 1928, *Bull. Misc. Info.*, Kew 1928:391)

Plectronia carinata Baker = *Plectronia acuminata* Baker
(W. B. Hemsley, 1916, *Journal of Botany* 54, suppl. 2, p. 147)

Vernacular name: bois dur blanc

HABIT. The plant is a shrub or small straggling tree with grayish-brown bark and slender branches. It reaches a height of 8 m. The stipules are triangular and up to 2.5 mm long.

LEAVES. The leaves are opposite and ovate with acuminate apices and cuneiform bases that are sometimes asymmetric. The leaves are also glabrous, with entire margins and may be as long as 12 cm. The five or six pairs of secondary veins are brochidodromous. The petioles are up to 2 cm long.

INFLORESCENCES. The inflorescences are axillary, up to 8 mm long, and on 1 cm long peduncles. The fascicles have five or six male or two or three female flowers.

FLOWERS.. The calyx is barrel-shaped, up to 1 mm long, and has five minute, ciliate lobes. The corolla tube is cylindrical, 2 mm long, white, and densely pubescent in the throat. The five lobes are reflexed. The male flowers have five anthers, are 0.75 mm long, and have a capitate stigma. The female flowers have minute atrophied anthers and trilobed stigmas.

FRUITS. The fruits are pendulous, brownish-pink drupes, with either two or three lobes and are up to 1.2 cm long.

DISTRIBUTION. Mahé, Praslin, and Silhouette

This rather straggly tree is locally common on Mahé at midaltitude, for example at La Reserve, and grows in areas of shady damp woodland. In some locations it grows between, or even on, granite boulders. Very few specimens are found on Praslin; *Canthium carinatum* is most abundant on Silhouette. Unless the dull pink three-lobed fruits are in evidence, the tree is rather nondescript and easily overlooked. The specific epithet *carinatum* means "keeled."

Other members of this family in the granitic islands are *Amaracarpus pubescens* subsp. *sechellarum*, *Canthium bibracteatum* (with red midribs to leaves), *Canthium sechellense* (with ovate coriaceous leaves to 15 cm), *Coffea canephora*, *C. liberica*, *Craterispermum microdon*, *Glionnetia sericea*, *Guettarda speciosa*, *Hedyotis goreensis*, *H. corymbosa*, *Ixora coccinea*, *I. finlaysoniana*, *I. hookeri*, *I. pudica*, *Mitracarpus hirtus*, *Morinda citrifolia*, *Mussaenda erythrophylla*, *M. frondosa*, *Oldenlandia corymbosa*, *O. goreensis*, *Paragenipa wrightii*, *Pentas bussei*, *Pentodon pentandrus*, *Psathura sechellarum*, *Psychotria pervillei*, *P. silhouettae*, *Rondeletia odorata*, *Rothmannia annae*, *Tarenna sechellensis*, *Timonius sechellensis*, and *Vangueria madagascariensis*.

ILLUSTRATION. Flowering habit, showing straw-colored, flush leaves, collected and painted on April 16, 1992, at 1×. Fruiting habit collected and painted in August 1989, at 1×. Herbarium sheets: Rosemary Wise 174, 178, 202 (OXF).

RUBIACEAE Jussieu

Canthium Lamarck

PLATE 38. *Canthium sechellense* (Baker) Summerhayes
(V. S. Summerhayes, 1928, *Bull. Misc. Info.*, Kew 1928:391)

Plectronia celastroides Baker   (Baker, 1877, *Flora of Mauritius*, p. 146)

Vernacular name: bois dur rouge

HABIT. The plant is a shrub with grayish-brown bark and grows as high as 3 m. The stipules are triangular, up to 3.5 mm long.

LEAVES. The leaves are opposite and ovate with rounded apices and cordate or obtuse bases. They are glabrous and coriaceous, have entire margins, and reach 6.5 cm in length. The five pairs of secondary veins are brochidodromous with domatia present on the under surface. The petioles are up to 1.5 cm long.

INFLORESCENCES. The inflorescences are axillary fascicles. They were not seen.

FRUITS. The fruits are globose, 12 mm long drupes, with the stigmatic remains persistent. The pedicels are up to 8 mm long.

DISTRIBUTION. Mahé and Silhouette

The main population of this very rare shrub is to be found high above 800 m, on Morne Seychellois (Lindsay Chong Seng, pers. comm.). A careful search could reveal more than the one solitary small bush that I found near the benchmark at the highest point of Congo Rouge. Other plants in this vicinity are *Syzygium wrightii*, *Hederorkis seychellensis*, *Glionnetia sericea*, *Northia seychellana*, *Roscheria melanochaetes*, and *Garnotia sechellensis*. Occasionally *Canthium* can be found at lower altitude, at 400 m, below Morne Blanc, (Annette Carlstrôm 1995, pers. comm.).

ILLUSTRATION. Fruiting habit; painted at 1×. Detail of domatia on undersurface of leaf; painted at 4×. Habit collected and painted on September 23, 1993. Herbarium sheet: Rosemary Wise 200 (OXF).

RUBIACEAE   Jussieu

Craterispermum Bentham
   This genus comprises 16 species distributed in tropical Africa, Madagascar, and Seychelles.

PLATE 39.   *Craterispermum microdon* Baker   (Baker, 1877, *Flora of Mauritius*, p. 145)
   Vernacular name: bois doux

HABIT. The plant is a tree that is glabrous in all parts and reaches 12 m in height. There are persistent, 5 mm long stipules at the nodes.

LEAVES. The leaves are opposite and lanceolate, with acute apices and cuneate bases. They are also coriaceous, dark green on the upper surface but lighter below, and up to 15 cm long with 8 cm long petioles. The 8–10 pairs of secondary veins are brochididromous.

INFLORESCENCES. The inflorescences are axillary.

FLOWERS. The flowers are sessile and white, usually occurring in pairs on flattened axillary peduncles, subtended by small cuspidate bracts. The calyx is up to 4 mm long, with five minute deltoid lobes. The corolla tube is up to 5 mm long and has five densely hairy valvate lobes that are 3.5 mm long. The five stamens are inserted at the throat.

FRUITS. The fruits are globose berries that are green when immature, becoming bright red at maturity. They are up to 5 mm long.

DISTRIBUTION. Mahé, Praslin, and Silhouette

Craterispermum microdon occurs at midaltitude, often growing as a small tree in open habitats (for example, beside the Le Niol path, just below the *Nepenthes pervillei* site). In the shady habitat of La Reserve, large trees are found at 400 m. At higher altitudes it is more common as an understory shrub. The specific name, *microdon*, refers to the small teeth. One of the most conspicuous characters of this species is the large persistent stipules present at the nodes. Medicinally it is said to have many uses. An infusion made from the leaves is reputed to bring on delayed menstruation.

ILLUSTRATION. Habit with both flowers and fruits; painted at 1×. Enlargement of node with axillary inflorescences; painted at 4×. Flowering habit collected and painted on June 17, 1991. Fruiting habit collected and painted on June 17, 1991. Herbarium sheets: Rosemary Wise 145, 191 (OXF).

RUBIACEAE Jussieu

Glionnetia D. D. Tirvengadum
  This is a monotypic genus from Seychelles.

PLATE 40. *Glionnetia sericea* (Baker) D. D. Tirvengadum
  (D. D. Tirvengadum, 1984, *Adansonia* 6[2]:197–206)

  Randia sericea (Baker) Hemsley (W. B. Hemsley, 1916, *Journal of Botany* 54, suppl. 2, p. 18)

  Ixora sericea Baker (Baker, 1877, *Flora of Mauritius*, p. 151)

  Vernacular name: manglier de grand bois

HABIT. The plant is a tree with spreading branches that grows to 6 m high and has deltoid, caducous 6 mm long stipules.

LEAVES. The leaves are opposite, oblong with pointed apices and attenuate bases, coriaceous, and glabrous. They may be as long as 15 cm. The 16 pairs of secondary veins are craspedodromous with parallel inter-secondaries and are finely reticulate on both surfaces. The midribs are usually magenta. The petioles are up to 2 cm long.

INFLORESCENCES. The inflorescences are terminal corymbs with clustered flowers.

FLOWERS. The flowers are creamy pink at first, becoming deeper pink and maroon, often with all stages present in the same cluster. The calyx is up to 6 mm long, is covered with adpressed hairs, and has five rounded lobes. The corolla tube may be as long as 7 cm, and has five spreading lobes that are up to 1 cm long. Both anthers and style are inserted in the tube.

FRUITS. The fruits are globose, vertically dehiscent capsules up to 8 mm long with persistent lobes.

DISTRIBUTION. Mahé and Silhouette

Glionnetia sericea grows in exposed habitats at altitudes above 600 m, for example, on the knoll at the summit of Congo Rouge, where it is found with stunted trees of *Northia seychellana*, *Syzygium wrightii*, *Rapanea seychellarum*, and the endemic grass, *Garnotia sechellensis*. In this habitat, *Glionnetia* is the dominant species. Smaller bushes are found on the cliff at the summit of Mt. Sébért, Mahé, that overlooks Seychelles International Airport. Both sites provide the requisite moist, humid conditions. On Silhouette, *Glionnetia* is found at Grand Congoman and on the higher parts of Mt. Dauban. The many clusters of fragrant, long-tubed flowers, which range in color from cream to pink to maroon (according to age), set against the dark evergreen leaves make this one of the most attractive of all the Seychelles plants. It has been repeatedly mentioned in publications that *Glionnetia* always exists alongside the pitcher plant, *Nepenthes pervillei*, a fact that is now disregarded. The vernacular name likens the leaves of the plant to those of the mangrove, *Rhizophora mucronata* (*manglier de grand bois* = "mangrove of the woods"). The generic name *Glionnetii* commemorates Mr. Guy Lionnet, a well-known naturalist and writer, living in Victoria.

ILLUSTRATION. Flowering habit and detail of fruits; painted at 1×. Flowering habit collected and painted on June 23, 1990. Fruiting habit collected and painted on June 24–25, 1990. Herbarium sheet: Rosemary Wise 127 (OXF).

RUBIACEAE Jussieu

Ixora Linnaeus

This genus comprises 300 species of trees and shrubs, mainly from Africa and Asia. All have white, yellow, orange, pink, or red flowers with long corolla tubes. Many are grown as ornamentals. The name *Ixora* is the Portuguese version of *Iswara*, the name of a Malabar deity to whom the flowers were offered.

PLATE 41.   *Ixora pudica* Baker   (Baker, 1877, *Flora of Mauritius*, p. 151)

Vernacular name: ixora blanc

HABIT. The plant is a tree that is glabrous in all parts and reaches a height of 7 m.

LEAVES. The leaves are opposite, ovate, and glabrous, have acute apices and cuneate bases, are coriaceous with entire margins, and may be up to 20 cm long. The 12 pairs of secondary veins are brochididromous. The petioles are up to 2 cm long and are often crimson at the base.

INFLORESCENCES. The inflorescences are dense, erect terminal corymbs, up to 8 cm long. The peduncles also are often crimson at the base.

FLOWERS. The flowers are white, very fragrant, and up to 5 mm wide. The calyx is puberulent, up to 1.5 mm long, and has four small deltoid lobes. The corolla tube is up to 5 mm long, with four spreading, 2.5 mm long lobes. The main difference between the male and the female flowers is that the two lobes of the stigma remain together in the male while those of the female flower are spreading.

FRUITS. The fruits are globose drupes, up to 7 mm long, which are green or green blotched with brown, becoming dark brown at maturity.

DISTRIBUTION. Mahé and Silhouette

When *Ixora pudica* is flowering, the pleasant scent is often the first indication that the plant is in the locality. Some specimens grow at the summit of Morne Seychellois, at 905 m (M. Kirkpatrick, pers. comm.). At lower altitudes, close to the summit of Copolia at 450 m, there is one tree to the left of the path in the area of open woodland. At this location it is found near a large tree of *Soulamea terminalioides*. Some other species in this community are *Dicranopteris linearis* (bracken fern), *Protarum sechellarum*, *Hypoxidia rhizophylla*, *Mimusops sechellarum*, and *Pandanus sechellarum*.

ILLUSTRATION. Flowering and fruiting habits; painted at 1×. Enlargement of flower; painted at 6×. Flowering habit collected and painted on June 30, 1990. Fruiting habit collected and painted on 5 July 1990. Herbarium sheets: Rosemary Wise 120, 121, 122, 175 (OXF).

RUBIACEAE   Jussieu

Paragenipa Baillon
  This genus comprises one species in Madagascar and one in Seychelles.

PLATE 42.   *Paragenipa wrightii* (Baker) F. Friedmann,
  comb. nov.

  Psychotria wrightii Baker   (Baker, 1877, *Flora of Mauritius*, p. 156)

  Randia lancifolia Hemsley   (W. B. Hemsley, 1916, *Journal of Botany* 54,
    suppl. 2, p. 17)

  Vernacular name: café marron grande feuille

HABIT. The plant is a shrub or small tree with grayish-brown fissured bark. It reaches a height of 5 m.

LEAVES. The leaves are opposite and elliptic or ovate, with rounded apices and cuneiform bases. They are coriaceous, glabrous, and up to 20 cm long. The venation is faint, with 12 pairs of brochidodromous secondary veins, and the tertiary veins are indistinctly reticulate. The petioles are up to 1 cm long.

INFLORESCENCES. The inflorescences are axillary fascicles bearing one to three flowers.

FLOWERS. The flowers are white, up to 1.5 cm wide, and on pedicels that are up to 4 mm long. The puberulent calyx is up to 1 mm long, and has five small acute lobes. The corolla tube is funnel-shaped and up to 9 mm long. It has five rounded, spreading lobes that are up to 6 mm long. The five 7 mm long anthers are exerted, with the filaments arising in the throat. The style may be as long as 6 mm and has a bificate stigma.

FRUITS. The fruits are red ovoid berries that reach 2.5 cm in length.

DISTRIBUTION. Mahé, Praslin, Silhouette, Félicité, and Curieuse

One of the most widespread endemics, *Paragenipa wrightii* commonly grows from sea level to 700 m, mainly in open habitats. It is one of the most vigorous regenerators in the shallow and impoverished soil on glacis. Its easy-to-recognize characteristics are the compact, often columnar, habit and the colorful flush leaves. These range from very light green to dull orange through purple. The specific epithet, *wrightii* commemorates Dr. Percival Wright.

ILLUSTRATION. Habit with both flowers and fruits, showing young flush leaves; mature leaves; painted at 1×. Flowering habit collected and painted on August 11, 1989. Fruiting habit collected and painted on August 11, 1989. No specimens pressed.

RUBIACEAE Jussieu

Psathera Commerson ex Jussieu
  This small genus consists of 89 species that are confined to Madagascar, the Mascarenes, and Seychelles.

PLATE 43. *Psathura sechellarum* Baker (Baker, 1877, *Flora of Mauritius*, p. 157)

Psychotria sechellarum (Baker) Summerhayes (V. S. Summerhayes, 1928, *Bull. Misc. Info.*, Kew 1928:392)

HABIT. The plant is a shrub up to 4 m high with furrowed branches and persistent, small lanceolate, bilobed stipules.

LEAVES. The leaves are opposite, obovate, glabrous, and coriaceous. They have entire margins and reach 20 cm in length. The 12–16 pairs of secondary veins are craspedodromous, and the tertiary venation randomly reticulate. The petioles are up to 1.5 cm long.

INFLORESCENCES. The inflorescences are terminal, much branched panicles that may be as long as 20 cm. They have persistent small, deltoid bracts.

FLOWERS. The flowers are subsessile, white tinged with pink, and up to 5 mm across. The calyx is campanulate and up to 2.5 mm long, with five small deltoid lobes up to 2 mm in length. The corolla tube is up to 5 mm long, and has five spreading valvate lobes up to 8 mm long. There is a band of dense hairs in the throat. The flowers either have the five stamens exerted with a 2.5 mm long style or inserted with a 4.5 mm long style. The filaments arise at the base of the tube.

FRUITS. The fruits are globose drupes that are red at maturity. They are up to 8 mm long and have rims formed at the apices by the persistent calyx teeth.

DISTRIBUTION. Mahé and Silhouette

  Psathura sechellarum is a rare, critically endangered, moisture-loving shrub that is found from mid- to high altitudes (500–700 m). Several individuals can be seen alongside the Congo Rouge–Le Niol path, in the same area as *Nepenthes pervillei*; however, the total population of *P. sechellarum* is possibly only about 30 plants. On the summit of Morne Blanc, associated plants are *Gastonia crassa*, *Syzygium wrightii*, *Psidium cattleianum*, *Hypoxidia rhizophylla*, and the stunted trees of *Pandanus sechellarum* and *Northia seychellana*. *P. sechellarum* is the only one of the genera to have terminal inflorescences and bifid stipules.

ILLUSTRATION. Flowering habit, detail of fruiting habit, and mature leaves; painted at 1×. Flowering habit collected and painted on November 2, 1990. Fruiting habit collected and painted on November 2–3, 1990. Herbarium sheets: Rosemary Wise 138, 168, 170, 179 (OXF).

RUBIACEAE   Jussieu

Psychotria Linnaeus

This large tropical genus comprises 1,400 species. The roots of some of the South American species are used as hallucinogens. Other species are grown as ornamentals. Many species have domatia that house ants.

PLATE 44.   *Psychotria pervillei* Baker   (Baker, 1877, *Flora of Mauritius*, p. 155)

P. affinis Baker   (Baker, 1877, *Flora of Mauritius*, p. 154)

P. dupontiae Hemsley   (W. B. Hemsley, 1907, *Bull. Misc. Info.*, Kew 1907:363)

P. pallida Hemsley   (W. B. Hemsley, 1916, *Journal of Botany* 54, suppl. 2, p. 19)

Vernacular name: bois couleuvre

HABIT. The plant is a shrub with terete branches and small deltoid stipules that soon wither after the leaves unfurl. It may grow as high as 5 m.

LEAVES. The leaves are opposite, glabrous, lanceolate, and coriaceous, with obtuse apices, acuminate bases, and entire margins. They may be up to 15 cm long. The 10 pairs of secondary veins are camptodromous. The petioles are up to 2 cm long.

INFLORESCENCES. The inflorescences are corymbose terminal panicles.

FLOWERS. The flowers are white, up to 5 mm wide, and on 1.5 mm long pedicels. The calyx is campanulate and up to 2 mm long, with five deltoid teeth. The corolla tube is as long as 6 mm, is densely pilose in the throat, and has five valvate, lanceolate, spreading lobes that are up to 2.5 mm long. The flowers have either five anthers exerted in the throat and a style up to 4 mm in length, or inserted anthers and a style as long as 7.5 mm.

FRUITS. The fruits are globose drupes that are green at first but turn black at maturity. They contain two or three pyrenes.

DISTRIBUTION. Mahé, Praslin, and Silhouette

Psychotria pervillei grows between 200 and 900 m. Small understory shrubs, although not common, are found on Congo Rouge and Morne Blanc. Several are found near to the benchmark at the summit of Brulée, La Reserve (at 501 m), together with a wide range of endemic species including *Gastonia crassa, Syzygium wrightii, Soulamea terminalioides*, and various orchids. Like many related members of the Rubiaceae, *Psychotria* tends to be infested with coccids, which may account for the low number of individuals that put it in a threatened category. The leaf shape is variable, depending on habitat and altitude. Infusions of the leaves are used medicinally as an appetite-inducing tonic, especially for elderly women.

ILLUSTRATION. Flowering and fruiting habits, young and mature fruits; painted at 1×. Flowering habit collected and painted on July 4, 1991. Fruiting habit collected and painted on July 5, 1991. Herbarium sheets: Rosemary Wise 135, 169 (OXF).

RUBIACEAE Jussieu

Psychotria Linnaeus

PLATE 45.   *Psychotria silhouettae* F. Friedmann
· (F. Friedmann, 1990, *Adansonia* 12[1]:65)

HABIT. The plant is a shrub that attains a height of 1.5 m and has bifid caducous stipules.

LEAVES. The leaves are opposite and glabrous, with acuminate apices and cuneiform bases. They may be as long as 15 cm. The 10 pairs of secondary veins are brochidodromous. The petioles are up to 3.5 cm long.

INFLORESCENCES. The inflorescences are branched terminal panicles.

FLOWERS. The flowers are white, up to 3 mm across, and on pedicels that are up to 1 cm long. The calyx is up to 0.8 mm long and has five small lobes. The corolla tube narrows toward the base and is up to 2.5 mm long. It has five spreading lobes with thickened tips and is up to 1.3 mm in length. The five anthers are inserted in the throat in a band of pilose hairs. The style is up to 2.5 mm long.

FRUITS. The fruits are globose drupes, white at maturity, and up to 6 mm long.

DISTRIBUTION. Silhouette

This extremely rare, critically endangered, understory shrub is known from one site on Silhouette Island only—the Pisonia forest high above Anse Mondon—where possibly only three or four rather impoverished individuals now exist. The principal differences between this and the related species on Mahé are the white fruits, the less coriaceous leaves, and the longer acuminate leaf tips.

ILLUSTRATION. Flowering habit collected and painted in August 1990, at 1×. Fruiting habit collected and painted on October 23, 1992, at 1×. Herbarium sheets: Rosemary Wise 172, 180 (OXF).

RUBIACEAE Jussieu

Rothmannia Thunberg

This genus comprises 30 tropical species that are restricted to southern Africa and one species in the granitic Seychelles. Many are grown ornamentally.

PLATE 46. *Rothmannia annae* (E. P. Wright) Keay
(R.W.J. Keay, 1958, *Bull. Jardin Botanique de l'Etat à Bruxelles* 28:50)

Gardenia annae Wright (E. P. Wright, 1871, *Trans. Royal Irish Academy* 24:575)

Vernacular name: bois citron (French); Wright's gardenia (English)

HABIT. The plant is a tree with smooth, grayish-brown bark, is glabrous in all parts, and reaches a height of 6 m. The stipules are inter-petiolar.

LEAVES. The leaves are opposite and lanceolate, with acute apices, cuneate bases, and entire margins. They are up to 1 cm long and are characteristically carried in threes. The venation is faint. The six pairs of secondary veins are brochidodromous. Petioles are up to 5 mm long.

FLOWERS. The flowers are heavily scented, solitary, axillary, and 4–5 cm wide. The calyx is up to 6 mm long, tubular, and swollen at the base, narrowing for top third. The five lobes are linear. The corolla tube is up to 6 mm long, funnel-shaped, greenish-cream, either plain or with pink mottles. There are usually five 2 cm long corolla lobes (occasionally four or six) that are white speckled with deep magenta in the throat; infrequently they are pure white. The male flowers have five sessile, long, narrow anthers that are up to 16 mm long and alternating with the corolla lobes, with a two-lobed stigma and a 4 cm long style. The female flowers, which are slightly smaller, have five, 12 mm long sterile anthers and a style as long as the corolla.

FRUITS. The fruits are hard ovoid to globose berries, olive green blotched with cream, and up to 6 cm long. These contain many seeds which germinate readily.

DISTRIBUTION. Aride. Possibly the plant once occurred on Praslin and Silhouette.

At present the number of trees of *Rothmannia annae* on Aride, the most northerly of the granitic islands, is estimated to be 1,200. Many consider this critically endangered plant to be the most beautiful of the Seychelles endemics. It is locally abundant at seven sites, which range from a few meters above sea level (in the fertile soil of the plateau) to the summit. After periods of heavy rain, all of the trees flower synchronously (about once a month in the rainy season—October to May), and the heavy scent of the flowers, which lasts for a few days only, almost overpowers the ever-present guano odor. Horne collected *Rothmannia* on Mahé (Herbarium sheet: Horne 512, 1874) and Praslin (Herbarium sheet: Horne 260, 1871), while Gardiner found it on Silhouette around 1905. The destruction of the trees by infestations of scale insects on these islands may be the reason why it is no longer found naturally in any other place than on Aride. Painting on Aride is not straightforward. Beside having over a million resident seabirds, it also has one of the densest populations of skinks in the world. These show no fear and wander freely over paints and paper.

I rushed over to Aride Island one windy July day, at the peak of the southeast monsoon, after a radio message was relayed via the police station at Grande Anse that *Rothmannia* was about to flower. This was in the early days of the project, when the stormy six-mile crossing between Aride and Praslin was by shallow wooden pirogues. I was handed an old plastic helmet, and my task was to bail out the water that seeped in through the bottom or crashed over the sides. This was no time to admire scenery or to think about seasickness!

The genus *Rothmannia* commemorates Johan Rothman (1684–1763), a Swedish physician, botanist, and teacher who encouraged Carl Linnaeus in botanical studies during his school days in Vaxjo. It was from him that Linnaeus learned Tournfort's system of classification. Edward Percival Wright (1834–1910), after whom the tree is commonly named, visited Seychelles in 1867.

ILLUSTRATION. Flowering habit, fruit, and detail of white-flowered shrub; all painted at 1×. Flowering habits collected and painted on August 2 and 8, 1985. Fruiting habit collected and painted on August 5, 1985. No specimens were pressed.

Rosemary Wise.

RUBIACEAE Jussieu

Tarenna Gaertner

This genus comprises 180 species from the Old World tropics. Some are used for timber.

PLATE 47. *Tarenna sechellensis* (Baker) Summerhayes
(V. S. Summerhayes, 1928, *Bull. Misc. Info.*, Kew 1928:391)

Webera sechellensis Baker   (Baker, 1877, *Flora of Mauritius*, p. 139)

Tarenna nigrescens auct. non (Hooker f.) Hiern   (W. B. Hemsley, 1916, *Journal of Botany* 54, suppl. 2, p. 17)

Vernacular name: bois dur blanc

HABIT. The plant is usually an understory tree that is glabrous in all parts and has smooth bark. It reaches a height of 5 m. The stipules are paired, linear, often caducous, and up to 12 mm long.

LEAVES. The leaves are opposite, ovate, and chartaceous and have acuminate apices, attenuate bases, and entire margins. They are as long as 14 cm. The 8–11 pairs of secondary veins are brochidodromous. The petioles are up to 1 cm long.

INFLORESCENCES. The inflorescences are terminal panicles with branched pedicels and are often pendulous.

FLOWERS. The flowers are white, sweet-scented, up to 2 cm wide. The calyx is tubular, up to 1.5 mm long with four lobes that are up to 0.8 mm long. In the male (bisexual) flowers, the corolla tube is as long as 1 cm with four slightly reflexed, rounded lobes. The four stamens are inserted between the lobes at the throat. The anthers are narrow, slightly curved upward, and up to 1 cm long. The style is up to 2 cm long with a bilobed stigma. Female flowers are smaller and have sterile anthers and a 1 cm long style.

FRUITS. The fruits are borne on pedicels, are ovoid, shiny, green, and up to 7 mm wide.

DISTRIBUTION. Mahé, Praslin, Silhouette, La Digue, Curieuse, and Félicité

This species is a midaltitude tree that is more common on Silhouette than any other of the islands. There are a few trees on Mahé that grow higher, near the summit of Congo Rouge. *Tarenna* is most frequently found growing in deep woodland. One tree, which grows with various palms in the area, spreads over the path near La Reserve, Mahé, where the path passes to the side of a massive vertical rock face, between viewpoints 1 and 2. Occasional trees exist on glacis.

ILLUSTRATION. Vegetative branch, inflorescences, and fruits; painted at 1×. Enlargement of flower; painted at 1×. Flowering habit collected and painted on October 31, 1991 and July 23, 1992. Fruiting habit collected and painted on December 1, 1991. Herbarium sheets: Rosemary Wise 124, 163, 164 (OXF).

RUBIACEAE Jussieu

Timonius Rumphius

This genus consists of 150 species ranging from Mauritius, Sri Lanka, Andamans, and Malesia to Australia and the Pacific.

PLATE 48.　*Timonius sechellensis* Summerhayes
(V. S. Summerhayes, 1928, *Bull. Misc. Info.*, Kew 1928:391)

Timonius flavescens (Jack) Baker, sensu Baker　(Baker, 1877, *Flora of Mauritius*, p. 144)

Vernacular name: bois cassant de montagne

HABIT. The plant is a shrub or small tree with many branches that grows as high as 8 m. The stipules are up to 2 cm long and caducous.

LEAVES. The leaves are opposite and elliptic or rhomboidal, with acuminate apices and deltoid bases. The upper surface is glabrous, and the lower has appressed hairs when young but becomes glabrous when mature. The eight pairs of secondary veins are brochidodromous, and the tertiary veins are scalariform. Domatia with tufts of white hairs are present in the axis of the veins. The petioles are up to 1.5 cm long.

INFLORESCENCES. The inflorescences are axillary cymes.

FLOWERS. The flowers are yellowish orange. The male flowers are on pedicels as long as 2.5 cm, with two triangular bracts up to 3 mm long and as many as 12 flowers. The flowers are sessile, with two smaller bracts. The receptacle is conical, surmounted by a calyx with four deltoid lobes. The corolla tube is up to 9 mm in length, pubescent on the outer surface, and has four 4 mm long spreading lobes. The one to three female flowers are on peduncles that are as long as 3 cm and have a globose receptacle surmounted by a smaller four-lobed calyx and a 4 mm long corolla tube.

FRUITS. The fruits are globose, fleshy drupes that are green when young and red to near black at maturity. They are up to 1 cm long.

DISTRIBUTION. Mahé, Praslin, and Silhouette

These small trees or, often, fastigiate shrubs are common at mid- to high altitudes. One of the first shrubs to be encountered at the beginning of the climb up Morne Blanc is a small bush of *Timonius sechellensis*, which grows right in the center of the path. Good field characters are the rhomboidal leaf shapes and small orange flowers. At other sites—for example, Bernica, where the habitat is lower and more exposed—the leaves are much larger, and the compact shrubs grow with *Diospyros seychellarum*, *Erythroxylum sechellarum*, *Pandanus multispicatus*, and several palm species. In more heavily wooded areas, at higher altitudes, *Timonius* loses the compact habit and is more commonly a tree with spreading branches. An infusion of the leaves is given to reduce fever.

ILLUSTRATION. Habit with both flowers and fruits and mature leaves; painted at 1×. Enlargements of flowers; drawn at 7×. Flowering habit collected and painted on June 20, 1990. Fruiting habit collected and painted on June 20–21, 1990. Herbarium sheets: Rosemary Wise 136, 140, 184 (OXF).

SAPINDACEAE Jussieu

This family comprises 145 genera and 1,325 species of trees, shrubs, climbers, lianas, and herbs that are found in the tropics and subtropics, although a few species are in temperate regions. Many species have edible fruits, including akee, the national fruit of the West Indies (*Blighia sapida*), litchi (*Litchi chinensis*), and rambutan (*Nephelium lappaceum*). In Brazil, a stimulating caffeine-rich drink, guarana, is made from the liana *Paullinia cupana*. The genus *Sapindus* has berries rich in saponins, which yield a soap substitute. Other species produce timber, oils, and fish poisons. Many more are grown as ornamentals. In the granitic Seychelles there are three indigenous genera and some cultivated introductions.

Allophylus Linnaeus

This genus consists of 1 polymorphic tropical species, subdivided into about 175 rather indistinct subspecies.

PLATE 49.   *Allophylus sechellensis* Summerhayes
(V. S. Summerhayes, 1928, *Bull. Misc. Info.*, Kew 1928:390)

Vernacular name: bois cafoul trois feuilles

HABIT. The plant is a small tree or scrambling shrub up to 5 m high with grayish-brown bark and slender branches. Stipules are absent.

LEAVES. The leaves are alternate, trifoliate, and glabrous with 2 cm long petioles. The leaflets are obovate, with the margin often crenate toward the apex. Terminal leaflets are up to 7 cm long. The four to six pairs of secondary veins are craspedodromous. Domatia occur in the axis of the veins on lower surface.

INFLORESCENCES. The inflorescences are axillary racemes that are as long as 10 cm.

FLOWERS. The flowers are unisexual and up to 2.5 cm wide. The calyx has four sepals, free almost to the base. The four white petals are up to 1.5 mm in length and have two small lobes on the inner surface that are obscured by the dense hairs. There are eight stamens that are up to 1.5 mm long and a bifid style.

FRUITS. The fruits are red drupes, globose or ovate, and up to 8 mm long.

DISTRIBUTION. Mahé, Praslin, and Silhouette

This is one of the rarest of the endemic plants, being found only at a few sites, mainly close to the sea and up to 100 m—for example, above Grand Barbe, Silhouette; in restricted areas in the extreme south of Mahé; and on L'islette, western Mahé, where it grows among semicultivated trees as a rather straggling shrub in a rocky area.

The red fruits, which are characteristic of this genus, are attractive to and are dispersed by birds, especially pigeons. The authority, Victor Samuel Summerhayes (1897–1974), was in charge of the orchid herbarium at the Royal Botanic Gardens, Kew, from 1924 until 1964. *Allophylus* comes from the Greek *allos*, meaning "other," and *phylon*, meaning "race" or "nation."

Other members of this family in the granitic islands are *Allophylus pervillei* (small tree with elliptic leaves and spiked inflorescence of green flowers, common in the reserve of the Black Paradise Flycatcher on La Digue), *Cardiospermum halicacabum* var. *microcarpum*, *Dodonaea viscosa*, *Filicum decipiens*, *Litchi chinensis*, *Nephelium lappaceum*, *Sapindus rarak*, and *S. saponaria*.

ILLUSTRATION. Habit with fruits and flowering shoot; painted at 1×. Flowering habit collected and painted on June 27, 1990. Fruiting habit collected and painted on June 28, 1990. Herbarium sheets: Rosemary Wise 117, 118 (OXF).

SAPOTACEAE Jussieu

This pantropical family is composed of 116 genera and 1,100 species of trees and shrubs. Gutta-percha is the coagulated latex of sapotaceous trees and is harder than rubber and not as flexible. It was originally used in the manufacture of golf balls and as an insulant. Chicle, which is used in the production of chewing gum, comes from *Manilkara zapota*. Edible fruits are obtained from many species, including *Achras zapota* and *Chrysophyllum cainito*. *Pouteria lucuma* was an important part of the diet of the Incas. It is still grown in the high Andes and exported to North America.

Mimusops Linnaeus

This genus comprises 57 species from tropical Africa, Seychelles, and Malesia to the Pacific. In Malaya *Mimusops elengi* is cultivated for its fragrant flowers.

PLATE 50. *Mimusops sechellarum* (Oliver) Hemsley
(W. B. Hemsley, 1916, *Journal of Botany* 54, suppl. 2, p. 23)

Imbricaria sechellarum Oliver   (Oliver, 1894, *Hooker's Icones plantarum*, t. 2315)

Vernacular name: bois de natte

HABIT. This plant is a tree that grows up to 30 m high and has fissured grayish-brown bark with white latex. The minute stipules are caducous.

LEAVES. The leaves are spirally arranged, sometimes clustered at ends of branches, ovate, coriaceous with emarginate apices and obtuse bases, dark or grayish green, and up to 15 cm long. The 12–14 pairs of secondary veins are camptodromous.

FLOWERS. The flowers are axillary, or in the axils of the leaf scars, and up to 1 cm wide. The calyx is up to 9 mm long and has two whorls of free sepals, the outer ones of which are valvate. The fleshy corolla tube is either hirsute or glabrous, is light green, and is shorter than the lobes.

FRUITS. The fruits are fleshy indehiscent berries with one to six seeds.

DISTRIBUTION. Mahé, Praslin, Silhouette, and Marianne

When the first settlers arrived, *Mimusops* was one of the more widespread tree species of the forest and river ravines. The excellence of the timber was soon recognized by the early inhabitants, who cut trees indiscriminately until the species became extremely rare. Seedlings have recently been reintroduced to Frigate Island (Ron Gerlach, pers. comm.). Examples of this very fine timber can be seen on Silhouette (the bar of the hotel and parts of the traditional old plantation house near the jetty, Grand Kas). There are stands of trees at Morne Poule Marron, the steep cliffs behind this house. The main populations on Mahé now grow in relatively inaccessible areas, for example, alongside *Medusagyne oppositifolia* on the steep glacis of Mt. Bernica and on the summit of Mt. Sébért. Isolated individuals survive at low altitudes (for example, alongside the Danzilles to Anse Major path, Mahé).

Other members of this family in the granitic islands are *Chrysophyllum cainito*, *Mimusops coriacea* (with obovate leaves to 15 cm. and globose golden edible fruits that are up to to 4 cm wide), *Northia seychellana*, *Pouteria obovata*, and *Pouteria campechiana*.

ILLUSTRATION. Flowering habit and details of fruits and seeds; painted at 1×. Flowering habit collected and painted on August 29, and September 6, 1989. Fruiting habit collected and painted on July 20, 1990. Herbarium sheet: Rosemary Wise 171 (OXF).

SAPOTACEAE   Jussieu

Northia Hooker

This is a monotypic genus from the granitic Seychelles. Dr. T. D. Pennington, Royal Botanic Gardens, Kew, in his generic monograph on the Sapotaceae (1991) explains: "In the protologue Hooker spelled the name *Northea* in the text, but *Northia* on the plate. Art. 75.2 of ICBN therefore applies, and the spelling which best suits the recommendations of Art. 73 is to be retained. Rec. 73B(b) recommends that when the name of the person ends in a consonant, the letters -ia are added in the formation of a generic name. The spelling *Northia* is therefore adopted here, as it was by Baehni (1965)."

PLATE 51.   *Northia seychellana* Hooker f.   (W. B. Hemsley, 1884, *Hooker's Icones plantarum*, t. 1473)

Northia confusa Hemsley   (W. B. Hemsley, 1916, *Journal of Botany* 54, suppl. 2, p. 361)

Northea hornei (M. M. Hartog) Pierre   (Pierre, 1890, *Notes Botaniques, Sapotacées*, fasc. 1, p. 11)

Vernacular name: capucin

HABIT. This plant is a tree that grows up to 20 m high and has reddish-brown bark containing white latex. Stipules are absent.

LEAVES. The leaves are spirally arranged, clustered at the ends of the shoots, elliptic or obovate, coriaceous, and as much as 30 cm in length. They are dark green on the upper surface and rust-colored and tomentose below. The midribs are prominent on both surfaces. The secondary veins are numerous, parallel, and craspedodromous, with a prominent marginal vein and many reticulate tertiary veins.

INFLORESCENCES. The inflorescences are axillary fascicles of 5–10 flowers.

FLOWERS. The flowers are bisexual and up to 12 mm wide. Pedicels are as long as 3 cm. The calyx is in two whorls of three free sepals, the outer ones of which are valvate. The corolla tube is carnose and up to 6 mm long. It has six lobes, which are contorted in bud and up to 4 mm long. Each lobe has two lateral segments. The six stamens, which are inserted at the top of the corolla tube, are in a single whorl. The flowers abscise circularly at the base of the corolla tube, below the insertion of the staminodes. These shed "rings" are found under flowering trees.

FRUITS. The fruits are indehiscent, globose, fleshy, and up to 10 cm wide. The single seed is as long as 8 cm and broadly ellipsoid. It has a shiny, chestnut-brown, woody testa and a rough-surfaced broad scar the length of the seed.

DISTRIBUTION. Mahé, Praslin, Silhouette, Curieuse, and Félicité

Northia seychellana is the dominant species in some of the higher sites on the islands above 600 m, for instance, in the mist forest of Congo Rouge, where the trees can be 12 m tall. In this community, associated species are the tree fern, *Cyathea sechellarum*, *Dillenia ferruginea*, *Verschaffeltia splendida*, *Roscheria melanochaetes*, *Hypoxidia mahéensis*, *Pandanus sechellarum*, and the saprophytic *Seychellaria thomassetii*. In more exposed areas, for example on the summits of Congo Rouge and Morne Blanc on Mahé and on high regions of Silhouette, the trees are stunted and may be less than 3 m high. At one time *Northia* probably grew at low altitude. (One remaining tree on Curieuse is at sea level.) From the time of the first settlers until 1905, *Northia* was one of the most common timbers to be exported from Mahé to Mauritius; it was used for roofing shingles and cartwheel spokes. As recently as the 1950s, *Northia* was felled extensively on Silhouette for construction on Mahé (Guy Camille, pers. comm.). Columns in the Grand Kas, La Passe, Silhouette, were fashioned from local wood in 1862. The vernacular name, capucin, refers to the resemblance of the seed to the head of a cowled Capuchin monk.

Many plants produce seeds that are dispersed by birds or bats capable of flying for long distances. On small islands there is the possibility that a high percentage would be lost by being dropped into the sea. One safeguard against this unnecessary waste is that the plant produces fruits with very large seeds. When no local disperser is capable of carrying them, the seeds fall from the trees and germinate near the parent plant.

The genus *Northia* was named by Sir John Hooker after the intrepid Victorian artist and traveler, Marianne North, who visited Seychelles for three months in 1883. Her painting of *Northia* and about forty others undertaken during her visit are on permanent exhibition in the Marianne North Gallery, Royal Botanic Gardens, Kew. The specific synonym is named for John Horne (1835–1905), who, after spending one year at the Royal Botanic Gardens, Kew, was employed in the Botanic Gardens, Mauritius, becoming director from 1865 until 1891.

ILLUSTRATION. Fruiting habit, seed, and immature fruits and flowers; painted at 1×. Flowering habit collected and painted on June 25 (buds) and May 1, 1990 (mature flowers). Fruiting habit collected and painted on June 21, 1990. Herbarium sheet: Rosemary Wise 206 (OXF).

SIMAROUBACEAE   De Candolle

This family consists of 22 genera and 170 species found throughout the tropics and subtropics. The family contains the medicinal genera *Brucea* and *Quassia* (for the treatment of dysentery and worms) and the ornamental *Ailanthus*, tree of heaven. The granitic Seychelles have one indigenous and two introduced genera.

Soulamea Lamarck

This genus comprises nine species, which occur in Malaysia, New Caledonia, Fiji, and Seychelles.

PLATE 52.   *Soulamea terminalioides* Baker   (Baker, 1877, *Flora of Mauritius*, p. 42)

   Vernacular name: colophant

HABIT. The plant is a tree that grows to 10 m in height and has grayish bark with distinct leaf scars. Stipules are absent.

LEAVES. The leaves are alternate, up to 40 cm long, spirally arranged, and oblong. They have mucronate apices and cuneiform bases, are coriaceous, and have entire margins. The petioles are as long as 7 cm. The leaves are clustered at the ends of the branches. They are silky when young but become glabrous when mature. The 20 pairs of secondary veins are parallel and camptodromous. The tertiary veins are closely reticulate.

INFLORESCENCES. The inflorescences are axillary racemes up to 8 cm long.

FLOWERS. The flowers are actinomorphic (radially symmetrical), and the male flowers are larger than the female. The three sepals are silky, imbricate, and 1 mm long. In male flowers the three yellow petals are reflexed and up to 1.5 mm long. The six 1.5 mm long stamens have extrorse anthers. The female flowers have 1 mm long petals and 0.7 mm long staminodes. The 2 mm long ovary is triangular and surmounted by three recurved styles.

FRUITS. The fruits are three-winged, pendulous capsules that are 3 cm long. They are light green when young, becoming brown and papery when mature.

DISTRIBUTION. Mahé and Silhouette

Soulamea terminalioides is a locally widespread tree, growing from around 100–500 m in altitude, often on rocky outcrops. The one large tree below the summit of Copolia, in the stretch of open woodland, is near *Ixora pudica* and *Mimusops sechellarum*. Trees are also found at higher altitudes on Congo Rouge, Casse Dent, and Mt. Sébért. On Silhouette, *Soulamea* grows on Mt. Laurant. The leaves are particularly distinctive, having shiny, dark green blades, and many conspicuous, parallel pale yellow veins.

The specimen of this was collected on September 3, 1989, during my first visit to Copolia. This was a memorable day. The wide sweeping glacis on the summit was such a delight because so many of the plants that I knew I would eventually be painting were there in front of me. It was Regatta Day and between the hilltops, I had a good view of the yachts tacking in Beau Vallon Bay. This site is typical of an inselberg, a steep-sided eminence rising from relatively level ground. Very few introduced species populate such areas, and the vegetation remains predominantly native.

Other members of this family in the granitic islands are *Brucea javanica* and *Quassia amara*.

ILLUSTRATION. Flowering habit collected and painted on September 4, 1989, at 1×. Fruiting habit collected and painted on August 22, 1989, at 1×. Herbarium sheet: Rosemary Wise 101 (OXF).

URTICACEAE Jussieu

This family comprises 52 genera and 1,050 species of a few trees, shrubs, lianas, and herbs from the tropics to temperate areas. Many species have stinging hairs. The economic uses are few. In Southeast Asia fibers from *Urtica* species are used in textiles. The granitic Seychelles have four indigenous genera.

Procris Commerson ex Jussieu

This genus contains 20 species distributed in the Old World tropics.

PLATE 53. *Procris insularis* Schroter   (H. E. Schroter, 1938, *Feddes Repert.* 45:288)

HABIT. This perennial herb, glabrous in all parts, has succulent stems, and grows to 80 cm in height. The stipules are up to 2 mm long.

LEAVES. The leaves are opposite, one of which is large and one of which is reduced and is often caducous. They are obovate, falcate, and asymmetric, with acuminate apices and attenuate bases. They are also membranous, have margins that are irregularly dentate, crenate, or entire, and grow to 24 cm in length. The midribs of young leaves have irregular, dark brown scales that are up to 1 mm across. The six to eight pairs of secondary veins are brochidodromous. The petioles are up to 1 cm long.

INFLORESCENCES. Male and female inflorescences are often both on the same plant. The male inflorescence is a panicle up to 5 cm long. The female one is a sessile, hemispherical capitulum.

FLOWERS. In the male flower the pedicel is articulated with the five imbricate perianth lobes, two of which are up to 2 mm long and larger than the other three. The filaments are fused to the bases of the lobes and the pistil is rudimentary. Female flowers have five spathulate tepals, again of different sizes, and dark brown scales that are up to 1 mm long.

FRUITS. The fruits are sessile achenes with persistent tepals.

DISTRIBUTION. Mahé, Praslin, and Silhouette

Procris insularis is a fairly common plant locally and occurs at and above 500 m on Mahé and Silhouette but lower on Praslin. It prefers shaded places and frequently grows in leaf litter on the top of rocks, often with *Gynura sechellensis* and *Malaxis seychellarum*, for example, on Morne Blanc, La Reserve, and Congo Rouge.

Other members of this family in the granitic islands are *Laportea aestuans*, *Pilea microphylla*, and *Pipturus argenteus*.

ILLUSTRATION. Habit with male inflorescence and habit with semi-spherical female inflorescences; painted at 1×. Detail of pedicels showing glands; painted at 3×. Enlargement of male and female flowers; painted at 10×. Flowering habit collected and painted on June 21, 1990. Fruiting habit collected and painted on June 21, 1990. Herbarium sheets: Rosemary Wise 141, 149 (OXF).

THE MONOCOTYLEDONS

ARACEAE Jussieu

This family consists of 106 genera and 2,950 species of shrubs, climbers, and herbs with a few epiphytes and free-floating aquatics. Most are tropical, but there are some temperate-region representatives. The swollen, starchy corms of some tropical aroids are important sources of food: *Alocasia indica*, *Amorphophallus campanulatus*, *Colocasia esculena*, *Cyrtosperma chamissonis*, and several species of *Xanthosoma*. The crystals of calcium oxalate contained in the corms are harmful until they are destroyed by baking or boiling. *Monstera deliciosa* (Swiss cheese plant), *Dieffenbachia* (dumbcane), *Dracunculus*, *Philodendron*, and *Anthurium* are all popular houseplants.

Protarum Engler

This is a monotypic genus from the Seychelles.

PLATE 54. *Protarum sechellarum* Engler (H.G.A. Engler, 1901, *Jahrbücher 30 Beibl.* 62:42)

Vernacular name: arouroute de l'Inde marron

HABIT. This perennial herb is usually solitary, rarely clump-forming, and has 12 cm long tuberous rhizomes ringed by closely spaced leaf scars. The petioles are smooth, blackish-purple to gray, and mottled and speckled with pink, black, and olive green.

LEAVES. The leaves are solitary and up to 25 cm long. Before unfurling they are enclosed by several cataphylls, which are deciduous. The leaves are divided into 7, 9, or 11 lanceolate and radially arranged leaflets, which are dark green but sometimes pinkish-silver on and around the midribs and main veins.

INFLORESCENCES. The inflorescences are solitary, either appearing synchronously with new leaves or without leaves, and are subtended by cataphylls. The peduncles are short and concealed by the cataphylls. The spathe is cowl-like, constricted toward the base, and is light gray inside, and pinkish-gray with darker speckles on the outside. The spadix is half the length of spathe and sessile.

FLOWERS. The flowers are unisexual and segregated in zones on the spadix. The female zone is basal and about 2 cm long. Between this and the 1.5 cm male zone is a 1.5 cm sterile zone. Above these is a round tipped conic appendage that is up to 4 cm long.

INFRUCTESCENCES. The infructescences are enclosed in persistent, enlarged basal portions of the spathes and have actively declinate peduncles.

FRUITS. The fruits are succulent, bright orange berries and mostly single-seeded.

DISTRIBUTION. Mahé, Praslin, and Silhouette

Protarum sechellarum occurs mostly in the mist forest at high altitudes, although some are found at lower elevations. On Copolia, isolated plants grow near the path, from 400 m upward. Occasionally they grow lithophytically. In all habitats the plant prefers shade to full sunlight. *Protarum* is now considered to be related to the cultivated taro, *Colocasia esculenta*, an isolated relict form with some primitive features such as divided leaves and female flowers with staminodes. The plants flower infrequently, possibly only once every two years, so the chance of seeing them is limited.

Other members of this family in the granitic islands are *Alocasia macrorrhiza*, *Amorphophallus paeoniifolius*, *Anthurium andraeanum*, *A. crystallinum*, *Caladium bicolor*, *C. argyrites*, *Colocasia esculenta*, *Dieffenbachia sequine*, *Epipremnum pinnatum*, *Monstera deliciosa*, *Philodendron bipinnatifidum*, *P. scandens*, and *Syngonium podophyllum*.

ILLUSTRATION. Fruit with section cut away to show arrangement of seeds, flower, and detail of base of flower showing spadix; all painted at 1×. Leaf with corm and leaf with pink coloration on leaflets; painted at 0.5×. Flowering habit collected and painted October 10, 1992. Fruiting habit collected and painted on October 22, 1992. Young plant, painted September 23, 1989. Young plant with speckled leaves painted October 16, 1992. Herbarium sheets: Rosemary Wise 105, 111 (OXF).

Inflorescence and fruit preserved in spirit at the Royal Botanic Gardens, Sydney, Australia.

CYPERACEAE Jussieu

This family consists of 115 genera and 3,600 species of herbs, mainly rhizomes, with a cosmopolitan distribution. Many species of sedge are cultivated worldwide for the fabrication of mats, sandals, and boats. Thor Heyerdahl's reed boats, which were used in his two *Ra* expeditions from Morocco to the Caribbean, were manufactured from *Cyperus papyrus*. The papyrus of ancient Egypt was obtained from the same species, which grows in Central Africa and the Nile valley.

Lophoschoenus Stapf

This genus comprises 11 species that are distributed in Seychelles, Borneo, and New Caledonia.

PLATE 55. *Lophoschoenus hornei* (C. B. Clarke) Stapf
(L. Gibbs, 1914, *Botanical Journal Linnean Society* 42:179)

Schoenus hornei C. B. Clarke   (T. Durand and H. Schinz, 1894, *Conspectus Florae Africae*, vol. 5, p. 657)

Asterochoete elongata Kunth   (Baker, 1877, *Flora of Mauritius*, p. 417)

Vernacular name: l'herbe rasoir

HABIT. The plant is a perennial rhizomatous erect sedge that grows to 1.25 m high.

LEAVES. The leaves arise from the basal tufts, are linear and up to 1 m long, and have denticulate margins. The culms are three-angled, unbranched below the inflorescence, and green with a band of brown above the nodes. Ligules are absent.

INFLORESCENCES. The inflorescences are panicles that are up to 45 cm long and have many arching branches that are up to 12 cm long and are subtended by linear bracts. The pedicels have subulate bracts at their bases and are up to 5 mm long. The spikelets have one or two flowers that are axillary to the glumes and up to 5 mm long. The outer glumes are deltoid, lanceolate, membranous, and 5 mm in length. The upper glumes are smaller. The rachis is flexuous, flattened, and three-ribbed. Achenes are oblong and minute and surrounded by seven or eight flattened pubescent bristles. These are several times longer than the achenes.

DISTRIBUTION. Mahé, Praslin, Silhouette, and Curieuse

This graceful, arching sedge is a common understory plant that grows at mid- to high altitudes, both in shaded areas such as Morne Blanc and in full sunlight on the glacis at the summit of Copolia. On the higher reaches of the Sans Souci inter-island road, plants occur alongside "citronelle" *Cymbopogon citratus*, often thriving in minute pockets of soil accumulating in cracks in the granite. The specific epithet commemorates John Horne, the director of Pamplemousses Botanical Garden in Mauritius. He visited and collected in Seychelles in 1871 and 1874.

The genus *Schoenus* was described by Charles Baron Clarke (1832–1906). He was a lecturer in mathematics at Cambridge University from 1857 to 1865 and superintendent of the Calcutta Botanic Gardens from 1869 to 1871. Clarke was president of the Linnean Society of London from 1894 to 1896.

Other members of this family in the granitic islands are *Bulbostylis barbata*, *Cyperus alopecuroides*, *C. articulatus*, *C. compressus*, *C. conglomeratus*, *C. difformis*, *C. exaltatus*, *C. halpan*, *C. papyrus*, *C. rotundus*, *Eleocharis dulcis*, *E. variegata*, *Fimbristylis complanata*, *F. cymosa*, *F. dichotoma*, *F. littoralis*, *Kyllinga alba*, *K. colorata*, *K. monocephala*, *K. polyphylla*, *Mariscus dubius*, *M. paniceus*, *M. pedunculatus*, *M. pennatus*, *M. tenuifolius*, *Mapania floribundum*, *M. seychellaria*, *Pycreus globosus*, *P. polystachyos*, *Schoenoplectus juncoides*, *Scleria sieberi*, and *S. sumatrensis*.

ILLUSTRATION. Flowering and fruiting habits and detail of stem; painted at 1×. Enlargement of flowers; painted at 10×. Flowering habit collected and painted on November 9, 1991. Fruiting habit collected and painted on November 9–10, 1991. Herbarium sheets: Rosemary Wise 134, 157, 167 (OXF).

CYPERACEAE Jussieu

Mapania Aublet

This genus comprises 50 species that are distributed in the tropics excluding Madagascar.

PLATE 56. *Mapania floribundum* Nees von Esenbeck ex Steud (T. Koyama, 1967, *Memoirs New York Botanical Garden* 50:69)

Thoracostachyum floribundum (Nees von Esenbeck) C. B. Clark (T. Durand and Schintz, 1894, *Conspectus Flora Africae*, vol. 5, p. 667)

Thoracostachyum angustifolium C. B. Clarke (C. B. Clarke, 1908, *Bull. Misc. Info.*, Kew 1908:52)

HABIT. The plant is a robust perennial rhizomatous sedge with three-angled stems and grows to 1.5 m in height.

LEAVES. The leaves are mostly basal and sheath the stem. The blades are linear and coriaceous with serrate margins and are up to 2 m long.

INFLORESCENCES. The inflorescences are terminal panicles that are up to 20 cm across. There are as many as 15 primary peduncles with a few pedunculate reddish-brown spikes, which are up to 9 mm in length.

FRUITS. The fruits are up to 4 mm long and are ovoid, shiny brown, and sometimes ridged.

DISTRIBUTION. Mahé, Praslin, Silhouette, La Digue, Curieuse, and Félicité

Very large clumps of this sedge border the paths at La Reserve, Mahé. It is a fairly common component of mid- to high altitude forests, for example, Trois Freres, Congo Rouge, and Morne Blanc. The majority of plants grow in moist shady habitats, but occasionally isolated ones are found in more exposed places. These probably are old plants that have survived after the forest was cleared.

Although the leaf width is very variable, it is distinct from *Mapania seychellaria* in that *M. floribundum* is generally more robust in all parts. At lower altitudes, in the Vallée de Mai, these two species often grow in close proximity at the sides of the paths. The differences between the two species are then apparent.

ILLUSTRATION. Flowering and fruiting habits and detail of leaf blade; painted at 1×. Enlargement of fruit; painted at 6×. Flowering habit collected and painted on June 7, 1991. Fruiting habit collected and painted on June 7, 1991. Herbarium sheet: Rosemary Wise 160 (OXF).

CYPERACEAE Jussieu

Mapania Aublet

PLATE 57. *Mapania seychellaria* D. A. Simpson
  (D. A. Simpson, 1992, *Revision of the Genus Mapania*)

HABIT. The plant is a perennial sedge with all leaves basal.

LEAVES. The leaf blades are linear, acuminate, and coriaceous, have serrate margins, and can be as long as 48 cm. The sheaths are lanceolate.

INFLORESCENCES. The inflorescences are lax panicles with three or four peduncles supporting several spikes on secondary peduncles. The spikes are elliptic, light brown, and up to 1.5 cm long.

FRUITS. The fruits are ovoid, light brown, and up to 5 mm long.

DISTRIBUTION. Praslin

Mapania seychellaria has only recently been described, and all collections to date are from the Vallée de Mai on Praslin. It is superficially very similar to *Mapania floribunda*, but the distinguishing features of this shade-loving sedge are the much narrower leaves, the stoloniferous habit, and the considerably smaller and sparser spikes and fruiting heads. All six of the endemic palms, the four endemic screw pines, and many other endemic and indigenous trees, including *Artocarpus heterophyllus*, *Adenanthera pavonina*, and *Averrhoa bilimbi*, are found in this habitat.

ILLUSTRATION. Fruiting habit; painted at 1×. Detail of leaf blade; painted at 4×. Fruiting habit collected and painted on September 21, 1993. Herbarium sheet: Rosemary Wise 204 (OXF).

GRAMINEAE Jussieu

This family consists of 737 genera and 7,950 species of herbs and bamboos with a cosmopolitan distribution, especially in the tropics, north temperate, and subarid zones. Many species of bamboo are used in handicrafts. The staple diets of most civilizations is provided by this family, including *Triticum aestivum* (wheat), *Hordeum* spp. (barley), *Avena* spp. (oats), *Saccharum officinarum* (sugarcane), *Panicum miliaceum* (millet), *Zea mays* (maize), *Oryza sativa* (rice), and many species of lawn and agricultural grasses.

Garnotia Brongniart

This genus comprises 29 species that range from Southeast Asia to the Pacific and one species in the granitic Seychelles.

PLATE 58. *Garnotia sechellensis* Hubbard C. E. Hubbard & Summerhayes   (V. S. Summerhayes, 1928, *Bull. Misc. Info.*, Kew 1928:394)

HABIT. The plant is a perennial grass that grows as high as 1.7 m and has an unbranched, slender, terete, glabrous stem with many nodes enclosed by sheaths.

LEAVES. The leaves are chartaceous and pubescent above the nodes, with the apex either villose pubescent or glabrous. The ligule is reduced to a ring of ciliate hairs that are 5 mm long. The lamina is linear or lanceolate linear, narrowing at the base, and has an acuminate apex that tapers to a sharp point. It also has distinct midribs and is up to 35 cm long. The panicles are erect and narrow, reaching 40 cm in length. The rachis is obtuse, quadrangular in section, and striate. Branches are suberect, grow to 10 cm long, and have lateral pedicels up to 4 mm long.

SPIKES. The spikes are linear lanceolate and up to 6 mm long. The glumes are chartacious, trinerved, and scabrid. The lower glumes are lanceolate and up to 5 mm long with a 2 mm long, sharp apical point. The upper glumes are membranous, trinerved, oblong lanceolate, acute with a short point, and up to 6 mm long. The palea are up to 4.5 mm and are transparent, linear, and binerved and have ciliate margins. The anthers are 2 mm long.

DISTRIBUTION. Mahé and Silhouette

Garnotia sechellensis is a very rare, critically endangered grass, which at one time was known only from inaccessible ledges and usually only seen through binoculars. Some rather straggly plants grow on the knoll at the highest point of Congo Rouge, both beside the upward path (along with *Psychotria pervillei*, *Syzygium wrightii*, *Psidium cattleyanum*, *Nepenthes pervillei*, and *Northia seychellana*) and on the shady, eroded northern side of the knoll. It also occurs on the upper areas of Morne Blanc. Grasses are poorly represented in mist forest vegetation in general. *Garnotia* is an Indomalayan and Polynesian genus with the species most closely related to *Garnotia sechellensis* occurring in Sri Lanka.

The authority, Charles Edward Hubbard (1900–1980), worked at the Royal Botanic Gardens, Kew, from 1920 until 1965, becoming deputy director from 1959.

Other members of this family in the granitic islands are *Aristida setacea*, *Arundo donax* (cultivated), *Axonopus compressus*, *Bambusa vulgaris*, *Bothrio-* *chloa pertusa*, *Brachiaria brizantha*, *B. mutica*, *B. subquadripara*, *B. umbellata*, *Chloris barbata*, *C. pycnothrix*, *C. virgata*, *Chrysopogon acidculatus*, *Coix lachryma-jobi*, *Cymbopogon citratus*, *C. flexuosus*, *C. martinii*, *C. nardus*, *C. pruinosus*, *Cynodon dactylon*, *Cyrtococcum oxyphyllum*, *C. trigonum*, *Dactyloctenium ctenoides*, *D. pilosum*, *Dendrocalamus giganteus*, *Dichanthium aristatum*, *Digitaria ciliaris*, *D. didactyla*, *D. horizontalis*, *D. radicosa*, *D. setigera*, *Echinochloa colonum*, *Eleusine indica*, *Enteropogon sechellensis*, *Eragrostis ciliaris*, *E. racemosa*, *E. subaequiglumis*, *E. tenella*, *Heteropogon contortus*, *Hyparrhenia rufa*, *Ischaemum heterotrichum*, *I. indicum*, *Lepturus radicans*, *Oplismenus compositus*, *Panicum brevifolium*, *P. maximum*, *P. repens*, *Paspalum conjugatum*, *P. nutans*, *P. paniculatum*, *P. scrobiculatum*, *P. vaginatum*, *Pennisetum polystachyon*, *P. purpureum*, *Perotis hildebrandtii*, *Rhynchelytrum repens*, *Rottboelia exalta*, *Saccharum officinarum* (cultivated), *S. spontaneum*, *aegyptiacum*, *Sacciolepis curvata*, *Setaria barbata*, *Sorghum arundinaceum*, *Sporobolus diander*, *S. pyramidalis*, *S. tenuissimus*, *S. virginicus*, *Stenotaphrum dimidiatum*, *S. micranthum*, *Thysanolaena maxima*, *Urochloa paspaloides*, *Vetiveria zizanioides* (cultivated), and *Zea mays* (cultivated).

ILLUSTRATION. Vegetative habit and inflorescence; painted at 1×. Leaves collected and painted on September 23, 1993. No other dates recorded. Herbarium sheet: Rosemary Wise 203 (OXF).

HYPOXIDACEAE   R. Brown

This family of 8 genera and 120 species of perennial herbs is from the tropics and warm areas, mainly in the southern hemisphere. This family is sometimes included in the Liliaceae (sensu lato).

Curculigo Gaertner

This genus consists of 15 species of perennial herbs from the southern hemisphere. In Indomalesia, fibers from *Curculigo latifolia* are used in making fishing nets.

PLATE 59.   *Curculigo sechellensis* Bojer ex Baker   (Baker, 1877, *Flora of Mauritius*, p. 368)

Vernacular name: coco marron

HABIT. This perennial tuberous herb has all leaves basal and grows up to 2 m high. The petioles are heavily spined and as long as 45 cm.

LEAVES. The leaves can be up to 4 m in length. They are broadly lanceolate, strongly ribbed, and bifid or sometimes simple at the apex and have spiny margins. The venation is parallel.

FLOWERS. The flowers are in dense central clusters, surrounded by the leaf bases. The perianth tubes are filiform, pilose, and up to 8 cm. The six perianth lobes are pale yellow and lanceolate. There are six stamens. Bracts are lanceolate, pilose, and up to 8 cm long.

FRUITS. The fruits are creamy white and woody, surrounded with the fibrous remains of the bracts.

DISTRIBUTION. Mahé, Praslin, Silhouette, and Frégate

Along with *Lodoicea maldivica, Curculigo sechellensis* was the only flowering plant to be described from the granitic islands in the eighteenth and early nineteenth centuries. Baker (1877) wrote that the leaves were used to wrap plugs of tobacco. At first glance this now threatened plant could be confused with a young palm, hence the vernacular name, coco marron, meaning "wild coconut." (*Curculigo* differs from palm species in particular by the parallel rows of sturdy black thorns on the petioles.) Enormous plants, up to 2 m high, border the paths at La Reserve, Mahé. The 10–12 cm high clumps of flowers and fruits are not easy to see even though they are at ground level because they are often covered by leaf litter and encircled by the leaf stems. This leaf litter provides the preferred habitat of the bronze house gecko, *Aleuronyx* sp., on La Misere, Mahé (Justin Gerlach, pers. comm.). M. Bojer, the authority for *Curculigo*, was a professor of botany at the Royal College of St. Louis, Mauritius. He published his book *Hortus Mauritianus, ou énumeration des plantes exotiques et indigènes qui croissent à l'île Maurice* in 1837.

Other members of this family in the granitic islands are *Hypoxidia mahéensis* and *H. rhizophylla*.

ILLUSTRATION. Flowers, fruits, and detail of spiny petiole; painted at 1×. Whole plant; painted at 0.17×. Flowering habit collected and painted on June 23, 1991. Fruiting habit collected and painted in October 1992. Herbarium sheets: Rosemary Wise 89, 158 (OXF).

HYPOXIDACEAE R. Brown

Hypoxidia Friedmann

This genus consists of two species, both of which are endemic to Seychelles.

PLATE 60. *Hypoxidia maheensis* Friedmann (F. Friedmann, 1985 [1984], *Adansonia* 6[4]:459)

HABIT. The plant is a perennial herb with tuberous rhizomes and all leaves basal. The petiole is brown, pubescent, and up to 65 cm long.
LEAVES. The leaves are narrow toward the petioles and are more obtuse at the apices. They are up to 20 cm broad and 85 cm long and are sparsely pubescent on the veins on the undersurface. The bracts are densely hairy, lanceolate, and as long as 8 cm.
FLOWERS. There are from two to four flowers, which are up to 6 cm long on densely hairy peduncles that reach up to 15 cm in length.
FRUITS. The fruits are cylindrical and angular, widening in the lower third, and up to 4 cm long.
DISTRIBUTION. Mahé

Far less common than *Hypoxidia rhizophylla*, *H. maheensis* is a plant of high altitudes (600–700 m) with a large population in the mist forest at Congo Rouge. Both species have variable leaf widths, but those of *H. maheensis* are noticeably much wider. Unlike *H. rhizophylla*, this species does not root from the leaf tips. The flowering habit is the same. Buds usually open in the afternoon and wilt the same day, making the chance of seeing them in the wild highly unlikely. *Hypoxidia maheensis* is endangered because of its very limited distribution and smaller populations.

ILLUSTRATION. Leaf; painted at 0.5×. Young leaf, flower, and fruits; painted at 1×. Bare of mature leaf in background; drawn at 1×. Flowering habit collected and painted on October 18, 1992, and October 1993. Fruiting habit collected and painted on October 18, 1992. Herbarium sheet: Rosemary Wise 192 (OXF).

HYPOXIDACEAE R. Brown

Hypoxidia Friedmann

PLATE 61. *Hypoxidia rhizophylla* (Baker) F. Friedmann
(F. Friedmann, 1985 [1984], *Adansonia* 6[4]:456)

Curculigo rhizophylla (Baker) Durand and Schinz (Baker, 1877, *Flora of Mauritius*, p. 308)

Hypoxis rhizophylla Baker (Baker, 1877, *Flora of Mauritius*, p. 369)

HABIT. This plant is a perennial herb with all leaves basal and tuberous rhizomes. Petioles are pubescent, yellow to beige, and up to 90 cm long.

LEAVES. The leaves are glabrous and ligulate, up to 10 cm across, and up to 1 m long. They often root from the leaf tip. The bracts are densely hairy, lanceolate, amplexicaul, and up to 4 cm.

FLOWERS. There are from three to five flowers, which are on short scapes at the leaf bases and are up to 15 cm across. The six perianth lobes are in two whorls, with alternate lobes wider. The color varies in different populations from dark purple, maroon, and light tan to the less common greenish yellow.

FRUITS. The fruits are conical with persistent perianths.

DISTRIBUTION. Mahé, Praslin, Silhouette, La Digue, and Curieuse

The flowers of both *Hypoxidia rhizophylla* and *H. maheensis* are rarely seen due to their ephemerality. Both species appear to flower synchronously, opening in the early afternoon and wilting that same day. The putrid smell, which is characteristic of fly-pollinated plants, differs slightly according to the color of the flowers. Dr. F. Friedmann has grown many in cultivation and recognizes at least ten varieties of *Hypoxidia rhizophylla*. Color and size appear to vary according to altitude (plants are found from 100 to 700 m). Often each clump will be composed of clones of new plants that have rooted from the leaf tips of the parent. The ability to root from the leaf tips and the narrower leaf blades distinguish *Hypoxidia rhizophylla* from *H. maheensis*. Due to their ability to grow at practically all levels, vegetative plants are a fairly common sight, usually in shade.

ILLUSTRATION. Flowers of various colors, fruits, flower buds, and plant habit; detail of petiole with dark coloration; all painted at 1×. Flowering habits collected and painted on October 18, 1992, and September 14, 1993. Fruiting habit collected and painted on October 20, 1992. Herbarium sheet: Rosemary Wise 159 (OXF).

ORCHIDACEAE Jussieu

This very large cosmopolitan family consists of 795 genera and 17,500 species of epiphytes and herbs, but rarely lianas. Many of the spectacular cultivated varieties are sold by florists, including *Cattleya, Cymbidium*, and *Vanda*. Flavorings are extracted from *Angraecum, Leptotes*, and *Vanilla*.

Agrostophyllum Blume

This genus comprises 60 species ranging from Seychelles, where there is one species, to the West Pacific.

PLATE 62. *Agrostophyllum occidentale* Schlecter (R. Schlecter, 1915, *Beihefte zum Botanischen Centralblatt* 33[2]:413)

HABIT. The plant is a perennial climbing epiphyte that lacks bulbs and reaches a length of 60 cm.

LEAVES. The leaves are in two ranks and have flattened blades up to 15 cm long. The apices are rounded, and the bases are folded and sessile.

FLOWERS. The flowers are in dense terminal clusters. They were not seen.

FRUITS. The fruits are green cylindrical capsules up to 6 mm long.

DISTRIBUTION. Mahé and Silhouette

Agrostophyllum occidentale is an uncommon climbing orchid dependent on humidity and damp habitats, such as those found above 600 m on Morne Blanc and Congo Rouge, Mahé. The terminally flowering plants grow on the moss-covered trees at these altitudes, favoring shaded positions. It is categorized as a threatened species.

Other members of this family in the granitic islands are *Acampe praemorsa, Angraecum eburneum* subsp. *brongniartianum, A. zeylanicum, Bulbophyllum intertextum, C. triplicata, Cirrhopetalum umbellatum, Cynorkis fastigiata, Dendrobium crumenatum, Disperis tripetaloides, Eulophidium pulchrum, Grammatophyllum speciosum, Graphorkis scripta, Hederorkis seychellensis, Malaxis seychellarum, Oeoniella aphrodite, Phaius tetragonus, Platylepis occulta, P. sechellarum, Polystachya concreta, P. fusiformis, Spathoglottis plicata, Vanda teres, Vanilla phalaenopsis*, and *V. planifolia*.

ILLUSTRATION. Fruiting habit collected and painted on October 21, 1992, at 1×. Herbarium sheet: Rosemary Wise 185 (OXF).

ORCHIDACEAE Jussieu

Angraecum Bory

This genus comprises 206 epiphytic species, found in tropical Africa, Madagascar, the Mascarenes, Seychelles, Sri Lanka, and the Philippines. In Mauritius, thé de bourbon and ice creams are flavored with extracts of *A. fragrans*.

PLATE. 63.   *Angraecum eburneum* Bory subsp. *brongniartianum* (Thouars) H. Perrier   (Bory, *Voyage dans les quatres principales îles des Mers d'Afrique*, 1801–2, vol. 1, p. 19)

Vernacular name: paille en queue (French); tropic bird orchid (English)

HABIT. This plant is a perennial, robust, epiphytic herb, with stems that are as long as 1.5 m.

LEAVES. The leaves are oblanceolate and coriaceous, with rounded apices and folded bases. They are up to 60 cm long.

INFLORESCENCES. The inflorescences are axillary racemes that may reach 75 cm in length. They have woody, suberect stems that are the same length as the leaves and bear widely spaced flowers. The bracts are dark brown, amplexicaul, ovate, chartacious, and up to 2 cm long.

FLOWERS. The flowers are fragrant and up to 6 cm wide. The pedicels are 3 cm long and twisted. Both the sepals and petals are white to pale green, free, ovate-lanceolate, with acuminate apices, spreading or reflexed up to 4.5 cm long. The labellum is cordate, white shading to yellow into the throat, and up to 3 cm long. The apex is rounded and hooded, and the base has a median lanceolate plate. The spur is slender and up to 15 cm long.

FRUITS. The fruits are spindle-shaped ribbed capsules that are up to 7 cm long.

DISTRIBUTION. Mahé, Praslin, and Silhouette

This beautiful orchid is the national plant of Seychelles and is often used in wedding bouquets. The individual clumps can be over a meter across and have many inflorescences. It is locally common, especially in rocky habitats, usually at higher altitudes. In the vicinity of viewpoint 3 on La Reserve, Mahé, *Angraecum* grows on boulders amid a wide range of endemic species and *Premna serratifolia*; however, many specimens grow with *Curculigo sechellensis*, *Vanilla phalaenopsis*, *Canthium bibracteatum*, and *Paragenipa wrightii* on an exposed glacis running down to sea level in southwest Mahé. Plants grow in more shaded conditions in the Vallée de Mai on Praslin. The species is used medicinally in Seychelles. A tea made from the orchid is said to reduce fevers, while an infusion soothes skin problems in children. At the age of nineteen, the authority, Colonel Bory de Saint Vincent (1780–1846) set out for Australia as a naturalist on a ship under the command of Captain Baudin. After a disagreement, he left the expedition at Mauritius and was employed by the government as a surveyor of the French possessions in the vicinity. The majority of his time was spent on Bourbon (Réunion), where he produced an excellent map of the island. The specific epithet commemorates the French naturalist, Brongniart.

A closely related species from Madagascar, *A. sesquipedale*, which was discovered early in the nineteenth century, has spurs that are as long as 45 cm. Charles Darwin suggested that the pollinator would have to have a proboscis of similar length, but it was not until 1903 that the moth was discovered. *Angraecum* is from the Malay word meaning "air plants" because of their epiphytic nature; *eburneum* is from the Latin word for "ivory white."

ILLUSTRATION. Flowering habit collected and painted on November 6–7, 1992, at 1×. Fruiting habit collected and painted on November 6, 1992, at 1×. No specimens pressed.

ORCHIDACEAE Jussieu

Hederorkis Thouars

This genus consists of three species, two in Mauritius and one in Seychelles.

PLATE 64. *Hederorkis seychellensis* Bosser (J. Bosser, 1976, *Adansonia* 16[2]:228)

Bulbophyllum scandens Rolfe (R. A. Rolfe, 1922, *Bull. Misc. Info.*, Kew 1922:23) not *Hederorchis scandens* Thouars (1822) nor *Bulbophyllum scandens* Kraenzl (1904)

HABIT. The plant is a robust, epiphytic, scrambling herb with squarish stems and no bulbs. It grows as high as 2 m.

LEAVES. The leaves are paired, flattened, ovate oblong, and coriaceous, with obtuse or acute apices. They are up to 18 cm long.

INFLORESCENCES. The inflorescences are curving, solitary or clustered, axillary racemes, up to 10 cm long. They consist of several cream or purple flowers on short pedicels. The bracts are ovate, have obtuse apices, and are up to 2 mm long.

FLOWERS.. Both the sepals and the petals are free, oblong with obtuse apices, and up to 12 mm long. The labellum is oblong and curved, and its apex is obtuse or indented. The lateral lobes are erect and narrow. The column is club shaped and up to 4 mm long. There is no spur.

FRUITS. The fruits are brown, ribbed, spindle-shaped capsules up to 2 cm long, with persistent perianth remains.

DISTRIBUTION. Mahé and Silhouette

This rare and endangered epiphyte grows at altitudes between 400 and 600 m. A few robust plants can be seen at the highest point of Congo Rouge. The stems coil around other plants. Flowers are seen infrequently, and these are usually pink, although yellow ones also exist (Dr. F. Friedmann, pers. comm.). The authority of the genus *Hederorkis*, Chevalier Aubert du Petit Thouars, published several large volumes on the vegetation of Madagascar and the Mascarenes between 1804 and 1822. He also made large general collections of plants that were distributed to many European herbaria.

ILLUSTRATION. The illustration was taken from photographs and painted at 1×. No specimens were collected.

ORCHIDACEAE Jussieu

Malaxis Solander ex Swartz
This genus comprises 300 subcosmopolitan species of terrestrial herbs.

PLATE 65.   *Malaxis seychellarum* (Kraenzlin) Summerhayes
(V. S. Summerhayes, 1953, *Kew Bulletin* 8:578)

Liparis seychellarum Kraenzlin

HABIT. The plant is a perennial epiphytic or terrestrial orchid that reaches 50 cm in height.
LEAVES. The leaves are spirally arranged, ovate, and up to 20 cm long, with bases amplexicaul to the stem. The margins are sometimes repand.
INFLORESCENCES. The inflorescences are erect racemes, bearing many flowers, and reach a length of 20 cm.
FLOWERS. The flowers are either yellow, green, or purple and are up to 4 mm long. The three sepals are 3 mm long. The petals are linear and 3 mm long. The labellum is ovate and up to 3 mm long. The spur is 4 mm long.
FRUITS. The fruits are slender green capsules, up to 2 cm long.
DISTRIBUTION. Mahé and Silhouette

One of the more common and widespread of the orchids from mid- to high altitudes, *Malaxis* prefers damp, shady areas. It is abundant in the mist forest of Congo Rouge, often growing in the thick mosses on trees and also a common inhabitant on Morne Blanc and La Reserve, growing with *Procris insularis* in humus accumulations on the top of rocks.

The authority of the genus, Daniel Solander (1736–1782), was the most traveled of all the students of Linnaeus. After leaving his native Sweden, he settled in London. His first appointment was assistant librarian at the British Museum, followed, at a later date, by keeper of the Department of Natural History. Many of his plant collections were made during the three years he spent with Captain Cook, sailing to Australia on the *Endeavour*.

ILLUSTRATION. Flowering and fruiting habit; painted at 1×. Enlargement of mature flower; painted at 4×. Flowering habit collected and painted on August 18, 1989. Fruiting habit collected and painted on August 18, 1989. Herbarium sheet: Rosemary Wise 86 (OXF).

ORCHIDACEAE Jussieu

Platylepsis Richard

This genus comprises 10 species that range from tropical Africa to Seychelles.

PLATE 66. *Platylepsis sechellarum* Moore (Baker, 1877, *Flora of Mauritius*, p. 340)

HABIT. The plant is a terrestrial perennial orchid that is up to 15 cm high. It has glandular stems that are pubescent at the top, with white imbricate scales.

LEAVES. The leaves are numerous toward the base of the plant, lanceolate, and amplexicaul. They may be up to 9 cm long.

INFLORESCENCES. The inflorescences are 8 cm long spikes with lanceolate, pubescent bracts.

FLOWERS. The sepals are oblong and up to 6 mm long. The petals are free and linear. The labellum is equal to the column, adnate to its base, obovate, obtuse, with papilla near the base. The column is curved. The pollinia are subpyriform and longitudinally grooved.

FRUITS. The fruits are white capsules up to 8 mm long.

DISTRIBUTION. Mahé and Silhouette

There is doubt that this can now be considered an endemic species (Dr. P. Crib, Kew, pers. comm.); however, the painting is included in a historical context because it occurs in the lists of Proctor (1974), Friedmann (1986), and Robertson (1989). This uncommon, endangered terrestrial orchid is found in the mist forest zones, between 400 and 900 m, growing on Mahé in association with *Northia seychellana*, *Pandanus sechellarum*, *Seychellaria thomassetii*, *Hypoxidia maheensis*, and *H. rhizophylla*.

The authority of the genus *Platylepsis*, Achille Richard, published *Monographie des Orchidées des îles de France et de Bourbon* in 1828.

ILLUSTRATION. Flowering habit; painted at 1×. Detail of flower; painted at 10×. Flowering habit collected and painted on June 16, 1991. Fruiting habit collected and painted on June 16, 1991. Herbarium sheet: Rosemary Wise 147 (OXF).

ORCHIDACEAE   Jussieu

Vanilla Miller

This genus comprises 100 species of often leafless epiphytes and lianas from the tropics and subtropics. *Vanilla planifolia*, introduced from Mexico, is grown commercially in Seychelles. In the absence of natural pollinators, each flower has to be hand-pollinated in order to produce the pods from which the flavoring is extracted.

PLATE 67.   *Vanilla phalaenopsis* Reichenbach   (Reichenbach, *Flore des Serres*, series 2, vol. 7, pp. 97–98)

Vernacular name: vanille sauvage

HABIT. The plant is a perennial scrambling herb with stout, leafless stems and aerial roots from the nodes.

INFLORESCENCES. The inflorescences are peduncled racemes, with many flowers and small triangular bracts.

FLOWERS. The flowers are white, shading to apricot into the throat. They are as wide as 8 cm. The sepals are oblong lanceolate and up to 8 cm long. The petals are the same length, but wider and undulate at the margins. The lip is entire, broad, obtuse or apiculate, and repand at the margin. It is up to 6.5 cm long. The column is clavate and up to 2.5 cm long.

FRUITS. The fruits are cylindrical green capsules that reach lengths of 16 cm.

DISTRIBUTION. Mahé, Praslin, Silhouette, and Félicité

Again there is doubt as to whether this is an endemic species. It is possibly identical to an African species but is included here in a historical context. At low altitudes this leafless climber is locally abundant, usually in dry, open areas. On the glacis between Danzilles and Anse Major, western Mahé, the snakelike stems wind round and over such shrubs as *Euphorbia pyrifolia*, *Canthium bibracteatum*, and *Paragenipa wrightii*. Not more than three of the beautiful white flowers with apricot-colored throats are open simultaneously on any one stem. The flowering occurs after periods of heavy rain. Like the cultivated *Vanilla planifolia*, *V. phalaenopsis* flowers only when it has grown higher than its support and the stems have become pendulous.

ILLUSTRATION. Flowering habit collected and painted on August 26, 1989, at 1×. Fruiting habit collected and painted on September 29, 1989, at 1×. No specimens pressed.

PALMAE Wendland and Jussieu

This family consists of 198 genera and 2,650 species from the tropics and subtropics. *Chamaerops humilis* extends into southern Europe. Some genera produce edible fruit, including coconuts (*Cocos nucifera*) and dates (*Phoenix dactylifera*). Copra is produced from the dried kernel of *Cocos nucifera*, and coir fibre from the husks. Sago, one of the staple foods of some areas in the Far East, is obtained from the processed pith of the sago palm, *Metroxylon* spp. The stripped stems of rattan canes (*Calamus* spp.) are used in furniture-making. Raffia is obtained from strips of the surface of young leaves of *Raphia*. The stimulant betel nut is obtained from the seeds of *Areca catechu*, which are chewed together with powdered lime and the inflorescences of *Piper*.

Deckenia H. Wendland

This genus is monotypic, occurring only in Seychelles.

PLATE 68. *Deckenia nobilis* H. Wendland (H. Wendland, 1870, *Gardeners Chronicle*, p. 561)

Vernacular name: palmiste (French); cabbage palm or palmiste (English)

HABIT. The plant is a solitary monoecious palm that reaches a height of 35 m. It has yellow spines on the stems when young but becomes unarmed at maturity and has conspicuous leaf scars. The tubular sheaths are erinaceous when young.

LEAVES. The leaves are pinnate and as long as 4.5 m, with the bases forming a smooth, stem-enclosing sheath. The leaflets are elongate, acuminate at the apex, tomentose when young, and regularly arranged. The petioles, which are spiny in juveniles, are caniculate adaxially and up to 30 cm long.

INFLORESCENCES. The inflorescences are solitary, infrafoliar, and protected in the bud by erinaceous bracts, which are held at right angles to the stem. There are numerous branches arranged in three orders. These become pendulous and may be up to 2 m long. The prophyll and peduncular bracts are similar and caducous.

FLOWERS. The flowers are in triads and are spirally arranged. The male flowers are globose, with three triangular sepals and petals. There are from six to nine stamens, and the pistilode is longer than the petals. The female flowers are globose, and the three sepals and petals are rounded and imbricate. The six staminodes are dentate and flank three stigmas.

FRUITS. The fruits are ovoid and black, up to 1 cm long. The stigmatic remains are conspicuous and basal.

DISTRIBUTION. Mahé, Praslin, Silhouette, La Digue, Curieuse, and Félicité

In the past, this was the Seychelles palm from which the growing meristem was removed, thus killing the tree, to produce the original "millionaire's salad." Although some restaurants still maintain that this palm is used, in reality it is the common coconut that is felled because *Deckenia* is a protected species. (The large terminal shoots of coconut palms are sometimes seen on sale in the market in Victoria.) The two spiny sheaths that enclose and protect the developing inflorescences are seen only on *Deckenia*, a good field character. These develop in the axis of the long leaf bases that encircle the trunk. When the leaf falls, the freed bracts move outward at right angles to the tree and are shed as the pendulous inflorescences unfurl. They remain on the ground under the palms, resembling hedgehogs. Providing that the depth of soil is sufficient, this stately palm is adapted to living in exposed areas, for example, the cliff faces of Bernica.

This palm was named after the German explorer of Africa, Baron von der Decken.

Other members of this family in the granitic islands, most of which are cultivated and mainly in the Botanic Garden, are *Acrocomia aculeata*, *A. catechu* (betel palm), *Borassus flabellifer*, *Brahea edulis*, *Caryota mitis*, *C. urens*, *Chrysalidocarpus lutescens*, *C. madagascariensis*, *Cocos nucifera* (coconut palm), *Corypha umbraculifera*, *C. utan*, *Cyrtostachys renda*, *Daemonorops* [?] *jenkinsoniana*, *Dictyosperma album*, *Elaeis guineensis*, *Hyophorbe lagenicaulis*, *Jubaea chilensis*, *Latania loddigesii*, *L. lontaroides*, *L. verschaffeltii*, *Licuala spinosa*, *Livistona chinensis*, *L. rotundifolia*, *Lodoicea maldivica*, *Nephrosperma vanhoutteana*, *Orbignya cohune*, *Phoenicophorium borsigianum*, *Phoenix dactylifera*, *P. loureirii*, *P. rupicola*, *Ptychosperma macarthurii*, *Raphia farinifera* (raffia), *Rhapis excelsa*, *Roscheria melanochaetes*, *Roystonea regia*, *Sabal minor*, *Syagrus romanzzoffiana*, *Thrinax parviflora*, and *Verschaffeltia splendida*.

ILLUSTRATION. Monochrome of young and mature palm. Flowers and fruits and seedling leaf; painted at 1×. Spiny bracts; painted at 0.5×. Enlargement of male flower; painted at 12×. Flowering habit collected and painted on November 3, 1991. Fruiting habit collected and painted on October 16, 1991. Herbarium sheet: Rosemary Wise 156 (OXF).

PALMAE   Wendland and Jussieu

Lodoicea Commerson ex De Candolle
    This genus is monotypic, occurring only in Seychelles.

PLATE 69.   *Lodoicea maldivica* (Gmelin) Persoon ex
    H. Wendland   (Kerch. Palm. 250)

Cocos maldivica Gmelin = *Lodoicea sechellarum* Gmelin
    (Labillardière, 1807, *Ann. Mus. Par.* 9:140)

Lodoicea callipyge Commerson ex Jaume St. Hilaire   (St. Hilaire, 1805,
    Exposition des familles naturelles, vol. 1, p. 96)

Vernacular name: coco de mer (French); double coconut (English)

HABIT. The plant is a dioecious, solitary palm up to 34 m high with faint
    leaf scars on the stems.
LEAVES. The leaves are costapalmate and marcescent, up to 10 m long with
    a 4.5 m wide blade, and segmented at the margins with pendulous and
    bifid lobes. On the lower surface, the midrib and veins are covered with
    a dense, mealy indumentum. The petioles are caniculate, channelled
    adaxially, and half the length of the blades.
INFLORESCENCES. The inflorescences are interfoliar. Male catkins arise from
    a short peduncle that is sometimes terminal and solitary and sometimes
    has two or three catkins. The female inflorescences are unbranched,
    and flowers are borne on zig-zagging rachilla.
FLOWERS. The clusters of staminate flowers are arranged spirally in de-
    pressions flanked by leathery bracts. Each has a small bracteole, three
    sepals forming a cylindrical tube, and a three-lobed corolla. There are
    from 17 to 22 stamens. Bracts sheath the female flowers, which are ses-
    sile, ovoid, and have two large bracteoles at the bases. The three sepals
    are imbricate and coriaceous, as are the three petals, which do not
    unfurl.
FRUITS. The fruits are ovoid, with a smooth epicarp and fibrous mesocarp.
    The endocarp is lobed and usually contains one, but occasionally two
    to four, pyrenes.
DISTRIBUTION. Praslin and Curieuse. This species was formerly on Round
    Island and Chauve Souris, both satellite islands off Praslin.

On Praslin, coco de mer is found in three locations—Vallée de Mai,
Anse Marie Louise, and Fond Ferdinand—with an estimated total in 1996
of 16,000 individuals (Carlström 1996). The Vallée de Mai is one of the
premier tourist attractions of the Seychelles, now a World Heritage Site, a
forest supporting all six of the endemic palms. Each of these monotypic
palms differs in its habitat requirements. This sole example of island floral
gigantism in the Seychelles prefers deep, well-drained soil. Undoubtedly
it is one of the most universally well-known plants and holds three botanical records. The leaves, which can be up to 10 m long, are the world's
longest, while the mature seeds, weighing up to 20kg are the world's
largest and heaviest. The female flowers are the largest of any palm.

For centuries, these strange fruits had washed ashore in India, on Sri
Lanka, and on the Maldives, where, as no one had seen the parent plant,
it was assumed that they came from an underwater palm that was growing
on a now submerged land link with the Indian subcontinent. This theory
gave rise to the common name, coco de mer, or coconut of the sea. All
fruits that washed ashore automatically became the property of the ruler.

Because of their extreme rarity, the fruits sold for astronomical prices. The
Hapsberg Emperor, Rudolph II (1576–1612) is said to have paid 4,000
guilders for one. Many legends arose due to the peculiar shape of the seed,
and it was considered to have aphrodisiacal properties.

Although Arab traders had certainly visited the Seychelles Islands for
many centuries, the first recorded landing was not until 1609, when the
East India Company expedition, led by Alexander Sharpeigh, visited
Mahé and North Island. On June 15, 1744, Captain Lazarre Picault explored Praslin, which he named Isle des Palme. He later wrote in his
journal of "Lattans bearing cotton," referring to the persistent fibrous
sheaths of the coco de mer, a palm which he obviously did not recognize.

In 1768, Barre, about whom little is known, a member of an expedition
led by Chevallier Marion du Fresne, recognized the "lattans." A colleague
on the same expedition, Ducheman, returned the following year and took
away a boatload of the fruits. Selling large numbers of these in India reduced the extreme rarity, and the previously high market value was lost.

The botanist Philibert Commerson visited Seychelles in 1766 and was
the first to produce a generic description, suggesting the name *Lodoicea*,
from the Latin *lodoicus*, in honor of Louis XV. Sonnerat's specific description of 1771 gave the name *Lodoicea maldivica*. This somewhat misleading
name, being the first, still stands. (The more suitable *Lodoicea sechellarum*
of 1917 has to follow the ruling and give precedence to the original name.)

A recent theory suggests that a coco de mer fruit could only reach the
Maldives if it fell in the sea in the month of July, because of the changeable
currents. The fruits are heavier than water, and it is questionable how long
the journey would take and in what condition they would be on arrival.
The fruits in fact can only float when the specific gravity is reduced, which
happens after the seed decays. One theory about how the seeds reached
the islands is that certain families, maybe over the span of many genera-
tions, held the secret of the whereabouts of these precious palms and
sailed to Seychelles to collect them for the ruling family.

When a mature fruit falls, it takes six months before the woody husk
disintegrates. Germination occurs two years later. The shoot appears between the lobes and extends for up to 4 m underground. The palms produce three or four new leaves annually and start bearing fruit after 25
years. Fruits take 7 years to mature and a cluster can weigh 400 lbs.
Individual seeds can be three- or four-lobed, as seen in the museum in
Victoria, but these are uncommon. The woody endocarps are often halved
and used as bowls and are known as "Praslin crockery." These are used not
only domestically but also are ideally shaped for bailing boats. Of the six
endemic palms, this is the only dioecious species, all the others bearing
both male and female flowers on the same inflorescences. There are equal
numbers of male and female palms in the Vallée de Mai; the male in
general is 7 m taller than the female. (The tallest tree in the Vallée de Mai
at present is 34 m high.) There is evidence that *Lodoicea* is tolerant of fire
and erosion. Palms have survived the severe and widespread fire at Fond
Ferdinand, Praslin in 1990.

ILLUSTRATION. Monochrome of young and mature palms. Female flowers and
    fruits; painted at 0.17×. Male catkin; painted at 0.5×. Detail of male flowers;
    painted at 1×. Enlargement of male flower; painted at 6×. Seed; painted at
    0.33. Flowering habit collected and painted on May 22, 1991 (male) and
    June 13, 1991 (female). Fruiting habit painted in July 1991. Herbarium
    sheet: Rosemary Wise 152 (OXF).

PALMAE   Wendland and Jussieu

Nephrosperma Balfour f.
   This is a monotypic genus, occurring only in Seychelles.

PLATE 70.   *Nephrosperma vanhoutteana* (Wendland ex Van Houtte) Balfour   (Baker, 1877, *Flora of Mauritius*, p. 386)
   Vernacular name: latanier millepatte

HABIT. The plant is a solitary tree palm that reaches a height of 14 m. It sometimes has small stilt roots. The leaf sheaths are up to 75 cm long, are mealy, and have sparse black spines, especially when the plant is young. The spadix can reach a length of 2.5 m.

LEAVES. The leaves are unequally pinnate and have orange rachises. They reach 3 m in length. The pinnae are glabrous, number as many as 40 pairs, have from one to four main veins, and are irregular in width. The terminal pinnae are confluent. The peduncles are up to 1.75 m long.

INFLORESCENCES. The inflorescences are erect, with the spirally arranged flowers in clusters of three—one female between two males.

FLOWERS.. The flowers are yellow. The male flowers have three imbricate sepals that split irregularly. The three valvate petals are four times the length of the sepals, and there are 40–50 anthers. The female flowers are globose, with three imbricate sepals and petals, six staminodes, and an obpyriform gynoecium with minute apical stigmas.

FRUITS. The fruits are globose, shiny orange red at maturity, and up to 1.5 cm long. They have lateral stigmatic remains.

DISTRIBUTION. Mahé, Praslin, Silhouette, Curieuse, and Ste. Anne

   Although *Nephrosperma* grows alongside the other endemic palm species in the Vallée de Mai, it is more generally a plant of low to midaltitude rocky areas. The creole name *millepatte*, meaning "millipede," is said to liken the sound of breezes moving through the pinnate leaves to the sound of the moving myriapod.
   The specific name commemorates the Belgian botanist, Louis Benoit Van Houtte (1810–1876), who traveled in Brazil, Guatemala, Honduras, and the Cape Verde Islands, collecting living plants.

ILLUSTRATION. Monochrome of young and mature palm. Seedling leaf, inflorescence and infructescence, and detail of leaf arrangement of mature leaf; all painted at 1×. Seedling collected and painted on June 8, 1991. Flowering habit collected and painted on July 16, 1991. Fruiting habit collected and painted on July 16, 1991. Herbarium sheet: Rosemary Wise 154 (OXF).

Rosemary Wise.

PALMAE   Wendland and Jussieu

Phoenicophorium H. Wendland
  This genus is monotypic, occurring only in Seychelles.

PLATE 71.   *Phoenicophorium borsigianum* (K. Koch) Stuntz
  (Stuntz, 1914, *Inventory of seed and plant imports*, no. 31, USDA)

  P. sechellarum H. Wendland   (H. Wendland, 1865, *L'Illustration Horticole* 12 [Miscellanée]:5)

  Stevensonia grandifolia J. Duncan ex Balfour   (Baker, 1877, *Flora of Mauritius*, p. 388)

  Vernacular name: latanier feuille (French); thief palm (English)

HABIT. The plant is a monoecious, solitary, tree palm that grows to a height of 15 m. The stems, which are conspicuously ringed with leaf scars, are armed with black spines when young but becomes sparsely spiny or spineless at maturity. The sheaths are tomentose, spiny when young, and up to 1 m long.

LEAVES. The leaves can be as long as 2 m. On young plants the lamina is entire and has a bifid apex. The mature leaves have lobes that are bifid at the apex and marginally edged with orange. The veins are prominent. The petioles are up to 50 cm long and have black spines.

INFLORESCENCES. The inflorescences are solitary and interfoliar, emerging below the crown, and branching to two orders. The flowers are in triads—one female flanked by two males.

FLOWERS.. The male flowers have three imbricate sepals, three keeled petals that are five times as long as the sepals, and 15–18 anthers. The female flowers are the same size as the males and globose. They have three imbricate sepals and petals, six staminodes and an asymmetrical gynoecium with three apical stigmas.

FRUITS. The fruits are ovoid and orange-red, and the stigmatic remains are sub-basal.

DISTRIBUTION. Mahé, Praslin, Silhouette, La Digue, Frégate, Curieuse, Félicité, and Ste. Anne

Phoenicophorium is a very hardy plant that often colonizes exposed, eroded land from sea level to 350 m. It is capable of withstanding droughts and full sun. In the forests, it is the most widespread of the endemic palms and is easy to distinguish by the rim of orange that borders the dissected margins of the leaves.

This was one of the first of the Seychelles palms to be transported overseas. In 1857, one that was growing in the Royal Botanic Gardens, Kew, was stolen, which gave rise to the common name, thief palm. In *The Flora of Mauritius and the Seychelles*, Baker referred to this palm as *Stevensonia grandifolia*. As a postscript to the description, he wrote, "We retain the name given to this plant by its discoverer, and published by him though without description. The name *Phoenicophorium*, subsequently given, and invented for the purpose of commemorating the disgraceful fact of a specimen of this palm having been stolen from Kew by a foreign employee, should surely be suppressed."

The pleated leaf surface of this palm collects leaf litter, which provides shelter for geckos and various invertebrates. The cut leaves are also dried in the sun and used for thatching.

ILLUSTRATION. Monochrome of young and mature palm. Inflorescence and infructescence, seedling showing dark spines, and detail of leaf margin; all painted at 1×. Seedling painted June 8, 1991. Flowering habit collected and painted on April 16, 1992. Fruiting habit collected and painted on July 26, 1990. Seedling collected and painted on July 30, 1990. Herbarium sheet: Rosemary Wise 155 (OXF).

PALMAE Wendland and Jussieu

Roscheria H. Wendland ex Baker
This genus is monotypic, occurring only in Seychelles.

PLATE 72. *Roscheria melanochaetes* Wendland ex Balfour
(Baker, 1877, *Flora of Mauritius*, p. 386)
Vernacular name: latanier hauban

HABIT. The plant is a monoecious, small, solitary tree palm that grows as high as 8 m. The slender stem, which occasionally has small stilt roots, is heavily armed when young with rows of stiff black spines. These become sparser at maturity.

LEAVES. The leaves are entire when young, flushing coral-red as they unfurl. The mature leaves are irregularly pinnate, up to 2.5 m long, and armed with spined sheaths.

INFLORESCENCES. The inflorescences are solitary and interfoliar when young but become infrafoliar after the leaves have been shed. They can reach a length of 1 m long. The branching is to four orders.

FLOWERS. The flowers are yellow. The male flowers are up to 1.25 mm in length with three imbricate sepals and three valvate petals, which are twice as long as the sepals, and six stamens. The female flowers are 2 mm in length, with three imbricate sepals, three imbricate, valvate petals, and six staminodes.

FRUITS. The fruits are globose, deep red at maturity, and up to 6 cm in length. The stigmatic remains are sub-basal.

DISTRIBUTION. Mahé, Praslin, and Silhouette

This is the smallest of the endemic palms and frequently has deep peachy-pink-colored flush leaves, which make it easy to identify at a distance. It is more common on Mahé, growing from mid- to high altitudes, but seldom below 500 m (Morne Blanc, La Reserve, and Congo Rouge), although there are a few trees at lower altitudes in the Vallée de Mai on Praslin.

It was named after Albrecht Roscher, a European traveler who was killed in Nyasaland. The specific epithet *melanochaetes* refers to the black spines on the trunks. Usually such armature reflects the need for the plant to protect itself against predators. In Seychelles, where the only native animals of any size used to be crocodiles and tortoises, the reason for the presence of these spines is open to conjecture.

ILLUSTRATION. Monochrome of mature palm. Inflorescence and infructescence; painted at 1×. Detail of rachis with male and female flowers; painted at 4×. Apex of young flush leaf to show coral-pink coloration; painted at 1×. Flowering habit collected and painted on May 19, 1991. Fruiting habit collected and painted on July 1, 1990. Herbarium sheet: Rosemary Wise 153 (OXF).

PALMAE   H. Wendland and Jussieu

Verschaffeltia Wendland
   This genus is monotypic, occurring only in Seychelles.

PLATE 73.   *Verschaffeltia splendida* H. Wendland
   (H. Wendland, 1865, *L'Illustration Horticole* 12 [Miscellanée]:6)
   Vernacular name: latanier latte

HABIT. The plant is a monoecious, solitary tree palm up to 30 m high with stilt roots forming a cone at the base. The trunk is ringed with leaf scars and has black spines at the base, on the leaf sheaths, and on the petioles when the plant is young. The spines are lost at maturity. The leaf sheath can be as long as 3.5 m.

LEAVES. The blades are obovate and notched at the apex. They are entire when young, but because of wind damage, are irregularly split when mature. The leaves may be as wide as 1.75 m and as long as 3m. The venation is pinnate. The petioles are semi-terete. The spadix is slender, pendulous, amplexicaul, up to 2 m long, and doubly branched. The peduncle is glabrous and compressed.

INFLORESCENCES. The inflorescences droop below the leaves.

FLOWERS. The flowers are yellow, spirally arranged, in clusters of three—one female between two males. The male flowers are globular and have three imbricate sepals, three valvate petals, which are twice as long as the sepals, and six stamens. The female flowers are larger and globular, with three imbricate sepals, three imbricate petals, which are valvate at the tips, and six staminodes. (The flowers were not collected.)

FRUITS. The fruits are globose, woody, red at maturity, and up to 2 cm long with the stigmatic scar sub-basal. The seeds are globular and woody with raised ridges.

DISTRIBUTION. Mahé, Praslin, and Silhouette

Verschaffeltia splendens is, by nature, a typical rain-forest species, preferring the higher, wetter regions from 300 to 600 m and frequently bordering streams. This palm is distinguished from the five other endemic species in that it has stilt roots and almost entire leaves and is often solitary. In the juvenile state, it is the only one of the six endemics to form a stem (and stilt roots) immediately after germination. The other five initially have a rosette of young leaves that do not form a trunk for some years. Good examples of *Verschaffeltia* can be seen in the Vallée de Mai, where the stilt roots are occasionally immersed in streams, and in the mist-forest areas of Mahé. Often the first indication of the presence of this tall palm is the scattering of woody, deeply ridged seeds over the ground. The genus is named after Ambroise Verschaffelt (1825–1886), a Belgian botanist and owner of a horticultural firm founded by his grandfather.

ILLUSTRATION. Monochrome of young palm. Seedling with needlelike spines and showing the developing stilt roots; painted at 1×. Fruits and seeds; painted at 1×. Flowering habit collected and painted on July 22, 1990. Fruiting habit collected and painted on May 21, 1991. Herbarium sheet: Rosemary Wise 162 (OXF).

PANDANACEAE R. Brown

This family consists of three genera and 675 species of trees, shrubs, lianas, and epiphytes that are found from the Old World tropics to New Zealand. Most of the species prefer coastal or marshy habitats, and some have edible fruits.

Pandanus Parkinson

This genus comprises 600 species from the Old World tropics. In Malaysia many cakes and savories are flavored with an extraction from *Pandanus*. In Africa the leaves are used for sleeping mats, baskets, hats, and thatch. *Pandanus odoratissimus* is cultivated as a fruit tree in the Marshall Islands.

PLATE 74. *Pandanus balfourii* Martelli (U. Martelli, 1905, *Webbia* 1:361)

Pandanus odoratissimus Balfour (non Linnaeus) (Baker, 1877, *Flora of Mauritius*, p. 401)

Vernacular name: vacoa borde de mer

HABIT. The plant is a tree that reaches a height of 8 m. The slender branches have clusters of terminal leaves in three ranks that form a semiorbicular crown.

LEAVES. The leaves are drooping and coriaceous, up to 1.5 m long, and armed with white spines on the midribs and on the margins.

INFLORESCENCES. The inflorescences were not seen.

FRUITS. The fruiting heads are on peduncles that are up to 20 cm long and have many bracts. They are pendulous, oblong elliptical, up to 25 cm long, and contain 70–90 spirally arranged drupes, tightly packed together with the top quarter of each free of its neighbors. An individual drupe is yellow at the base, shading upward to red, and with a green truncate apex. This is divided into sections by shallow grooves. Each section is capped with sub-reniform stigmas with short mucros.

DISTRIBUTION. Mahé, Praslin, Silhouette, La Digue, Frégate, North, Curieuse, Aride, Félicité, Cousin, and Cousine

Sauer (1967) lists 57 species of coastal plants. Of these, only one, *Pandanus balfourii*, is endemic to Seychelles. Having no economic use, the trees have survived in many locations. They can be seen by the roadside in several places on Mahé, including on the northwest peninsula, near the Sunset Beach Hotel, and in the far south, near Takamaka. Preferring low habitats, *P. balfourii* is seldom found above 150 m. The common name of pandans, screw pine, refers to the spiral arrangement of the leaves. The specific epithet commemorates Dr. I. B. Balfour, who described the palms and pandans for Baker's *Flora of Mauritius and the Seychelles*.

Other members of this family in the granitic islands are *Pandanus hornei*, *P. multispicatus*, *P. sanderi*, *P. sechellarum*, and *P. utilis*.

ILLUSTRATION. Monochrome of mature tree. Fruit and segment of mature fruit; both painted at 1×. Fruiting habit collected and painted on July 16–18, 1991. No specimens were pressed.

PANDANACEAE   R. Brown

Pandanus Parkinson

PLATE 75.   *Pandanus hornei* Balfour f.   (Baker, 1877, *Flora of Mauritius*, p. 397)

Vernacular name: vacoa parasol

HABIT. The plant is a tree that grows to 20 m high. The smooth stems have annual scars and stilt roots at base and frequently branch into threes.

LEAVES. The leaves, which occur in three ranks, are coriaceous, darker green above, and up to 3.25 m long. The blades taper to fine points. The margins have many red appressed spines. On the midrib the spines extend from the middle to the tip.

INFLORESCENCES. The inflorescences are pendulous with unisexual flowers. (They were not seen.)

FRUITS. The fruiting heads are globose, pendulous, and up to 30 cm across. The glaucous drupes are five- or six-angled, widening to domed apexes, with the top third free and green and the lower part orange. Each is up to 14 cm long and has prominent reniform styles.

DISTRIBUTION. Mahé, Praslin, Silhouette, and Curieuse

An easy way to identify this midaltitude tree is by the fairly constant division of the trunk and branches into threes. Many of these elegant, moisture-loving trees can be seen on Praslin beside the main road below the Vallée de Mai in the direction of Grand Anse. Just beyond this area, which also has other screw pines, is the waterfall immortalized in the painting of Marianne North. The specific epithet commemorates John Horne, who collected and described many plants during his visits to the islands in 1871 and 1874.

ILLUSTRATION. Monochrome of mature trees. Fruit, segment of mature fruit, and detail of leaf margin showing red teeth; all painted at 1×. Fruiting habit collected and painted on October 22, 1991. Seed collected and painted on October 16, 1993. No specimens were pressed.

PANDANACEAE   R. Brown

Pandanus Parkinson

PLATE 76.   *Pandanus multispicatus* Balfour f.   (Baker, 1877, *Flora of Mauritius*, p. 403)

Vernacular names: vacoa de montagne, vacoa millepatte

HABIT. The plant is a shrub that is often decumbent and has aerial roots that branch freely. It is up to 4 m high.

LEAVES. The leaves are terminal, in three ranks, broad, and tapering to a fine point. They are up to 1.75 m long and have white spines on the lower midrib and margins.

INFLORESCENCES. The inflorescences were not seen.

FRUIT. The fruiting heads are in the axis of persistent bracts. There are six to eight heads arranged in dense erect spikes containing 200–400 tiny drupes.

DISTRIBUTION. Mahé, Praslin, Silhouette, Frégate, and Curieuse

This rather invasive pandan is often the dominant species on midaltitude glacis. Unlike the other Seychelles pandans, with their erect habits, this one is more usually seen as a branched and sprawling groundcover plant. On the summit of Copolia, it competes with *Nepenthes pervillei*, *Dianella ensifolia*, and *Lophoschoenus hornei*. On parts of Bernica, it is the dominant species and covers large areas of the glacis. Crossing these can be quite a painful experience with such spiny leaves at ankle level. Here its main associates are *Deckenia nobilis*, *Mimusops sechellarum*, *Medusagyne oppositifolia*, and *Diospyros seychellarum*. On the slopes of Curieuse that were formerly denuded by fires, *P. multispicatus* is one of the foremost colonizers. The specific epithet alludes to the many spikes of the inflorescences.

ILLUSTRATION. Young fruit, dead peduncle, and detail of leaf margin; all painted at 1×. Fruiting habit collected and painted on April 6, 1992. Herbarium sheet: Rosemary Wise 193 (OXF).

PANDANACEAE   R. Brown

Pandanus Parkinson

PLATE 77.   *Pandanus sechellarum* Balfour f.   (Baker, 1877, *Flora of Mauritius*, p. 402)

Vernacular name: vacoa marron

HABIT. The plant is a tree up to 14 m high. Many aerial roots, which are frequently as long as 10 m, arise from the crown.

LEAVES. The leaves are terminal, in three ranks, light green, and coriaceous and taper to fine points. The midribs are prominent and spiny. The margins have minute pink suberect spines. The few bracts are caducous.

INFLORESCENCES. The inflorescences were not seen.

FRUITS. The fruiting heads are subglobose, pendulous, and up to 30 cm wide. They contain 50–70 drupes, each of which is five- or six-angled and widens toward the pyramidal apex with the top third free. The fruits are green at the top, purple or chestnut below, and up to 12 cm long. The number of prominences on the apex equals the number of stigmas.

DISTRIBUTION. Mahé, Praslin, Silhouette, and La Digue

Very often the main trunk of *Pandanus sechellarum* disappears and the tree is supported solely by the stilt roots. When the pandan is growing on the edge of a cliff, as at La Reserve, Mahé, the roots grow down over the side until they are able to stabilize the plant in the soil below. These, at 10 m, are probably the longest examples of roots of this species in Seychelles. The somewhat phallic appearance of the growing tip of the stilt roots of this pandan not surprisingly gave rise to a local legend. Infusions prepared from these tips and drunk by local men are said to improve their virility! The endocarp of the fallen drupes disintegrates, and the persistent woody fibers spread to give the characteristic "shaving brush" appearance. The fruit illustrated here was collected by the foresters in the Vallée de Mai (with full permission from World Heritage) and was transported back to Mahé by air. Painting this enormous fruit kept me occupied for the next three days and almost depleted my paint box of several pans of yellow, blue, and brown paint! When confronted with a subject as "chunky" and sculptural as this, any delicate style of painting has to be abandoned, and paint was laid down, layer after thick layer.

ILLUSTRATION. Monochrome of small tree. Fruit, segment of mature fruit, and detail of leaf margin showing pinkish-white teeth; all painted at 1×. Fruiting habit collected and painted September 22—25, 1993. Seed painted in October 1989. No specimens were pressed.

TRIURIDACEAE Gardner

This family consists of 6 genera and 42 species of tropical herbs.

Sechellaria Hemsley

This genus has only one species each in Madagascar, Tanzania, and Seychelles.

PLATE 78.   *Seychellaria thomassetii* Hemsley   (W. B. Hemsley, 1907, *Annals of Botany* 21:74)

HABIT. This plant is a saprophytic herb that is minutely pilose and has erect, filiform, purple stems. It is up to 12 cm high.

LEAVES. The leaves are scalelike and ovate lanceolate. Each has an acute apex and may be up to 3 mm long.

FLOWERS. The flowers are either white or reddish-purple and borne in racemes with 6–10 flowers on each stem. The upper flowers are male and the lower ones female, sometimes with irregular, quasi-hermaphroditic flowers between. The male flowers have from four to six perianth segments, each one being ovate lanceolate with an obtuse apex. They are sometimes papillose, imbricate, and reflexed at anthesis. Alternative segments are slightly smaller. The three stamens are opposite to the larger segments and have four-lobed anthers that dehisce transversely. The staminodes are opposite the smaller segments. The female flowers do not have staminodes. They have 30–35 free, flesh-colored carpels, each with a central papillose style.

FRUITS. The fruits are fleshy aggregates that occur in a globose head that is up to 1.5 mm wide. Individual fruits are 1 mm long.

DISTRIBUTION. Mahé, Praslin, and Silhouette

This tiny saprophytic herb is not uncommon locally but is not easy to see due to its diminutive size and dull coloration. But once one gets accustomed to the type of habitat in which it grows, the plants become more noticeable. *Seychellaria* prefers the shady, damp mist-forest conditions and frequently, but not always, grows saprophytically on decaying leaves of *Pandanus sechellarum*. Dr. M. Kirkpatrick has recently found plants on Praslin, and a white form exists on Copolia. This latter color variation may be the result of lower-altitude conditions, or the inflorescences may have been very old and leached of color.

There are no related species in Seychelles.

ILLUSTRATION. Plant habit; painted at 1×. Enlargement of mature male flower with reflexed perianth segments and dark anthers; painted at 20×. Young male flower with cream anthers; painted at 20×. Fruit; painted at 20×. Individual segments of the fruit; painted at 80×. Female flowers; painted at 20×. Detail of spike with female flowers; painted at 10×. Flowering habit collected and painted on June 9, 1991. Fruiting habit collected and painted on June 9, 1991. Herbarium sheets: Rosemary Wise 150, 151 (OXF).

GLOSSARY

See also drawings of leaf shapes and margins at end of this section.

Abaxial. Dorsal; facing away from the axis.

Achene. A small, dry, indehiscent, single-seeded fruit.

Acuminate. Narrowing gradually to a point.

Actinodromous. Three or more primary veins diverging radically from a single point.

Actinomorphic. Regular; divisible into two equal parts in several planes.

Acute. Pointed.

Adaxial. Ventral; facing towards the axis.

Adnate. Joined to another part.

Aestivation. Arrangement of folded parts within a bud.

Alternate. Leaves arranged singly at different levels.

Amplexicaul. Clasping and partially encircling the stem.

Adroecium. Male sex organs; stamens.

Angiosperm. Plant with ovules enclosed in an ovary.

Annual. Completing a life cycle within one year.

Anther. Pollen-containing part of stamen.

Anthesis. Period when flower is expanded and pollination occurs.

Antrorse. Turned toward the apex.

Apetalous. Flower without petals.

Apex. Tip.

Apiculate. Ending in a short, sharp point.

Aril. Outgrowth of funicle, covering seed.

Aristate. Having a stiff bristle or awn.

Ascending. Directed upward at a sharp angle.

Attenuate. Tapering gradually to a sharp point.

Auricle. Small, ear-shaped appendage.

Axil. Angle formed by stem and upper surface of leaf.

Axillary. In the axil.

Beak. Prominent terminal projection.

Berry. Fleshy, indehiscent fruit with seed immersed in pulp.

Bifid. Cleft or divided into two before apex.

Bipinnate. Pinnate with each pinna itself pinnate.

Bisexual. Having both male and female parts in same flower.

Bivalved. Having two valves.

Blade. The expanded part of a leaf.

Bowl. Trunk of tree below lowest branch.

Bract. Reduced, modified leaf subtending flower or inflorescence.

Bracteole. Small bract.

Brochidodromous. Secondary vein forming a series of loops near margin with next.

Bulb. Underground organ, bearing leaf scales and buds.

Bullate. Blistered or puckered.

Buttress. Projecting flange from lower trunk of tree.

Caducous. Falling off early.

Calyptra. Caducous cover to a floral bud or to a circumscissile capsule.

Calyx. Outer perianth, with free or united sepals.

Campanulate. Bell-shaped.

Camptodromous. Secondary vein united near margin with next to form an arch.

Caniculate. Channeled.

Canopy. Collective term for crowns of trees in forest.

Capitate. In a head, headlike.

Capitulum. A close head of sessile or almost sessile flowers.

Capsule. Dry, dehiscent fruit that splits when ripe.

Carnose. Fleshy.

Carpel. Organ containing one or more ovules, separate or joined to form ovary.

Caryopsis. Dry, one-seeded, indehiscent fruit of a grass.

Cataphyll. Thin, rudimentary, sheathing leaf that encloses new shoot.

Catkin. Pendulous inflorescence of unisexual apetalous flowers.

Cauliflorus. Flowers arising from dormant buds on stems or trunks.

Chartaceous. Having a papery texture.

Chlorophyll. Green pigment of plants.

Ciliate. Fringed with hairs.

Circumscissile. Opening by a circular vent.

Cladodromous. Secondary veins freely ramified toward the margin.

Class. Taxonomic rank below phylum.

Clavate. Club-shaped.

Clone. Plants reproducing vegetatively from one parent; genetically identical.

Column. Stamens and styles fusing into a single structure.

Compound. Composed of two or more similar parts.

Concave. Hollowed.

Confluent. Merging together.

Congested. Tightly packed.

Connate. United with a similar part or organ.

Connective. Strip joining the anther cells in stamens.

Conspecific. Belonging to one and the same species.

Contorted. Twisted; imbricate aestivation with segments overlapping at edges.

Convex. Rounded, reverse of concave.

Cordate. Heart-shaped.

Coriaceous. Leathery.

Corolla. Inner perianth with free or united petals.

Corona. Circle of appendages between stamens and corolla.

Corymb. Flat-topped racemose inflorescence with pedicels of different lengths.

Costa. Midrib of a whole leaf rather than of leaflets.

Costapalmate. Shaped like the palm of a hand with a short midrib (costa).

Cotyledon. First leaves of embryo; are present in the seed.

Craspedodromous. Secondary veins running directly to margin.

Crenate. With rounded marginal teeth.

Crenulate. Finely crenate.

Culm. Hollow flowering stem of grasses.

Cultivar. Variant developed in cultivation.

Cuneate. Cuneiform. Wedge-shaped.

Cuspidate. Having a rigid point.

Cyathium. Inflorescence of *Euphorbia*.

Cyme. Inflorescence with central flower opening first, with opposite or forked branches.

Declinate. Curved downward.

Decumbent. Lying on the ground.

Decurrent. Continuing downward into axil or internode.

Decussate. Leaves in opposite pairs, each pair at right angles to the last.

Dehiscence. Splitting open at maturity to release contents.

Dehiscent. Splitting along definite lines.

Deltoid. Triangular.

Dentate. Toothed.

Denticulate. Minutely toothed.

Dichotomous. Divided into two equal forks.

Dicotyledon. Plant with two seed leaves present in embryo.

Didynamous. Pairs of stamens of two different lengths.

Digitate. Palmate leaf with leaflets arising from same point at top of petiole.

Dimorphic. Occurring in two different forms.

Dioecious. Male and female flowers on separate plants.

Domatia. Small depressed structures on lower surface of leaf, in axils of veins, enclosed by tissue or hairs.

Drupe. Fleshy fruit with seeds enclosed by woody endocarp.

Emarginate. Margin notched at apex.

Emergent. Crown rising above the canopy.

Endemic. Occurring naturally in one geographical area only.

Endocarp. Innermost layer of pericarp.

Entire. Smooth margin, without teeth, lobes or notches.

Ephemeral. Living for a very short time.

Epicarp. Outermost layer of pericarp.

Epiphyte. Plant growing nonparasitically on another.

Erinaceous. Hedgehog-like.

Eucamptodromous. The secondary veins do not reach the margin but join the adjacent ones with a series of cross veins.

Exserted. Protruding.

Exocarp. Combined epicarp and mesocarp of fruit.

Exotic. Plant from another region introduced to an area to which it is nonnative.

Exstipulate. Without stipules.

Extrorse. Anthers facing outward.

Falcate. Sickle-shaped.

Fastigiate. Sloping to a point.

Family. Group of related genera.

Filament. Anther stalk or thread.

Filiform. Threadlike.

Flexuous. Having alternate opposite curvature.

Fruit. Seed-containing structure in angiosperms.

Funicle. Stalk connecting ovule to placenta.

Fusiform. Spindle-shaped.

Genus. Taxonomic group of related but distinct species.

Glabrous. Lacking hairs.

Gland. Secretory structure.

Glaucous. Blue-green in color with whitish bloom.

Globose. Round, spherical.

Glume. Bract, paired at base of spikelet in grasses and single subtending flowers in sedges.

Gymnosperm. Plant with seed not enclosed by an ovary.

Habit. General appearance of plant.

Hastate. Arrowhead-shaped but with basal lobes turned outward.

Herb. Plant with nonwoody stem, sometimes woody at base.

Hilum. Scar on seed coat where seed was attached to funicle.

Hirsute. Hairy.

Hispid. Having stiff, bristlelike hairs.

Hygrophile. Moisture-loving plant.

Imbricate. Overlapping.

Immersed. Sunken.

Imparipinnate. Pinnate, with a terminal leaflet.

Incised. Deeply cut.

Indehiscent. Not opening at maturity.

Indigenous. Native to area; not introduced.

Indumentum. General term for hairs or scales on plant surface.

Inflorescence. Arrangement of flowers on the floral axis.

Infrafoliar. Occuring below the leaves.

Infructescence. Fruits developing from an inflorescence.

Internode. Stem between nodes.

Introrse. Anthers facing inward.

Involucre. Whorl of bracts beneath an inflorescence.

Keel. The two united lower petals of a papilionaceous flower.

Labellum. Lowest and usually largest petal of an orchid.

Lamina. Leaf blade.

Lanceolate. Lance- or spear-shaped.

Latex. Milky juice.

Lax. Loose, not compact.

Leaf. Outgrowth from stem consisting of petiole and lamina.

Leaflet. Leaflike segment of a compound leaf.

Legume. A pod with two sutures.

Lenticel. Corky breathing pore in bark.

Liana. Woody climber.

Ligule. Strap-shaped corolla in Compositae. Scale at top of leaf sheath in grasses.

Linear. Long and narrow and with parallel sides.

Lithophytic. Growing on rocks or stones.

Lobe. A division of an organ, usually rounded.

Midrib. Middle, principal vein of leaf.

Malesia. Phytogeographic region, including Malay Peninsula, Malaysia, the Philippines, Indonesia, and New Guinea.

Marcescent. Withering without falling off.

Marginate. Having a well-marked border.

Mesocarp. Fleshy part of succulent fruit.

Monocotyledon. Plant with one seed leaf present in embryo.

Monoecious. Having male and female flowers on the same plant.

Monopodial. Having one main stem or trunk, bearing lateral branches.

Monotypic. Genus with a single species.

Mucilaginous. Slimy.

Mucronate. Terminating in a short, straight point.

Nectar. Sweet fluid secreted from nectary.

Nectary. Gland secreting nectar.

Node. Point on stem where leaves arise.

Nut. Dry, indehiscent, one-seeded fruit with woody pericarp.

Obconical. Apex located below point of attachment.

Oblanceolate. Spear-shaped but reversed.

Oblong. Leaf length greater than width; sides often parallel.

Obovate. Egg-shaped, but widest near apex.

Obtuse. Apex blunt or rounded.

Operculum. Lid of circumscissile fruit or insectivorous pitcher.

Opposite. Leaves paired at nodes on either side.

Order. Taxonomic group consisting of closely related families.

Oval. Broadly elliptical.

Ovary. Part of plant containing ovules.

Ovate. Egg-shaped in section.

Ovule. Structure within ovary that develops into seed after fertilization.

Palea. Upper of two bracts enclosing grass flower.

Palmate. Leaf divided into leaflets that radiate from petiole.

Panicle. Inflorescence with many branches.

Papilionaceous. Having the flower structure of a member of the Fabaceae family.

Papillose. Having short, rounded hairs.

Pappus. Tufts of hair on fruits of Compositae; derived from modified calyx.

Parallelodromous. Two or more primary veins originating at the leaf base, running parallel, and converging at the leaf apex.

Paripinnate. Pinnate without terminal leaflet.

Pedicel. Stalk of a single flower.

Peduncle. Stalk of an inflorescence.

Peltate. Having the stalk attached near the middle of the leaf blade.

Pendulous. Hanging down.

Perianth. Outer nonreproductive parts of flower: calyx and corolla.

Pericarp. Wall of fruit that develops from ovary wall.

Perennial. Plant that lives for more than two years and flowers annually.

Persistent. Remaining attached.

Petal. A segment of the corolla.

Petiole. Leaf stalk.

Petiolule. Leaflet stalk in pinnate or compound leaf.

Pilose. Having soft, scattered hairs.

Pinna. Leaflet of a pinnate leaf.

Pinnate. Separate leaflets either side of stalk or rachis.

Pistil. Female organs of flower; consists of ovary, style, and stigma.

Pistilode. A sterile gynoecium.

Placentation. Pattern of attachment of ovules to ovary.

Pollen. Grains containing male reproductive cells; stored in anthers.

Pollination. Act of transferring pollen to stigma.

Pollinia. Cluster of pollen grains, as in orchids.

Prophyll. A bracteole.

Pseudobulb. Thickened bulblike stem in some orchids.

Pubescent. Having short, soft hairs.

Puberulent, puberulous. Sparsely pubescent.

Pyrene. Nutlet or kernel; stone of a drupe.

Pyriform. Pear-shaped.

Raceme. Inflorescence having flowers borne on pedicels along unbranched axis.

Rachis. Principal axis of inflorescence or compound leaf.

Ray floret. Outer part of compound flower.

Receptacle. The apex of a stem from which all parts of a flower arise.

Recurved. Curved backward.

Reflexed. Curved abruptly backward.

Repand. Slightly wavy.

Reniform. Kidney-shaped.

Repand. Slightly wavy.

Reticulate. Having a network pattern.

Revolute. Rolled-backward.

Rhizome. Horizontal, rootlike stem, on or under ground, with buds, shoots, and roots.

Rhomboid. Diamond-shaped.

Rosette. Circular arrangement of leaves.

Rugose. Wrinkled.

Sagitate. Arrowhead-shaped.

Saprophytic. Living on dead or dying plant or animal tissue and devoid of chlorophyll.

Scabrid. Rough in texture.

Scalariform. Resembling rungs of a ladder.

Scale. Reduced leaf, often membranous, covering buds and bulbs.

Scape. Leafless stalk, bearing one or more flowers, arising from ground.

Scarious. Thin and dry.

Sepal. One segment of calyx.

Sericeous. Silky, with appressed hairs.

Serrate. Margin with sawlike teeth.

Sessile. Lacking a stalk.

Sheath. A tubular covering.

Shrub. Woody plant with several main stems, smaller than a tree.

Spadix. Flower spike with thickened, fleshy axis.

Spathe. Large bract subtending and enclosing inflorescence.

Species. Group of closely allied, mutually fertile individuals.

Spicate. Spike-like.

Spikelet. One or more grass flowers subtended by a pair of glumes.

Spinous. Spiny.

Spur. Hollow, slender extension of calyx or corolla.

Stamen. Male sex organ of plant, consisting of filament, anther, and connective.

Staminal tube. Tubular structure formed when stamens are fused together.

Staminode. Sterile stamen, often reduced or modified.

Standard. The uppermost petal of a papilionaceous flower.

Stigma. Apex of style; receptive area for pollen grains to alight and germinate.

Stipule. Leaflike or scalelike outgrowth at base of petiole.

Stolon. Lateral, horizontal stem at ground level that roots at nodes to produce new plants.

Striate. Having parallel lines, grooves, or ridges.

Style. Apical part of gynoecium that bears stigma at tip.

Subglobose. Somewhat globose.

Subspecies. Taxonomic group below species, with minor morphological differences; usually separated ecologically or geographically.

Subulate. Awl-shaped.

Succulent. Fleshy.

Syconia. A multiple, hollow fruit, such as a fig.

Taxon. A member of any taxonomic category.

Tepal. A petal, sepal, or unit of undifferentiated perianth.

Terete. Circular in cross-section.

Tomentose. Feltlike, with covering of dense, short, soft hairs.

Trifoliate. Having three leaflets.

Truncate. Appearing cut off, or square.

Type specimen. Designated representative of taxon that is pressed, mounted, and preserved in a herbarium.

Umbel. Flat-topped inflorescence with pedicels arising from same point on peduncle.

Undulate. Having a wavy margin.

Valvate. Meeting but not overlapping.

Variety. Taxonomic category below species and subspecies that denotes population-based variation.

Vein. Strand of vascular tissue in leaf blade.

Venation. Arrangement of veins in leaf blade.

Viscid. Sticky.

Whorl. A ring of leaves, bracts, or floral parts.

Xerophyte. A plant adapted to living in dry areas.

Zygomorphic. Irregular flower that can be divided into equal halves in one plane only.

Leaf Shapes

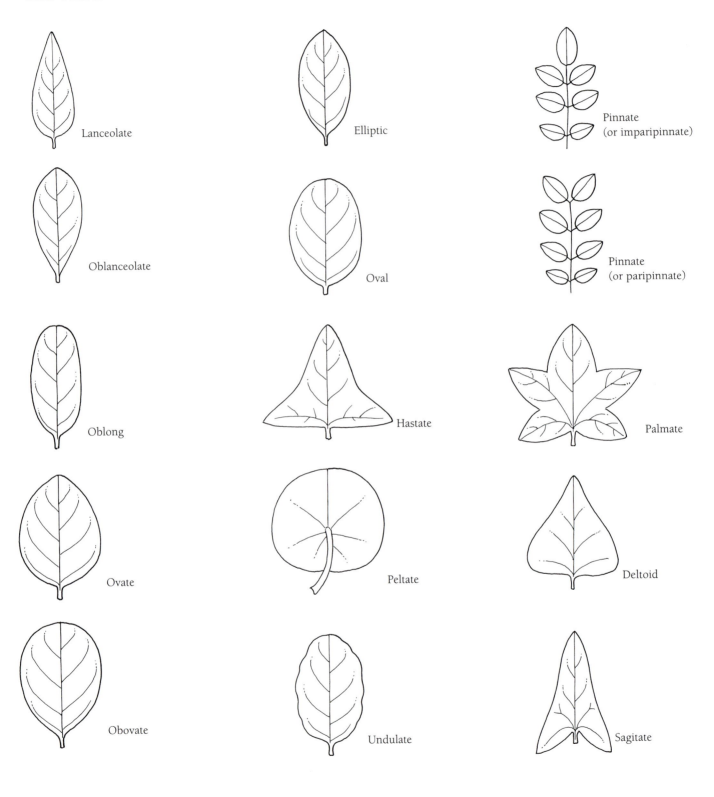

Lanceolate

Oblanceolate

Oblong

Ovate

Obovate

Elliptic

Oval

Hastate

Peltate

Undulate

Pinnate
(or imparipinnate)

Pinnate
(or paripinnate)

Palmate

Deltoid

Sagitate

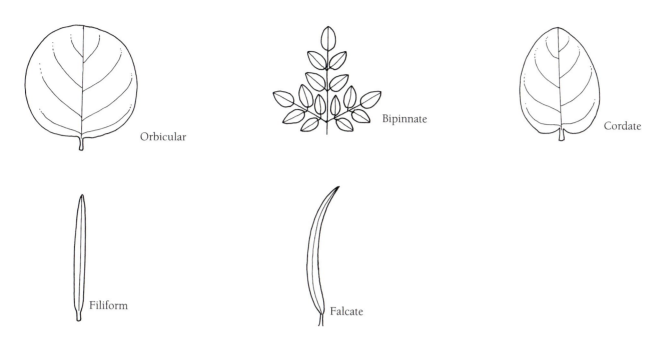

Orbicular

Bipinnate

Cordate

Filiform

Falcate

LEAF SHAPES: APEX AND BASE

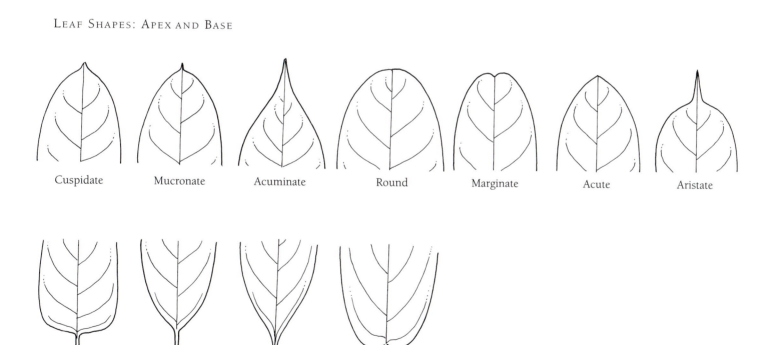

Cuspidate

Mucronate

Acuminate

Round

Marginate

Acute

Aristate

Truncate

Cuneate

Decurrent

Cordate

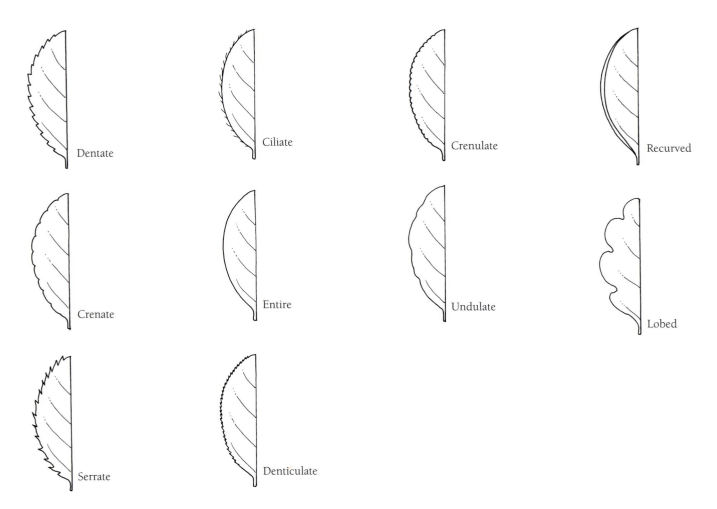

Dentate

Ciliate

Crenulate

Recurved

Crenate

Entire

Undulate

Lobed

Serrate

Denticulate

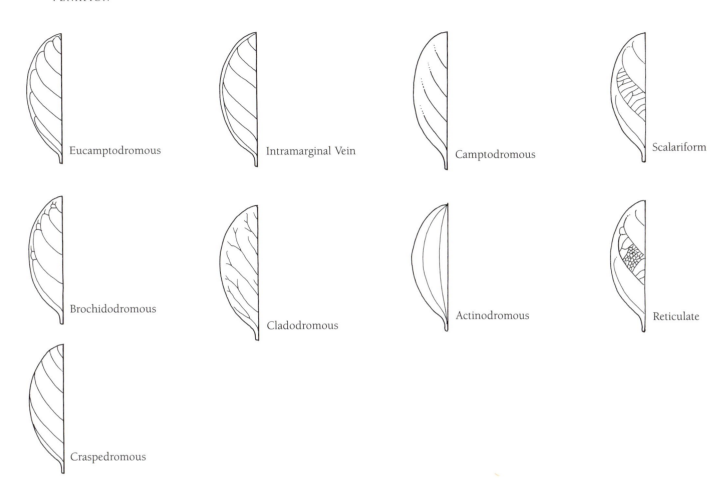

Eucamptodromous

Intramarginal Vein

Camptodromous

Scalariform

Brochidodromous

Cladodromous

Actinodromous

Reticulate

Craspedromous

REFERENCES

Bailey, D. 1961. *List of the flowering plants and ferns of Seychelles.* Seychelles: Government Printer.

Baker, J. G. 1877. *Flora of Mauritius and the Seychelles.* London: L. Reeve.

Baum, D., et al. 1985. *Oxford University Biological Expedition to the Seychelles.* Unpublished report.

Blunt, W. 1971. *The compleat naturalist.* London: Collins.

Carbognin et al. 1887. *Sechelles images.* Bologna: GMR Group.

Carlström, A. 1996. *Endemic and threatened plant species of the granitic Seychelles.* Seychelles: Ministry of Foreign Affairs, Planning, and Environment.

Carpin, S. 1996. *Odyssey illustrated guide to Seychelles.* Hong Kong: The Guidebook Company.

Fay, M. F., Swensen, S. M., and Chase, M. 1997. Taxonomic affinities of *Medusagynae oppositifolia. Kew Bulletin* 52 (1): 111–20.

Fleischmann, K., et al. 1996. Inselbergs in the sea: Vegetation outcrops on the islands of Mahé, Praslin, and Silhouette (Seychelles). *Bulletin of the Geobotanic Institute* 62: 61–74.

Friedmann, F. 1986. *Flowers and trees of Seychelles.* Seychelles: Dept. of Finance.

————. 1994. *Flore des Seychelles: Dicotylédons.* Paris: Editions de l'Orstom.

Gerlach, J., et al. 1990. *Oxford University Silhouette Expedition.* Unpublished report.

Gibson, H. S. 1938. *A report on the forests of the granitic islands of the Seychelles.* Seychelles: Government Printer.

Heywood, V. H., ed. 1978. *Flowering plants of the world.* Oxford: Oxford University Press.

Hemsley, W. B. 1916. Flora of Seychelles and Aldabra. *Journal of Botany* 54 (suppl. 2): 1–24.

Hickey, L. J. 1973. Classification of the architecture of dicotyledonous leaves. *American Journal of Botany* 60 (1): 17–33.

I.U.C.N. 1987. *Directory of Afrotropical protected areas.* Gland, Switzerland: I.U.C.N.

Jeffrey, C. 1962. *The botany of Seychelles: Report by the visiting botanist of the Seychelles Botanical Survey, 1961–1962.* Kew: Royal Botanic Garden.

Lionnet, G. 1986. *Coco de mer.* Mauritius: L'île aux Images Editions.

Lötschert, W., and Beese, G. 1981. *Collins guide to tropical plants.* London: Collins.

Kingdon, J. 1990. *Island Africa.* London: Harper Collins.

Mabberley, D. 1987. *The plant book.* Cambridge: Cambridge University Press.

McAteer, W. 1991. *Rivals in Eden.* Lewis, Sussex: The Book Guild.

Pavard, C. N.d. *Seychelles from one island to another.* Seychelles: GMR Group.

Pennington, T. D. 1991. *The genera of Sapotaceae.* Kew: Royal Botanic Garden and New York: New York Botanical Garden.

Proctor, J. 1974. The endemic plants of the Seychelles: An annotated list. *Candollea* 29: 345–87.

Rawlins, R. 1956. The general in the garden. *Blackwood's Magazine* (July): 1–10.

Robertson, S. A. 1989. *Flowering plants of Seychelles.* Kew: Royal Botanic Garden.

Robertson, S. A., Wise, R., and White, F. 1989. *Medusagyne oppositifolia. Kew Magazine* 6: 166–71.

Sauer, J. D. 1967. *Plants and man on the Seychelles coast.* Madison: University of Wisconsin Press.

Savage, A. J. P., and Ashton, P. S. 1983. The population structure of the double coconut and some other Seychelles palms. *Biotropica* 15 (1): 15–25.

Stearn, W. T. 1992. *Botanical Latin.* 4th ed. Newton Abbot: David and Charles.

Stoddart, D. R. 1984. *Biogeography and ecology of the Seychelles Islands.* The Hague: Junk.

Summerhayes, V. S. 1931. An enumeration of the angiosperms of the Seychelles Archipelago. *Transactions Linnean Society London* 19: 261–99.

Swabey, C. 1961. *Forestry in the Seychelles: Report of a visit by the forestry advisor in 1959.* Mahé, Seychelles: Government Printer.

———. 1970. The endemic flora of the Seychelles Islands and its conservation. *Biological Conservation* 2 (3): 1–34.

Vesey-Fitzgerald, D. 1940. On the vegetation of Seychelles. *Journal of Ecology* 28: 465–83.

Warman, S., and Todd, D. 1984. A biological survey of Aride Nature Reserve, Seychelles. *Biological Conservation* 28: 51–71.

White, F. 1983. *The vegetation of Africa.* Paris: UNESCO.

Wise, R. 1986. *Seychelles 1985–86: A botanical illustrator's report.* University of Oxford, unpublished report.

INDEX TO COMMON AND CREOLE PLANT NAMES

GENERAL INDEX